AMERICAN WHITETAIL

AMERICAN WHITETAIL

Deer Hunting Tips and Resources

Everything You Need to Know
About Whitetail Deer Hunting

Revised Edition

Terry F. Townsend

THE DERRYDALE PRESS
Lanham • New York • Plymouth, UK

Knowledge ⬦ Patience ⊜ Success

Published by The Derrydale Press
An imprint of The Rowman & Littlefield Publishing
Group, Inc.
4501 Forbes Boulevard, Suite 200, Lanham,
Maryland 20706
http://www.rlpgtrade.com

Estover Road, Plymouth PL6 7PY, United Kingdom

Distributed by National Book Network

British Library Cataloguing in Publication Information Available

Library of Congress Cataloging-in-Publication Data
Townsend, Terry F., 1946–
   American whitetail : deer hunting tips and resources : everything you need to
know about whitetail deer hunting / Terry F. Townsend. — Rev. ed.
      p. cm.
   Includes bibliographical references.
   ISBN 978-1-58667-118-1 (pbk. : alk. paper) — ISBN 978-1-58667-119-8
(electronic)
   1. White-tailed deer hunting. I. Title.
   SK301.T684 2011
   799.2'7652—dc22

                                                              2011010706

The paper used in this publication meets the minimum requirements of American National Standard for Information Sciences—Permanence of Paper for Printed
Library Materials, ANSI/NISO Z39.48–1992.

Printed in the United States of America

TESTIMONIALS FROM HUNTING PROFESSIONALS

Terry: good book, well done. For the entry-level deer hunter all the way to the expert, *American Whitetail Deer Hunting Tips and Resources* is loaded with information. I cannot think of a single aspect of the sport that has been overlooked. This is quality reading with plenty of pictures and illustrations. A quality possession with years of enjoyable reading.

—*John L. Sloan, outdoor writer and hunting guide*

American Whitetail Deer Hunting Tips and Resources is a very thorough and complete guide for the budding deer hunter and a great refresher course for the veteran woodsman. Terry Townsend has done his homework and put decades of experience into this very informative book.

—*Brenda Valentine, "First Lady of Hunting"*

American Whitetail Deer Hunting Tips and Resources is the most informative book on the American whitetail I have read in years. From the field to the freezer, Terry Townsend captures every aspect of the sport we love. His love of the hunt and his respect for the animal and its environment is unmistakable. I used to say all you needed on a hunt were the three Bs: binoculars, bullets, and brains. I now make it the four Bs: binoculars, bullets, brains, and this book.

—*Terry Higginbotham, owner and chief researcher at HuntStats.com—We Know When to Hunt!*

Jimmy Holt, a native Nashvillian, is probably the best-known outdoor personality in Tennessee. He has hosted *The Tennessee Outdoorsmen* television show for more than thirty years, written the outdoor pages for *The Tennessean,* and hosted his own radio show in Nashville. He also writes regularly for hunting and fishing magazines.

For many years now, I have read and listened to deer hunters as they told stories about their hunting trips into the woods in search of the whitetail deer. Terry Townsend's story is the latest I have had the pleasure of reading and his book, *American Whitetail Deer Hunting Tips and Resources* is the most interesting and complete deer hunting information I have read. He talks the talk, takes you into the woods, makes you smell the great outdoors and then has you soaking wet as you climb into your tree stand. He talks about sighting in your weapon, setting up a hunting camp, reminds you to contact landowners before you enter their property. If you are interested in deer hunting and need information about hunting gear and accessories, helping juvenile hunters, camouflage, and much, much more *American Whitetail Deer Hunting Tips and Resources* will provide it. Chapters revealing information on scrapes and rubs, the rut, deer tracks and field dressing can also be found, detailing the do's and don'ts.

—*Jimmy Holt, Tennessee outdoorsman & outdoor writer*

Terry Townsend has given you the opportunity to engage in a comprehensive look at hunting the most elusive creature in North America, the whitetail, in his new book *American Whitetail Deer Hunting Tips and Resources*. Some books offer strategies and tips, but Terry's work goes beyond that. He helps you build a foundation for better hunting, even to the point of what to do after you harvest the animal. I can tell you this: any hunter would be a better hunter by taking advice from a man who's well-seasoned in the ways of the whitetail, and that's Terry Townsend.

—*Jason Cruise, author of* The Heart of the Sportsman: Into the High Country
Executive Editor, The Sportsman's Bible, *Founder, Tennessee Outdoor Network*

I have been reading a book about deer hunting that I could not put down. Terry Townsend has written the most complete book I have seen in my thirty-something years of hunting. No matter what your level of hunting experience is, *American Whitetail Deer Hunting Tips and Resources* is very helpful to all, and I highly recommend it.

—*Bryan White, Texas Hunting Leases*

I have over forty years of outdoor experience, of which most of those years have involved hunting, and Terry's book, *American Whitetail Deer Hunting Tips and Resources*, is strongly suggested for both the new hunter and the experienced. Even with my experience level, I learned many new ways to do things, and when an author can do that, he has a best-seller on his hands! Excellent book!

—*Gary L. Benton, author of* Simple Survival: A Family Outdoor Guide

As a long-time deer hunter, outfitter, and TV show producer, I've seen a great need for this kind of book. Most of today's hunters are ill prepared physically, mentally, and equipmentally for success. *American Whitetail Deer Hunting Tips and Resources* could stop short a lot of hunting disappointments for the average deer hunter.

—*Donald R. Blizzard, founder of Whitetail Adventures, Inc.*

Terry Townsend's book, entitled *American Whitetail Deer Hunting Tips and Resources*, is by far the most complete source for virtually every aspect of whitetail deer hunting that I've seen. It's obvious that the years Terry spent writing the book were time well spent. Whether you are a first-time whitetail hunter or a seasoned veteran of forty-six years like me, Terry's book will enlighten you with new ideas and concepts to improve your hunting skills. From cover to cover, this book is jam-packed with information relating to whitetail hunting, and it's a must-have for anyone who hunts whitetail deer.

—*Howard J. Lux, owner of Lux's Wildlife Management National Sales Manager— Wildlife Buffet*

Terry F. Townsend has crafted the finest and most complete how-to book on hunting in *American Whitetail Deer Hunting Tips and Resources* that we have ever seen. It is truly everything you need to know about whitetail deer hunting.
American Whitetail Deer Hunting Tips and Resources is very well organized, fully illustrated, easy to read, and a great reference tool for deer hunters of any level.
Combining thirty-five years of deer hunting experience with over six years of research, Terry has created a masterpiece worthy of every deer hunter's library.

—*David Salman, president of Tracker Outdoors*

American Whitetail Deer Hunting Tips and Resources by Terry F. Townsend: wow! I have read at least fifty books dedicated to whitetail deer in my lifetime. This one is by far the best. It has great information for everyone who wants to start hunting, from the seasoned deer hunting veteran to everyone in between. The book is well written and contains everything I could ever think of, and more—and I have hunted whitetail deer for over twenty-five years, and thought I knew all there was to know about them. I found the book very interesting and highly recommend it to everyone who hunts deer. Great job, Mr. Townsend!

—*John E. MacEwan—president of International Hunting Land Association, Inc.*

American Whitetail Deer Hunting Tips and Resources by Terry Townsend is the most comprehensive book on whitetail deer hunting I have ever read. It is packed full of good information and is a must for any deer hunter. *American Whitetail Deer Hunting Tips and Resources* is put together with great detail and great pictures, and the resources at the back are a big help. If you are a whitetail deer hunter, you need to read this book. I have been hunting for twenty-eight years, and I learned some new things from *American Whitetail Deer Hunting Tips and Resources*. Thank you for writing an excellent book. My two boys are reading it now.

—*Jerry Wilson, Wilson Game Calls*, www.wilsongamecalls.com and www.deer-calls.net

American Whitetail Deer Hunting Tips and Resources by Terry Townsend is the most comprehensive book on deer hunting I have ever read. Not only is it informative, it is also fun to read.

—*Tom Tann, Big Buck 4n2 Rattling Antlers*, www.bigbuckrattlingantlers.com

The author of a new book, *American Whitetail Deer Hunting Tips and Resources*, Terry F. Townsend, of Columbia, TN, has stepped on board with TNdeer.com. His book on whitetail tips and resources is chock full of good information for the deer hunter. Even at nearly five hundred pages, it is still small enough to add to any backpack for a trip to the woods. Tips on how to be successful every year at everything from putting venison in the freezer to reading deer sign in the woods will guide even novice deer hunters. As a matter of fact, I recommend this book to any current deer hunter who has a youngster who is interested in deer hunting. There are many pictures explaining exactly what the text is about. Graphics and maps are included.

The new book, just completed late last year, will benefit any deer hunter. Newcomers to the sport can read thousands of great tips, while the seasoned hunter can read many things he has learned yet forgotten as time progresses.

There are four main sections to the book *American Whitetail Deer Hunting Tips and Resources*. Mr. Townsend takes you all the way from before the hunt to what to do after you have the deer back to camp. Tips on scouting, what to look for and where, shot placement, understanding good deer management, dealing with scent control, tree stand setup, and the different methods of hunting this great wild animal lace across pages with a leafy gray background that adds to the book's appeal and makes it less noticeable in the hands of a hunter reading it on stand.

There is also a section for scoring and aging your deer. Recipe pages and links to websites are included.

Be watching for a link to appear soon where you can order a copy of this wonderful book. It will make a great addition to any hunter's library of good reads. But I like the feature that it is still small enough to pack along on a hunt and enjoy reading on stand during those lull hours of non-deer movement. As a matter of fact, my personal copy went to stand with me several times this past season! I enjoyed refreshing my mind of many of things I read from within this book while waiting on the monster buck that never showed. I reckon I will have to read up on prescouting and do a better job of stand placement next season.

Thank you, Terry, for this neat book you have taken the time to put together as a true American whitetail hunter.

—*Mary Morris, wildlife photographer*

Writing this book was one of the most fulfilling experiences of my life and I hope you enjoy reading it as much as I enjoyed writing it.

IN HONOR & LOVING MEMORY

**JAMES LOYAL
MCCLANAHAN**
March 2, 1928–
November 16, 2001

**WILL BENTON
MCCLANAHAN**
April 24, 1981–
January 15, 2003

**HUNT SPENCE
MCCLANAHAN**
January 24, 1950–
February 21, 2003

DEDICATION AND APPRECIATION

I would first like to give thanks to my Lord and Savior, Jesus Christ, for allowing me this portion of my life with clarity of thought and the ability to write this book.

I wish to dedicate this book to the three most important people in my life: my wife, Linda; my daughter, Melanie; and my mother, Mary Brown Townsend, recently deceased. All three of these ladies played a major role in the accomplishment of this book. My wife was always there for me and provided encouragement and editing skills plus her photography contributions. My daughter's contribution was invaluable with her many hours of formatting and artistic efforts that made the first two editions of this book the high-quality publication that it is. My mother instilled in me those qualities necessary to take on this undertaking and persevere throughout, and also gave me encouragement and physical contributions to the book.

I appreciate very much the years I had with my now-deceased father, Clarence Aubry Townsend. He took me on my first hunt and opened the door for my ever-growing love of hunting.

I had a very close relationship with my now-deceased grandparents, Frank and Eula McClanahan. Together, they instilled very deeply in me the genuine love of family and value of down-home country living that has always drawn me back to the country and to deer hunting.

I wish to express my sincere appreciation for my late uncles Hunt and Loyal McClanahan for reinforcing my love for hunting as a young boy and providing me with wonderful places to hunt throughout my life.

I have to extend my appreciation to various members of my family and friends who have provided me with their companionship on so many different hunts over the years. These include my late cousin Spence; my cousins Barry, Ricky, Mike, and Stan; my brothers-in-law Don and Tommy; my son, Ronnie; my nephews Dustin, Tommy, and Hunt; and my close friends Larry, Brian, Mark, David, Willard, Scott, Artie, Greg, Carl, Jim, Craig, Jeff, Grover, Frank, Jack, Andy, and Mack. To all of you, I wish to thank you for some of the most wonderful experiences of my life. In your own ways, you all played a role in the development of this book.

I want to express a special thank-you to my aunt Mary Carolyn McClanahan; my late uncle Loyal and uncle Hunt McClanahan, my late aunt Anne Stutts; my late aunt JoAnn McClanahan; my late cousin Spence McClanahan; my cousins Barry Stutts, Ricky Stutts, Mike Stutts, and Stan McClanahan; and my friends Donnie Faulk, Larry Bell, Artie Slinker, Greg Slinker, Jack and Andy Gannon, and David Dick. You all made your properties available to me for deer hunting over the years and I am indebted to you all for all the experience I received as a result of being able to hunt on your properties.

I must acknowledge all of those wonderful people who so graciously contributed their beautiful whitetail and related photos to this publication: Peter Eades, nature photographer, for providing this book's cover photo, as well as others; Mary Morris, wildlife photographer, for her contribution of most of the full-page photos, as well as others; Dennis Goldsby, for permission to use photos from his website www.tndeer.com; Howard J. Lux (Wildlife Buffet), for his photo contributions to the "Food Sources" chapter of the book; Kevin Lammi, nature photographer (Northland Images); Linda Townsend; Eric Van Eck; Matthew Choate; Larry Bell; Kurt Welch (The Deer Domain); Larry Gilbert; Jack Izard (The Deer Domain); Jerry Vanis (The Deer Domain); Rick Long (Whitetail Hunter); CamTrakker ("The Big Buck Surveillance System"); and Trailcam.com.

My appreciation goes out to all of the other people who contributed photos or photography work to the book: my wife, Linda Townsend; my daughter, Melanie Townsend; my mother, Mary Brown

Townsend; my aunt Mary Carolyn McClanahan; my late uncle Loyal McClanahan; my late cousin Spence McClanahan; and Barry Stutts, Ricky Stutts, Mike Stutts, Anne Stutts, Jerri Stutts, Kathie McClanahan, Tommy McClanahan, Tammy Halfpap, Tommy Parker, Cindy Parker, Canita Campbell, Artie Slinker, Greg Slinker, Larry Bell, Steven Graham, and Jim Davis.

I want to say thank you to Fred Halfpap and Gary Benton for their generous input and all their technical assistance to this publication's website: www.awdhr.com.

My sincere appreciation to my friends Don and Helen League. Don represents USGS and was solely responsible for my acquiring permission to use information of theirs for the chapter "Aging Your Deer."

Thanks to Chris Tonkinson (Boone & Crockett Club and Pope & Young Club) and Glen Hisey (Pope & Young Club) for permission to use the actual score charts and adjoining instruction sheets.

To all the family, friends, and associates who have expressed an interest and encouragement over the past few years since the inception of the idea for this book, I say thank you.

Photo © by Mary Morris

CONTENTS

PREFACE

The original idea for this book was to attempt to lay down guidelines or helpful tips for young or inexperienced hunters. By inexperienced, I don't mean just hunters who occasionally go deer hunting, but also those who actually go a great deal but are fairly unsuccessful. I know from experience that a large number of hunters go into the woods with no real knowledge of what to look for or where to go. Some of them figure that the deer live in the woods, so "I'll go into the woods and shoot one." Whitetail deer hunting is a great deal more complicated than that. Over the years, I've been fortunate enough to harvest some nice deer, but I learned a long time ago that there is a big difference in being a successful deer hunter and being a big trophy buck hunter. To be a trophy buck hunter, you must spend a great deal of time and money on that one buck. Unless you harvest him by accident by being in the right place at the right time, you have to do a great deal of homework for that one particular buck. All trophy buck hunters first became successful deer hunters. Now, I have never had the time or money necessary to be a trophy buck hunter. My idea of being a successful deer hunter is to be able to put as much venison as I want on the table each year for my family while maintaining a good sense of deer management and abiding by all state laws and good hunting ethics. I truly love the venison almost as much as the actual hunt. There are certain deer to harvest and certain deer not to harvest, and the information in this book will explain all of this. If you are not a veteran deer hunter, begin by just trying to become a good, successful deer hunter. Concentrate on the trophy bucks only after you get the knowledge under your belt. That's where the information in this book comes in. One of the quickest ways for a new—or just an unlucky—deer hunter to get discouraged and quit deer hunting all together is to go several times and not see deer. If you go deer hunting and at least see deer most of the time, then you are doing certain things right, and sooner or later you will see a buck. Being able to see deer when you go deer hunting will keep you motivated until you begin harvesting them. This book contains hundreds of helpful tips to help you do just that. I have tried to cover, at least to some degree, everything from planning your first hunt of the year to actually preparing the venison for the table (along with twenty-five great venison recipes for you to try). As you are reading this book, keep in mind that what may work for certain hunters doesn't necessarily work for all hunters. Every hunter has his or her own bag of tricks, and you have to fill your trick bag with those that work for you. This book contains all of the tricks you'll need to become a consistently successful whitetail deer hunter.

The information found in this book is based on my forty years of whitetail deer–hunting experience as well as on my own research. This information is intended as guidelines to help get you on the path to learning all you can about the whitetail deer. You must realize that the whitetail will change his habits, do the unexpected, and flat-out surprise you. He is going to respond to all types of condition changes, and you will be left trying to figure out what changed and how he reacted to it in order to outsmart him. It is my sincere wish that all who read this book will feel that it was a worthwhile experience.

INTRODUCTION

For as long as I can remember, my favorite place to be has been in the woods. I enjoy the solitude, the peace and quiet, and the sounds that only the woods reveal when you are truly open to your environment. I love the absence of all of the sounds of the city: traffic, machines running, horns blowing, people shouting. Getting away from civilization makes me appreciate sounds like dewdrops falling sharply from leaves as a gray squirrel jumps from one limb to another on his route to begin his day. Or maybe it's the rustling of a chipmunk in the leaves just before he dashes into a hollow log and then peeps out of a knothole that gets my attention. I have learned to love the sounds of a flock of wild turkey flying down from their roost and the sounds they make to one another as they calmly feed through the woods; I love the sounds made by a covey of quail as they peacefully feed their way across the forest floor. Even the woodpeckers add to the harmony of it all as they inspect the various trees. Occasionally I may hear a pack of coyotes on a distant ridge just before daybreak, exposing just how real and wild it all can be in the woods. I love to watch and listen to all the different types of birds that are constantly around me, seemingly with no fear at all. Often, as I walk to my stand before daylight, a lonely old owl will let me know that I may fool the deer, but I haven't fooled him.

One of the most exciting sounds you can hear, however, is the sound of a whitetail buck calling from a distant hillside, or the sound of his approaching footsteps in the leaves—or perhaps the clashing around of his horns on the surrounding limbs and small trees. On a cold, brisk November morning, on the fringes of a secluded field next to a woodline, suddenly you see a flash of white or a glare in the sunlight. It's a big old whitetail buck with his breath steaming from his nostrils and his rack and body shimmering in the sunshine. You are all too aware of just how alert he is, ready to take flight in a second's notice at the first hint of danger. If the sight of something like this doesn't get your heart to racing and get you hooked on hunting for the whitetail deer, then this book just isn't for you. This book is a stepping stone on your pathway to learning all you possibly can about the whitetail deer, and it will make you much more qualified and successful at hunting him. We will never learn all there is to know about the whitetail deer. I do feel very strongly, however, that the primary difference between a good, successful whitetail deer hunter and a poor one is directly related to the difference in the amount of knowledge they have about the animal versus the amount of knowledge they actually put into use. The more knowledge you absorb, retain, and put into play in your deer-hunting strategies, the more successful you will become. In an effort to be as thorough as possible in each chapter of this book, it was necessary to reemphasize certain information. Many aspects of the whitetail will apply to different chapters, so you will find various information in more than one chapter of the book for learning purposes. I felt this was advantageous for the total overall effect of the chapter—as well as because repetition is a very effective way of learning.

SECTION I

◆

BEFORE THE HUNT

Photo © by Mary Morris

BEFORE THE HUNT

Many years ago—more than I care to remember—I went on my first deer hunt. I was 18, and my uncle was introducing my cousins and me to whitetail deer hunting. Until he brought up the idea, none of us had ever even seen a whitetail deer in the wild, that we could recall—naturally, we knew what they looked like, but we had just never crossed paths with one.

It was a weekend hunt, and I was using a borrowed rifle. It was midwinter and very cold, and I wore everything I could put on. The stand that my uncle had picked out for me was several hundred yards away from our camp, and my uncle failed to tell me to take my time getting there. Being excited about the hunt and anxious to shoot my first deer, I was in a hurry. I was in such a hurry to arrive at my stand on time that I was quite wet from sweat when I did get there. I guess I must have thought the deer would be at the stand waiting on me. In spite of how fast I was walking, I still happened to notice a section of corrugated tin that had blown off a nearby old barn, most covered by the tall grass in the field.

I finally arrived at the stand, soaking wet, and climbed up into it. I tried to get situated before daylight. I remember feeling good about not being too cold, but failing to associate this false feeling of warmth with the speedy walk to get to my stand. The longer I sat there, the colder I got, and my wet clothes became a real burden. What I had hoped would be a wonderful experience was turning out to be one of my most miserable experiences to that point. I was shaking and moving around, trying to stay warm, when suddenly I heard a single tap on metal followed by two more extremely quick taps. I sat there trying to figure out what this sound could have been when suddenly, the answer came to me.

I remembered the piece of tin partially hidden in the tall grass on my way to the stand. I visualized a deer walking in the tall grass and accidentally stepping on the tin. I figured the deer, after stepping on the tin with the first foot (thus the first beat on the metal), would quickly kick himself away or off of the tin with his two hind legs (thus the next two beats on metal). With this theory in mind, I decided to remain very alert and watch in the direction of the tin. About five minutes later, a nice seven-point buck walked up out of a creek bed on the far side of the field in the direction of the old barn and the tin. When I spotted him, I froze in amazement and was surprised that I had been able to perfectly read the situation. I'm not boasting, but merely pointing out a perfect example of beginner's luck. The buck turned broadside to me and basically posed for the shot. I harvested my first buck and got hooked on whitetail deer hunting for life at the same moment, although I didn't realize it then. I was so excited about my first buck that I lost the cold feeling. This first hunt meant more to me than I could ever express, then or now, and was truly one of those golden moments in my life. I wish this type of success to all new beginner deer hunters, so that they may become lifetime whitetail deer hunting enthusiasts as I have. Everyone needs a release, something that takes him or her away from the everyday grind of work and responsibilities, and whitetail deer hunting has been my escape. In these first few chapters, I relate many of the concerns you must deal with prior to the actual hunt—things you should do from the time you decide to go deer hunting until you actually leave with your weapon to hunt.

Photo © by Mary Morris

Photo © by Mary Morris

PREPARATION FOR THE HUNT

I get a tremendous amount of pleasure out of merely preparing for my hunts. I start focusing my attention on hunting season several months ahead of time so I don't forget anything. There are certain things that have to be done far ahead of the actual season, like applying for vacation time, leasing a piece of hunting property, doing substantial preseason scouting, and getting permission to hunt a certain area before someone else beats you to it. I think through a typical weekend hunting trip and try to imagine every situation that could arise. This process offers me the least degree of likelihood that I will forget something. Keep in mind that it is much better to have something along that you don't need than it is to need something that you don't have. You will develop your own method of getting ready for a hunt and beginning organizing this process, as I have done. If you wait until the last minute and merely throw things together, you not only will be half-prepared, but also will probably enjoy the trip less as a result.

I use two standard lists each time I begin to prepare for my trip. One list is the basic items that I need for a one-day outing, while the other is everything I like to carry with me for the entire trip. Both of these lists are found in chapter 3. If you plan to be gone for the entire weekend or longer, you will also want to make up a grocery list and plan each meal out on paper.

Be sure that all of your clothing is cleaned, descented, and placed in plastic bags, ready for hunting. Know what the weather forecast is, so you can plan to dress accordingly. It's better to have too many clothes than not enough, and essential to have the right type of clothing to accommodate the weather. It's important to wear fresh, clean clothes out each time you go on a hunt—the longer you wear the clothing, the more your scent saturates the fabric.

It is extremely important to sight in your weapon and know how it performs. You must have it clean and in perfect, working order so that it will be a mere extension of yourself when the time comes. Bring along enough ammo, arrows, and other weapon accessories as needed. You should focus a great deal of attention in this area.

Check all of your hunting and camping equipment to be sure that it is all in good working order. Your deer stand is one of the most important pieces of equipment—make sure it is safe to use at all times. Keep your cutting tools (knives, hatchets, axes, saws, etc.) sharp and cleaned. Be sure that light sources (flashlights, lanterns, etc.) are working properly, and that you have extra fuel and batteries. If you plan to camp and do some cooking, your cooking stove will need to be cleaned and ready for service.

If you have a hunting camper like I do, be sure to stock it with all the items you feel you will need throughout the season. Naturally, you will restock food and clothing from hunt to hunt, but many things should be available all season as you need them.

My home away from home during deer season.

Service up your four-wheeler and get it ready. If you use one, you know what a valuable piece of equipment it can be to a deer hunter.

A very valuable piece of equipment to a deer hunter.

You will need to remember certain items that may be necessary should you kill a deer. These include a carcass net, rubber gloves, an ice chest, ice, reuseable plastic storage bags, trash bags, rope, and a gambrel stick (or a piece of a tree limb between the two hind legs to hang your deer).

Take whatever precautions are necessary to be sure that your vehicle is ready for the trip. Be sure that it is serviced and fueled, that the tires have been checked, and that everything is in good working order. You don't want an automobile problem to ruin your trip. I drive a four- wheel-drive vehicle, but I still carry a come-along and chain and a couple of boards in case I should get my vehicle stuck. You should definitely do this if you don't drive a four-wheel-drive vehicle.

Make any necessary phone calls to the landowner or farmer to make them aware of your plans to be on their property on a specific date, and let them know approximately what time you plan to arrive. You must have a clear understanding with them about your hunting plans on their property, based on their restrictions or requirements.

Whatever you do, don't forget your license and any other necessary permission slips or permits. You certainly don't want to shoot a

nice deer and then find out that you left your license at home, especially if you live a great distance away from where you hunt.

If there are things at home or work that need to be taken care
of while you are away on your trip, be sure to make the necessary
arrangements to have these taken care of. This could be something as
simple as having your pets looked after or something as important as
mailing a bill or picking up a loved one at the airport. You may need
to leave a key out for the neighbor to be able to get inside to water
your plants or feed your fish or cat. Think all of these things through
so that your mind will be free to concentrate on your hunt.

If you hunt alone, always try to have some type of emergency plan
worked out with your spouse or some other loved one in case you
don't show up or call by a certain time. It's a good idea to have a cel-
lular phone with you (turned off) in case of an emergency. It's also
good to have a clear understanding of the route you normally take to
wherever you hunt, so that, if necessary, someone can know where
to start looking for you. It's also a good idea for a loved one to have
a general knowledge of the area you hunt in order to be able to find
you in case of an emergency. Always carry a first-aid kit with you on
your trip.

Some people need certain prescription medication, eyeglasses,
insulin shots, certain foods, and so on. Include these items when
going on your trip, or you'll just have to go back and get them.

Photo © by Mary Morris

Photo © by Mary Morris

PROPER HUNTING ATTIRE

Place a great deal of importance on your hunting clothes and all other articles of clothing you should have with you on your trip. If you forget to take something you need, your trip could be ruined. Since you must dress for comfort, think through an entire day of hunting and night in camp, and then the total trip in general. Imagine yourself in each hypothetical situation, including rain, cold weather, warm weather, and even snow, depending on the time of year. You must dress for comfort, so with each hunt, you must evaluate potential weather changes in order to be ready for them. For example, if you anticipate rain, be sure to have rain gear along; if you expect the weather to start out cold and then warm up, don't wear long johns, but do wear extra outer clothing that can be discarded if you get hot. The temperature could always drastically change, or a sudden storm could come up, so you need to be prepared. In addition to weather changes, you must also dress for quietness and camouflage or concealment. Try not to wear any type of clothing that is abrasive or that will make a lot of noise when you move in the woods.

Wear good camouflage—preferably mixed patterns—to break up your image. Mixed patterns help you blend into the surroundings better. There are certain things not to do, such as wearing fall patterns in the dead of winter when all of the leaves are off the trees, or wearing snow camo if there is no snow. You must be sure not to wear or carry anything shiny that will reflect the sunlight; this is a dead giveaway to a deer. If your weapon has any type of finish that will reflect the sunlight, use a gun sock, camouflage wrapping, or some other type of camouflage to conceal it. Dress to fit in with where you will actually be hunting and the cover that will be around you.

There is no limit to the amount of money you can spend on camouflaged clothing. You have options such as leafy wear for a 3D effect, fleecewear for added warmth and quietness, Scent-Loc clothing to help contain your body odor, and many, many different fall and winter camo patterns for mixing and matching. There are all types of blaze orange patterns, snowsuits, and all of the above in insulated or noninsulated jackets, pants, coveralls, shirts, caps, and so on. I recommend that you purchase your camouflage clothing a size or two larger than normal so that over the years of normal wear and numerous washings, they will still fit. This way, when you start adding that middle-age spread, or if you need to add an extra layer of clothing underneath, you won't feel confined.

When you are selecting your outer wear, such as your heavy jackets, parkas, coveralls, winter caps, and so on, consider what they contain to keep you dry and warm. While Thinsulate is probably the preferred choice for warmth since it is one-and-a-half to two times warmer than down and other polyester insulations when equal thicknesses are compared, there are other options to consider for keeping dry. Some are quieter than others—check them out carefully. Gore-Tex is probably my favorite because of my style of hunting, although saddle cloth is quieter and takes advantage of waterproof laminates to ward off moisture.

The clothing you take along for warm-weather hunting should include a hunting shirt and trousers for each day you plan to hunt, along with underwear and socks for each day, plus one extra change in case you get one set wet. Take two or three caps depending on how long you plan to hunt. You should have a couple pairs of camouflage gloves and a camouflaged mask unless you prefer to use camo paint for your face and hands. You should take along a lightweight pair of coveralls and a lightweight jacket, and I usually throw in one heavy shirt or jacket in case the weather should take a drastic turn. Be sure to carry your rain gear and an extra pair of hunting boots in addition to the ones you normally wear in case you get one pair wet.

If you are packing for a cold-weather hunt, take the same items that you would take on a warm-weather hunt, plus a pair of long johns for each day, as well as an extra pair in case you get one wet. You will want your heavier shirts and trousers plus a few good, warm sweatshirts; heavy coveralls and heavy jackets; two or three winter caps; a couple pairs of good, heavy, insulated gloves; and a good, warm facemask. Take your heaviest winter boots, as well as an extra pair in case you need it. Always have at least one pair of wet-weather boots along. Be sure to take enough thin cotton socks and thick wool socks.

Be sure to wash your clothing in an unscented detergent. There are many unscented household detergents on the market that seem to work just fine, in addition to specialized hunting soaps. Don't forget to wash the small items, such as your facemask, gloves, and cap. After washing all of your hunting clothes thoroughly, place them in a plastic bag with some type of cover scent to give them a natural odor such as might be found in the area where you will be hunting. Depending on where I will be hunting, I might use an earth scent, some pine needles, or oak leaves. You can use anything to help naturalize the odor to the area where you will sit and wait for your deer. Remember to wash off the bottoms of your hunting boots with an unscented soap; after they have dried, apply a cover scent to the boots' bottoms. Each time you go back into your hunting camp, you will probably pick up foreign scents on the soles of your boots. Kerosene, Coleman fuel, cigarettes, tobacco, and any other things that may end up on the ground in camp that we may not think about are likely to end up on our boots. Always try to clean the bottoms of your boot soles before each hunt unless you pull them off as you leave the woods and wait until you reenter the woods to put them back on. Some hunters do this regularly, but doing so has always been difficult for me to remember, so I just try to remember to clean mine. Never wear your hunting boots in any situation other than when you are actually hunting. For example, don't wear them to the gas station, where you walk on concrete that has had gasoline and other substances spilled on it.

Take more than one cap with you on the trip so you can wear a clean cap when the other accumulates too much odor. I like to change caps at least daily, because humans perspire a great deal through our heads. In warm weather, wear lightweight caps to help reduce the perspiration through your scalp. In extremely cold weather, wear warm, waterproof caps to protect you from the elements. I prefer a Gore-Tex/Thinsulate combination: the Thinsulate keeps me warm, and the Gore-Tex keeps me dry. I have earflaps on my winter caps for when the weather becomes too unbearable, but normally I do not use them; I sacrifice a little comfort in this area for the additional hearing capability. I don't like to compromise my sense of hearing, and I recommend this approach to anyone else who can deal with his or her ears being exposed.

Wear a thin pair of cotton socks under a thick pair of wool socks inside a very good pair of cold-weather boots. I prefer Sorrel boots, the warmest boots I have ever used. They are fairly lightweight, and their rubber soles, with a thick, padded insert, are rated for 100° below zero. For years, my feet got cold—and if my feet got cold, then the rest of me was uncomfortable, too. It's hard to stay warm when any part of you is cold. If your feet are cold or wet, you will be fidgeting around in an effort to stay warm and not be able to concentrate on your hunting. Since I discovered the Sorrel boots, I have had no problem staying warm each year. I cannot emphasize enough the importance of a very good pair of cold-weather boots. This is one item where you should spare no expense. If you are so cold that you have to fidget around to stay warm, you may as well have stayed in hunting camp for all the good you will do hunting. During bow season, when the weather is warm, you will want to wear a lightweight pair of hunting boots with a lightweight pair of cotton socks. There are pros and cons for rubber and leather. You should use what you feel works best for you based on your own body chemistry. Some people's feet sweat more than others, and what works for some won't necessarily work for all. Some argue that rubber boots hold odor and that each step forces the odor out the top of the boot, making rubber boots more likely to give your odor away to the deer. Others say leather boots absorb much of the odor to pass on to the deer: the more the leather absorbs, the stronger the odor the boot puts off. I personally prefer a lightweight leather boot for warm-weather hunting, because my feet tend to sweat less in them, and because leather boots are generally more comfortable to walk in for long periods. Just always remember to use a good cover scent on your boots. What boots you choose to wear are entirely up to you.

At the end of hunting season, be sure to thoroughly wash all of your hunting clothes and put them away together in one place, simultaneously checking to see whether anything needs to be replaced or repaired. Well prior to next year's hunt, you will want to take care of anything in the way of clothing that needs to be purchased, repaired, or replaced.

Photo © by Mary Morris

HUNTING GEAR AND ACCESSORIES

Deer hunting, like anything else you do in life, requires a great deal of planning. Taking the time to sit down at the kitchen table or your office desk and make a list of everything you can imagine that you will need will pay off later. Mentally walk yourself through every aspect of your hunting trip, and as you do, note each item you see yourself needing. It's better to have more than you need than to not have something that you need very badly. Keep this list and reuse it year after year. You will gradually be adding items to the list, and eventually you'll have everything covered.

1. Every deer hunter should have his or her own personal list of gear and accessories to take along on his or her hunting trip. While many of these items are based on personal preferences, needs, and hunting techniques, there are several basic items that everyone should have along. Here are some things to be sure to have at your disposal if you are on a hunting trip lasting longer than a single day. The first list is compiled of items that you will want to take along with you into the field on your actual hunt.

   A. Your weapon and any necessary accessories: for example, your bow, mechanical release, tab, glove, bow string wax, ample supply of bolts or arrows properly matched to your bow, broadheads, and quiver. If you are muzzleloader hunting, you need your rifle, projectiles (balls, bullets, or sabots), powder, primer caps, primer cap dispenser, ball starter, and quick loads. You may need a ball puller (depending on what type of rifle you use), as well as any tools necessary to break the gun down in the field for an emergency cleaning and reload, shoulder strap, scope covers, gun sock, and a ramrod. If you are rifle hunting, you want your rifle, ammunition, a sling, scope covers, and a camouflaged gun sock.

B. Butt-pack (fanny-pack) or, depending on how many items you plan to take, backpack

C. Field glasses

D. Flashlight, a small spare light, and extra batteries

E. Sharp knife with a sturdy handle for field-dressing purposes

F. 25 to 30 feet of quarter-inch nylon cord or rope

G. Compass

H. License, kill tag, permission slips, maps, and so on

I. Small pair of pruning shears or small limb saw

J. Pair of rubber gloves

K. Plastic bags

L. Deer calls, rattle bag, or horns

M. Any scents or lures you choose to use

N. Camouflage gloves and facemask or camo paint

O. Safety belt or harness

P. Wind check dust or other means of checking the wind

Q. Toilet tissue

R. Any medically required items such as glasses, hearing aids, or medicine

S. Munchies, beverages, cough drops, lozenges, and so on

T. Whistle, in case of an emergency

U. Blaze orange tape or glow tacks for marking blood trails and other things

V. Mosquito headnet if weather is warm

W. Portable climbing stand for those spur-of-the-moment hunting situations

X. Miscellaneous things like unscented insect repellent, hand- or footwarmers, range-finder, game finder, small toolkit, small first-aid kit, poncho or rainsuit, small camera, snake chaps, snakebite kit, handy wipes, and so on

The following is a list of recommended items to have along on your camping trip that you will probably need but will not necessarily take into the field with you when you are actually hunting.

A. Means of cooking: camper with stove, Coleman or gas stove, grill for campfire, extra cooking fuel, and so on

B. Cooking paraphernalia: pans, plates, bowls, glasses, cups, forks, spoons, knives, butcher knife, spatula, coffeepot, and so on

C. Groceries: paper towels, toilet tissue, dishwashing liquid, bar soap, toothpaste, charcoal, starter fluid, ice, water, water dispenser, salt and pepper, any preferred spices for cooking, hot or mild sauce, steak sauce, butter, cooking oil, mayonnaise, mustard, coffee, cream, sugar, juices, soft drinks or other beverages, butt-pack items like munchies, food for quick meals and cooking meals, and so on.

D. Lanterns, flashlights, matches, and any other light source you prefer to take

E. Ice chests for keeping food cold, but also for if you kill a deer and the weather is too warm for the meat

F. Folding chairs or seats of some type

G. Foldout table of some type

H. Portable toilet seat

I. Tarp or rain-proof protection to cover camp area if not in a camper or tent

J. Zeroing-in items, such as targets, tape, or tacks to attach your target in place; sandbags; rifle rest of some type; ammunition or projectiles; adjustment tools; field glasses; spotting scope; and so on

K. Cleaning kit for weapon and plenty of cleaning rags and oil

L. Bedding, including pillow, sleeping bag, blankets, quilts, sheets, towels, and washcloths

M. Toiletries: toothbrush, hair brush or comb, cotton swabs, eyeglass cleaner, and so on

N. Knife-sharpening kit, sharpening stone, or tool

O. Firestarter logs in case the weather is wet and you want a fire of some type

P. Alarm clock with an extra backup alarm clock

Q. Extra batteries for any battery-operated item

R. Items for skinning your deer: gambrel stick, nylon rope, pulley, block and tackle, or some way to hang your deer for skinning purposes, a good skinning knife, a container for water to wash any hair or excess blood or dirt, trash bags to place the meat in to keep it clean, ice chest and ice to keep it cool until you can get it to a cooler

S. Butchering your deer is normally not done on the trip, but circumstances could necessitate this task, and it never hurts to be prepared: a good sharp butcher knife, smaller knife for cutting the meat away from the bone and trimming any unwanted fat, cutting board, small bone saw, plastic wrap, freezer wrap, and plastic bags (for storing your deer)

2. Place a great deal of importance on the quality of the hunting gear you invest in. If you choose the proper gear, you can get a lifetime of use out of much of it, especially if you take proper care of it. There is a wide variety of just about anything you might need in the way of gear, so you need to compare items and try to pick what will work best for you. Don't be afraid to take advantage of money-back guarantees and thirty-day free trials and, if something is not doing what it was designed and promised to do, to send it back for a full refund and try another. But don't fall for gimmicks—and ask a lot of questions about the item. If a bottle of deer scent states that it is 100 percent guaranteed to be pure doe-in-estrous urine, feel comfortable that it is what it is claimed to be and not from a herd of goats. Check the company out and find out if they have ever been

reported to BBB or consumer affairs. Ask other hunters about certain companies and products. Other hunters can be one of the best sources of all so long as you keep in mind that what works for some doesn't necessarily work for all.

3. Be totally familiar with your state's requirements concerning wearing blaze orange during hunting season. There are many cases of people getting accidentally shot that could have been prevented had they been wearing the required amount of blaze orange during hunting season. To find this information out, contact your state's wildlife resources agency or your game and fish department. Either of these agencies should be able to help you. The proper amount of blaze orange or reflective clothing is a must during gun season with as many hunters as there are in the woods these days—many of them inexperienced.

4. Use topography maps, aerial photographs, your own notes based on your scouting, and conversations with friends, hunters, farmers, landowners, and others. Speak with the fish and game department, wildlife resources agency, forestry services, and so forth about this year's hunt and any interesting property location. Study and cross-reference all of this material in an effort to select the best possible hunting locations. This briefcase or folder of information is a vital part of your hunting gear and should always be taken along on any hunt lasting longer than a single day.

5. Always keep your equipment in good, working order. Be sure to clean, oil, and adjust your equipment as often as necessary. There are many outdoor conditions that could affect your weapon, such as light moisture, fog, dew, drizzling rain, humidity, and dust, to name a few. If anything gets wet while you are out hunting, be sure to clean and oil it as soon as you get back to camp. Your weapons especially require a great deal of care, and what type of weapon you're using determines just how much care is involved. Muzzleloader rifles, for example, should be cleaned after each day's hunt and prepared for the next day's hunt. If you didn't fire it during the day, it's a good idea to go ahead and discharge it when you get back to camp

and clean it thoroughly. This way, the next morning, you can pop two or three caps to be sure it is clear and load a fresh, dry load of powder and ball or bullet, giving you more confidence in your weapon for the hunt. Keep your blade edges sharp and well oiled at all times. Your broadheads should be sharpened on a regular basis and only used with sharp blades. Be sure your flashlight has strong batteries so you don't get halfway to where you are going and run out of light. Take precautions to make sure that all screws, nuts, bolts, and other fasteners on your tree stand, bow, guns, and so on are all tight and safe to use. These are just a few examples of some of the attention you must devote to your equipment. Use common sense and read your instruction manuals for proper care and maintenance.

6. You can greatly improve your accuracy and overall enjoyment of the hunt by using a good scope on your rifle or muzzle-loader. There are many good scopes on the market, and you'll just have to experiment and research the best one for you. Some scopes have wide fields of view as opposed to the more standard circular fields, and some have a much clearer field of view than others. Some are more conducive to low-light situations than others. You may choose a variable scope with a manual power adjustment, or a fixed-power scope. If you still want the capability of open sights in a rare situation, you will need see-through mounts for your scope. Try to select a scope that is waterproof, fog-proof, and shock-proof. Be sure to add lens covers to your scope; for these, I suggest the flip-up type, which remain on your scope at all times. When you need to sight or shoot, you just flip the covers up and out of your field of view. When you purchase your scope, it is a good idea to take your rifle in and have them mount and boresight your scope for you unless you want to purchase a boresight yourself. The boresighting should get your first shot on the target so you can fine-tune the scope adjustment from there.

7. It is important to have a sling on your weapon for more than one reason. If you shoot a deer and have to drag it out, you will need to be able to throw your weapon over your shoulder, leaving both hands free. The more you walk throughout the

day's hunt, the heavier your weapon becomes, and the more you depend on your sling. In some cases, the sling also helps with shot placement.

8. Always know how your weapon shoots before taking it on a hunt. Spend whatever time with it in the field necessary to become comfortable with your own capability with it. Get it zeroed in as perfectly as you can, and then—only then—are you ready to take it on the hunt. Take all your weapons out prior to hunting season each year to check and see if they are still zeroed in from the previous year. I can't imagine sitting on a deer stand and having any confidence at all if I have not previously checked my weapon on the range or somewhere else suitable.

9. Certain weapons can be quite loud, and it is extremely important to soundproof them in every way possible. Some bows are bad about this, so the use of various materials—Velcro, cloth camouflage tape, rubber, and so on—can quiet them down, as can oiling or tightening certain screws. As you make your draw, as you make your release, and as you shoot the weapon, try to concentrate on any noise to determine where it is coming from. Once you locate the problem, try to use whatever means necessary to silence the problem. A gun sock will muffle most of the sounds that your gun makes, since most of these noises are due to hitting the rifle against another object; the gun sock will cushion the hit and quiet it down. Your tree stand can be very noisy, especially during setup or takedown. Practice putting it up and taking it down to get so proficient at it that you can even do it in the dark (as you will often have to) and to pinpoint excessive noise locations. Apply whatever materials necessary to wherever necessary on the stand to solve the problem. When you have your stand packed up and on your back, be sure it doesn't rattle.

10. It is very important to practice with the same projectiles that you plan to hunt with. Many hunters practice shooting their bow with field points to keep their broadheads sharp for hunting, but the arrows or bolts will fly differently with broadheads

than with field points. Always practice with the same broadheads that you plan to hunt with. The same strategy applies to ammunition: be sure to zero in or check your weapon with the same type and grain of ammunition that you plan to use in the field. Any deviation can make a difference and cost you that buck. When muzzleloader hunting, be sure to use the same number of grains of powder that you practice with or zero your gun in with, as well as the same grain and type of ball or sabot or whatever you will be using in the field. You should check your weapon far ahead of opening day of deer season to be able to solve any problems you might have with the weapon. If a part is worn or broken or defective for any reason, you need time to repair or replace it before you need it for the hunt.

11. Prior to hunting in the rain, take some preventive maintenance steps, such as lubricating any movable parts on your weapon. When you are hunting in the rain, take precautions to keep your weapon as dry as possible. Keep the muzzle pointed toward the ground to try to keep water from going down the barrel. If you are muzzleloader hunting, it is imperative that you keep your powder dry; otherwise, you are just wasting your time, since wet powder won't ignite. Keep your quick loads and powder dispenser in a resealable plastic bag to keep them dry, and do the same for your primer caps and projectiles. If you expect to be hunting in the rain, take along a lightweight camo rain poncho to hold over your gun to keep it dry, or tuck your gun up under your normal rain gear—but keep your powder dry. Keep your bowstring waxed and any movable parts well lubricated.

12. If you build a permanent stand between two or more trees, when the wind blows, the stand may rub against one or more of the trees, drawing attention to you. If you build permanent stands, try to keep the boards far enough apart to prevent them from rubbing. If necessary, use pieces of rubber between the stand and the tree itself and between any joints that might make noise. This potential noise factor is one disadvantage to building permanent stands.

HUNTING AND OUTDOORS INVOLVEMENT

One of the reasons we hunt is because we are outdoor enthusiasts and just plain love to be outdoors. We enjoy associating with other people who share this same feeling. There are many outdoor activities that satisfy our outdoor desires. Many of us prefer to hunt and fish, just as others like to play outdoor sports, camp, hike, cycle, ride horses, climb mountains, and so on. We hunters need to practice what we preach and not only get involved in hunting activities ourselves, but also try to get others to share our love of hunting and get involved. We need to get our youth involved to a much greater degree than we have in the past. They need to be formally and accurately

Good friends and family on a successful hunt. How much better can it get?

introduced to proper gun and archery safety. They need to be properly taught the basic fundamentals of good marksmanship with guns and bows. There are not enough activities to guide youths in this direction. They need to know about our forefathers and their struggles for survival.

Try to stay tuned into your state's wildlife management programs, especially those programs that affect the game that you love to hunt each year. State wildlife management programs are constantly being modified and upgraded to the benefit of the game as well as the hunter. There are many organizations out there that are working for the benefit of the game as well as the hunter, whether directly or indirectly. These organizations include local state wildlife resources agencies, fish and game departments, the Quality Deer Management Association, Ducks Unlimited, the National Rifle Association, the National Wild Turkey Federation, Quails Unlimited, Doves Unlimited, National Wildlife Rehabilitators, and others. Do your part to support these organizations by joining those you can, and encourage others to do so. They are out there working for us, and need all the support we can give them.

Many states host a whitetail/turkey show or exhibit of some type each year. In Tennessee, it is called the Volunteer State Hunting Classic and is held one weekend a year. I have been attending for several years now and feel that it is a great opportunity for serious deer hunters to stay tuned into current technology in the field of whitetail deer and turkey hunting. There are manufacturers of all of the latest products available on the market, as well as a variety of seminars that offer a great deal of excellent knowledge on the subject of hunting the whitetail deer and wild turkey. There is always a great deal of information available on other types of big game hunting, too. Many outfitters and guide services set up booths or displays at these shows. There are competition archery shoots, trophy mount contests and displays, national trophy buck exhibits, outdoor photography contests, and a great deal more for the entire family. On top of all this, you also get an opportunity to talk deer hunting to a wide variety of other hunters and speakers. You can certainly learn a great deal if you apply yourself and take advantage of what is available to you.

Find out if your state offers an all-women outdoor conference or something similar each year, as Tennessee does. This conference is strictly for ladies interested in outdoor activities such as hunting, fishing, camping, map reading, compass reading, wild game cooking, canoeing, outdoor photography, bird watching, and much more, and is put on by the Tennessee Wildlife Resources Agency. My wife has been attending this for the last few years and gets excited about it each year. She enjoys it very much and has made a lot of new friends as a result. If your state does not offer this type of conference, find out who to talk to in hopes of getting one started in your own state.

My wife, partner, and best friend on one of our outings.

Check to see if your state offers a good hunter safety program for young hunters. This is one of the best ways I know to familiarize new young hunters with all of the safety aspects of hunting with a weapon in the great outdoors. They also learn about good hunting ethics and how to hunt responsibly, with a strong emphasis on firearm safety. The things that our youths learn from us and from programs such as this will impact their lives for all of their hunting years and hopefully prolong the number of years they will get to enjoy hunting.

Ronnie and Stephanie with a show of success.

If your state has a juvenile hunt each year set aside just for youths, get involved to the point of taking one of your own kids, or if you do not have kids yourself, take another less fortunate youth on this hunt. In Tennessee, the youths must first go through the hunter safety program before they can acquire a license. This hunt is strictly for young hunters, and even though an adult must accompany them, no one else is allowed to hunt during this period, just the youths.

Get involved in juvenile hunts for the benefit of youths.

Get involved in your state Hunters for the Hungry program and encourage others to do the same. This is a way that we hunters can contribute to those less fortunate than we are, and it's also a tax deduction for you.

My late cousin Spence and I with meat for the hungry.

If you own property of your own or have a close relationship or influence with someone who does, implement a wildlife management program on this property to help improve the quality of the wildlife or deer in the area. There are many good programs available and companies to check with for this endeavor. Your own state wildlife association would be helpful with advice in this area, as would the Quality Deer Management Association. Refer to chapter 16, on deer management.

My cousin Rick plants a new food plot for the deer.

Photo © by Mary Morris

CAMOUFLAGE

The whitetail deer has three extremely powerful senses, not the least of which is his keen sense of sight. It is very difficult to fool the whitetail deer, but one of the best tools we have to combat this sense is good camouflage. In order to combat his other senses, we must deal with the sight problem. If we can at least keep ourselves concealed from his vision, we can focus more attention on combat-

ing his keen senses of smell and hearing. There are many companies manufacturing camouflage clothing and many other camouflage items, right down to your weapon itself. The camo that you select is a personal preference, but some strategy should be used in your selection. Going deer hunting without the proper degree of camouflage is almost pointless. I say *almost* because you could get lucky—but the odds are against you. You have to blend into your surroundings in every way possible.

You want to blend into your area as much as possible through the use of good camouflage clothing on all parts of your body. Some hunters prefer camouflage paint on

Your camo should help you blend into your surroundings.

their face and hands, while others, including myself, prefer camo gloves and a camo face mask or net.

The camouflage that you select should blend into the surroundings based on the time of year and the terrain that you hunt in. If you are hunting in early fall, such as at the beginning of bow season, there is still a lot of foliage, so you need a lot of greens and browns. In mid-winter, when all the leaves are off the trees, the woods appear more black and gray. If you are hunting in an area with a lot of snow, you want some type of snow camo. It is good to mix and match camo patterns, and by doing so, you break up your silhouette even more than by just using the same camouflage.

The proper choice of camouflage is extremely important.

Be sure that every part of your body and anything you carry into the field with you is camouflaged with some type of camo pattern. If something you take with you is not camouflaged, at least be sure that it does not reflect sunlight or stand out in a way that would attract a deer's attention. Be aware of the fact that rifle scopes, prescription glasses, jewelry, and other such items can reflect the sunlight, calling attention to you and alerting the deer. Anything that shines will be visible for a great distance.

If the barrel or other metal portions of your rifle, muzzleloader, bow, or shotgun have a sheen to them, use a gun sock or camo wrapping to cover any shiny parts.

There are a large number of camouflage manufacturers and many more camo patterns available. Try to select a pattern and style that is quiet, durable, and compatible with the area that you plan to hunt to offer you the greatest degree of concealment and comfort. Be careful not to select something that will not blend into your surroundings and thus make you stand out to a deer.

Your rain gear should also fit the above requirements. It is a good idea to have a lightweight camo poncho that you can roll up and put in your pack for those days when rain is only a possibility.

In addition to your clothing and weapon, be sure that your stand and any accessories that go with it are also properly camouflaged. Just remember that you want to keep hidden from the deer everything that you take into the woods or field.

Use the woods, trees, and foliage to your best advantage in addition to your own personal camouflage. Set up your stand in such a way as to use your personal camouflage in harmony with the natural camouflage.

Strive to become one with your surroundings.

Wherever possible, place your stand on a tree with multiple trunks, or climb up to a point on your tree where the limbs help to conceal your presence.

Pay close attention to the background or the area behind you so that it does not highlight your presence. Remember that you want to blend in, or "not be there," so to speak.

Let your background determine your camo whenever possible.

Here are some examples of various camouflage patterns that are available from many sources. Many of these patterns are very similar, so you need to use quality comparisons. These various camos apply to different types of terrain that you will be hunting in at different times of the year.

Photo © by Mary Morris

SAFETY

It doesn't matter what type of activity you are doing: you should always try to be as safe as possible while doing it. There are certain activities, hobbies, sports, jobs, and so on that are much more dangerous and more likely to cause you physical harm than others. Whitetail deer hunting, or any other type of hunting for that matter, requires a weapon of some sort, and any weapon requires total awareness of weapon safety. You must place safety above all else when doing anything that could cause harm, and any type of weapon can cause harm. There are many aspects of hunting that require your utmost attention to safety at all times. Whether you are handling your weapon, climbing into a tree stand, walking through snaky or dangerous terrain, or building a camp fire, you must think safety at all times.

Keep safety at the top of your list of priorities. Safety first is and always will be your best policy. You should get into the habit of focusing on the safety aspect of anything that you do when you are hunting, but especially when you are whitetail deer hunting.

Even though I prefer to hunt alone most of the time because I tend to have better luck this way, it is definitely safer to have a hunting buddy along in case something should happen and you require help. You could fall from your stand and break a bone, get snakebit, have a heart attack or suffer some other illness or condition, have a vehicle breakdown, or experience any number of other things that might cause you to require help. If you don't have a hunting buddy along, make sure that someone knows where you plan to hunt so that if

Good friends can add a great deal of enjoyment to your hunt, as well as an element of safety.

something were to happen, they would know where to come looking for you.

Always bring certain medical items on the hunting trip with you. Take your standard first-aid kit, including some fine-pointed tweezers, antiseptic, and handy wipes, in addition to any special medicine you may require, such as heart medication, insulin, and any other necessary pills. Take an extra pair of glasses or contacts in case yours get broken, as well as a snakebite kit, and anything else that specifically applies to your personal health or safety.

It is extremely important to learn your hunting area well so that you don't have to worry about ever getting lost. Learn the general structure of the area, such as where the old logging roads are and how they lie in relation to direction. Locate the water sources, food sources, bluffs, exceptionally large trees, old and dead trees, power line clearings, fences, and anything else that would serve as a landmark to reorient you should you get lost. Familiarize yourself with the boundaries of the property you have permission to hunt on. It is not safe to wander onto someone else's property while hunting, since someone else may be hunting and could accidentally shoot you. And, by respecting boundaries and property lines, you are helping hunter–landowner relations, too.

An old logging road not only adds to your hunting possibilities but also makes for a good landmark to help you keep your bearings.

Make a mental note of the location of any exceptionally large trees, especially oaks, in your hunting area, along with their exact locations.

Note the location of any farm road on the property as well as how it runs.

Be extremely careful during preseason scouting and bow season not to get snakebit. This is the time of year when snakes are active, and when you are most likely to encounter a poisonous snake. Keep a snakebite kit with you and wear a good pair of snake chaps when doing your scouting or walking to your stand during warm temperatures. When I do any scouting during this time of year, in addition to wearing snake chaps, I have a good long stick in my hand that I use to check any thick area in front of me before I step there. There are a variety of poisonous snakes whose home ranges vary throughout the United States. I wanted to include a photo of as many of these as I could to aid in the recognition of one, should a problem arise. I have also included valuable information necessary in case of an emergency situation or an actual snakebite. This information was taken from "The Snakebite Emergency" webpage, at www.xmission .com/ ~ gastown/herpmed/snbite.htm.

Pay attention to and remember the location of any cedar or pine groves in your hunting area, as well as any other refuge or sanctuary-type areas.

WHAT TO DO IF BITTEN BY A VENOMOUS SNAKE

1. Allow the bite to bleed freely for fifteen to thirty seconds.

2. Cleanse and rapidly disinfect the area with a Betadine pad (assuming you're not allergic to iodine or shellfish).

3. If you get bitten on the hand, finger, foot, or toe, wrap the leg or arm rapidly with a three- to six-inch ACE or crepe bandage past the knee or elbow joint, immobilizing it. Leave the area of fang marks open. Apply an extractor immediately if possible. Wrap the area no tighter than one would for a sprain. Make sure that pulses are present.

4. Apply a Sawyer Extractor until there is no more drainage from the fang marks. The extractor can be left in place for thirty minutes or more if necessary. It also aids in keeping the venom

from spreading by applying a negative pressure against the tissue where the venom was initially deposited and creating a gradient that favors the movement of venom toward the Sawyer's external collection cup.

5. If the extractor is not available, apply hard, direct pressure over the bite using a four- by four-inch gauze pad folded in half twice. Tape it in place with adhesive tape.

6. Soak the gauze pad in a Betadine solution if available, and if you're not allergic to iodines.

7. Strap the gauze pad tightly in place with adhesive tape.

8. Overwrap the dressing above and below the bite area with an ACE or crepe bandage, but not too tightly. Wrap it no tighter than you would for a sprain. Make sure pulses are present.

9. Wrap an ACE (elastic) bandage as tight as one would for a sprain but not too tight.

10. Check for pulses above and below the elastic wrap. If pulses are absent, the wrap is too tight, so unpin and loosen it.

11. Immobilize the bitten extremity with a splint if one is available.

12. If possible, try and keep the bitten extremity at heart level or in a gravity-neutral position. Raising it above the heart level can cause antivenin to travel into the body. Holding it down below heart level can increase swelling.

13. Go to the nearest hospital or medical facility as soon as possible.

14. Try and identify, kill, and bring along (if safe to do so) the offending snake. This is the least important thing you should do. Visual identification or description usually suffices, especially in the United States.

15. Bites to the face, torso, or buttocks are more of a problem. Disinfect and prep (shave) the area with a razor provided in the extractor kit. Use the extractor device until there is no further drainage possible, and then apply a pressure dressing with a gauze pad and tape. ACE/crepe bandaging can not be applied to such bites. A pressure dressing made of a gauze pad may help if a Sawyer Extractor is not available.

16. Antivenin is the only and best treatment for snakebites, and you must get as much as is necessary as soon as possible. Antivenin administration should not be delayed. Up to twenty vials may be needed to neutralize the effects of a rattlesnakebite and other crotalid venoms in North America. Children may need more than this, as envenomation is apt to be much more serious in a small person compared to a larger one.

WHAT NOT TO DO IF BITTEN BY A VENOMOUS SNAKE

1. Contrary to advice given elsewhere, do not permit the removal of pressure dressings, Sawyer, or an ACE bandage until you are at a facility ready and able to administer the antivenin. As soon as the dressings are released the venom will spread, causing the usual expected problems of venomous snakebites. The hospital must be prepared to administer the antivenin.
2. Do not eat or drink anything unless approved by medical sources.
3. Do not engage in strenuous physical activity.
4. Do not apply oral (mouth) suction to the bite.
5. Do not cut into or incise the bite marks with a blade.
6. Do not drink any alcohol or use any medication.
7. Do not apply hot or cold packs.
8. Do not apply a narrow, constrictive tourniquet such as a belt, necktie, or cord.
9. Do not use a stun gun or electric shock of any kind.
10. Do not remove dressings or elastic wraps until you arrive at the hospital and antivenin is available.
11. Do not waste time or take any risks trying to kill, bag, or bring in the offending snake.

* Remember that ACE or other wide bandaging must not be wrapped so tight as to cut off systemic venous or arterial circulation. Properly applied, such bandages will not compromise the systemic circulation.

WHAT TO TELL THEM AT THE HOSPITAL

1. Ask the staff to contact the poison control center immediately.
2. Locate the nearest antivenin resource. For North American species, call Wyeth at 610-688-4400.
3. Ask the staff to use physician consultants available through poison control.
4. Alternatively, contact snakebite consultants through the Jacobi Medical Center's (in Bronx, New York) emergency hotline at 1-718-430-6494.
5. Any questions may be directed to sgrenard@siuh.edu, or more expediently if necessary, to 718-227-6234, or beeper (emergencies only) 917-354-8289. After three tones, enter your callback number, being sure to include your area code and country code (if necessary); then push the pound sign.
6. Questions on snakebites may be posted to the Venom List. If you are not a member please, go to the Venom List website or write the moderator to be subscribed at venom@icomm.ca.

OTHER DOS AND DON'TS

1. Never hike, camp, work, or collect specimens in areas where there are venomous snakes unless accompanied by at least two companions: one to stay with the victim and the other to go get help. All parties should know what to do.
2. If you come across any snake in the field and don't know positively what it is or isn't, do not approach it, try to examine it, or photograph it (unless you have a long telephoto or zoom lens). Move away from it as expediently as possible.
3. If you work with venomous snakes in a public or private collection or in a museum or university laboratory, never open their cage without a companion nearby who is familiar with snakebite first aid.

4. A telephone with an outside line should always be located in the room or area where venomous snakes are located in case there is a need to call for help.

5. Never handle or attempt to handle venomous snakes without at least one trained companion present.

6. If you are not an experienced venomous snake handler, don't try handling or catching them without first obtaining extensive experience and training from someone who is trained.

7. If you maintain a private or laboratory collection of live, venomous species, keep all the cages under lock and key; rooms where such cages are located should have a double door and vestibule, be completely visible through glass paneling from the outside, and be off-limits to all but authorized personnel. If a snake appears missing from a cage, you may be able to locate it before entering the room in preparation of resecuring it. Such rooms should be completely sealed: no open or screened windows and no mouse holes or pipe holes through which a snake could escape. Sink drains should be also be capped and toilets, if present, always kept covered.

8. If you deal with venomous snakes, always make sure you have or know where to locate a supply of the specific antivenin for the species you are involved with.

PLEASE READ THE FOLLOWING DISCUSSION:

The Snakebite Emergency website suggests the use of containment or sequestration of injected venom at or near the bite site using broad (3–6" wide) compression bandaging such as a crepe or an ACE-type elastic bandage. This is the standard, worldwide-accepted first-aid treatment for bites by elapid snakes such as cobras, coral snakes, and many Australian species. This method has delayed the onset of serious snakebite symptoms for as long as twenty-four hours in Australia, where victims of deadly bites were that far from medical assistance. The method remains controversial in the United States, although a number of top snakebite experts have recently recommended its use in crotalid bites in printed references appearing in peer-reviewed journals.

Some feel that the use of containment or sequestration for certain types of North American pit viper (rattlesnake, moccasin and copperhead) bites increases the risk of disfiguring local tissue injury, which, while not necessarily life-threatening by itself, may necessitate skin grafts and extensive repair and treatment once the acute, life-threatening phase of the event has passed. Some experts feel the spread of venom to vital organs can be life-threatening and that you have no way of knowing how life-threatening a snakebite is in the first moments of the event. Therefore, users of this method must recognize that there is a trade-off.: containment as a life-saving measure at the risk of local tissue damage which while not necessarily life-threatening, could be disfiguring, painful and/or which could require prolonged and extensive follow-up treatment.

We urge readers who decide to use this method on any type of snakebite to do so as a life-or-death decision and to make this decision in recognition of the above information. In addition, some U.S. crotalid bites, particularly from large species, result in widespread damage to limbs even when bites were to digits on hands or feet. Thus the wide-area, low-pressure wraps can prevent the spread of venom and more widespread damage. Again, some experts feel that this increases the intensity of more localized damage.

While snakebite mortality without these dressings may be low, we have been appraised of too many unnecessary and tragic deaths and widespread disfigurement without its use and in general advocate its use when properly applied. Disfiguring local injury can be limited to a much smaller area compared to crotalid (pit-viper: rattlers, copperheads, cottonmouths) snakebites where this type of containment has not been used. Compression bandages are standard in Australia, but Australia sustains mostly elapid bites, although some have some serious local tissue or muscle effect as well. The venom of the king brown snake, a widely distributed species (Pseudechis australis) targets skeletal muscle tissue. Bites from cobras also have local effects through direct-acting cardiotoxins, so containment can save lives from bites by these snakes.

We strenuously oppose the offhanded dismissal of containment, which has been successfully used in Australia for nearly twenty years, by a few experts in the United States. Denial of the value of this method by these experts has resulted in the death of professional and hobbyist handlers of cobras and other elapid snakes who erroneously were led to believe that the method should not be used because of the incorrect claim that local tissue destruction is the only effect of containment. A number of advocates of the method have been bullied and threatened by a few others who are opposed to this treatment because they say there is no proof of its value in rattlesnakebites, but they can point to no studies which disprove its worth, whereas there have been safety animal studies done using diamondback rattler venom on pigs and monkeys demonstrating that containment prevents the spread of venom and suppresses widespread swelling.

VENOMOUS SNAKES OF THE UNITED STATES

EASTERN COTTONMOUTH, South Carolina.

FLORIDA COTTONMOUTH

FLORIDA COTTONMOUTH, northeast Florida

FLORIDA COTTONMOUTH, Appalachicola Forest

The cottonmouth snake is a type of water moccasin that lives in swampy areas of the Southeastern United States and parts of Illinois, Kansas, Oklahoma, and Texas.

SOUTHERN COPPERHEAD,
Georgia, Florida Panhandle

NORTHERN COPPERHEAD, Kentucky.
The northern copperhead ranges
from West Massachusetts to
Southern Illinois and Western
Tennessee, south to Alabama and
Georgia. It is more common in West
Virginia than the rattlesnake.

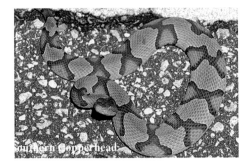

SOUTHERN COPPERHEAD,
South Carolina

BROAD BAND COPPERHEAD. The
broad band copperhead is located
in West and Central Texas through
North-Central Oklahoma, on up into
Kansas. Photo © by Jeremy Coates

TRANS-PECOS COPPERHEAD. The trans-pecos
copperhead ranges across the Trans-Pecos region
of West Texas from Val Verde and Crockett Counties
through the Big Bend and Davis Mountain region,
southward into the Mexican states of Coahuila and
Chihuahua.

ALBINO WESTERN DIAMONDBACK
RATTLESNAKE

EASTERN DIAMONDBACK
RATTLESNAKE, North Florida. The
eastern diamondback rattlesnake is
at home in the palmetto flatwoods
and dry pinelands of the South.

EASTERN DIAMONDBACK
RATTLESNAKE, Georgia

RED DIAMOND RATTLESNAKE,
Southern California. The red diamond
rattlesnake is limited to Baja and
Southern California; from Riverside/
San Bernardino area southwards in
Peninsular Ranges and on their desert
slope; inhabits brushy areas, often with
rocks. Photo by Chris Brown.

WESTERN DIAMONDBACK
RATTLESNAKE, Oklahoma. Luther
C. Goldman, U.S. Fish & Wildlife
Service. The western diamondback
rattlesnake ranges from the southern
tip of Nevada, across Arizona
south of the line from Lake Mead
and the Mongollon Rim, and into
Southeastern California, northeast
of Baja California. The range spans
eastward to Oklahoma, Arkansas,
and south to Central Mexico.

WESTERN DIAMONDBACK
RATTLESNAKE, Texas.

CANEBRAKE RATTLESNAKE, Florida. The canebrake rattlesnake is a close relative of the timber rattlesnake and intergrades with its northern cousin in many areas.

CANEBRAKE RATTLESNAKE, South Georgia

GRAND CANYON RATTLESNAKE. The Grand Canyon rattlesnake is predominantly found in the Grand Canyon. Photo © by Mike Mahanay, GrandCanyonTreks.org

TIMBER RATTLESNAKE, West Virginia. The timber rattlesnake is a top predator in the forest ecosystems of eastern North America.

TIMBER RATTLESNAKE

MOJAVE RATTLESNAKE, Arizona. The Mojave rattlesnake ranges from Southwestern Utah, South Nevada, and the Mojave Desert region of California to Central Mexico. Frequents desert flats with scrub vegetation.

© Gary Nafis

HOPI RATTLESNAKE, Arizona. The Hopi rattlesnake inhabits rocky outcrops and talus slopes. They may den in mammal burrows, crevices, and caves (sometimes in large numbers). They can be found in Northeastern Arizona and extreme Northwestern New Mexico. Photo by Gary Nafis, http://www.californiaherps.com/.

Photograph by Jim Rorabaugh, USFWS

ARIZONA BLACK RATTLESNAKE. The Arizona black rattlesnake is a western rattlesnake found from Central Arizona to Western New Mexico. Photo by Jim Rorabaugh, U.S. Fish & Wildlife Service.

BANDED ROCK RATTLESNAKE, Texas. The banded rock rattlesnake usually lives at higher altitudes in dry, rocky areas. It is found in Western and Central Mexico, North to Central New Mexico, and Southeastern Arizona.

MOTTLED ROCK RATTLESNAKE, Texas. The mottled rock rattlesnake is found in the far southeast corner of New Mexico, Southwestern Texas, and South to Central Mexico.

SOUTH PACIFIC RATTLESNAKE, California

TIGER RATTLESNAKE, Arizona. The tiger rattlesnake is found only in rocky canyons, hillsides, and ravines in deserts or grasslands and are most active after rains. They are nocturnal and begin foraging when the sun goes down. These snakes can be found in isolated populations through most of Sonora Mexico northward to South-Central Arizona.

DUSKY PYGMY RATTLESNAKE, Florida. The pygmy rattlesnake is quite common throughout the Eastern United States and especially the Southeast, all the way down through Florida.

PANAMINT SPECKLED RATTLESNAKE. The panamint speckled rattlesnake is a desert dweller common to Southern Nevada and adjacent California.

NORTH PACIFIC RATTLESNAKE, Oregon

WESTERN PYGMY RATTLESNAKE, Photo © by Terry Hibbitts

PRAIRIE RATTLESNAKE, Oklahoma. The prairie rattlesnake can be found from the Great Plains region of North America from Southeastern Alberta and Southwestern Saskatchewan to Northeastern Sonora, Northern Chihuahua, and West-Central Texas and from the Rocky Mountains eastward through the central portions of North and South Dakota and North-Central Nebraska to extreme Western Iowa, Western Oklahoma, and Central Kansas. It has spread to the west through gaps in the Rocky Mountains to Eastern Idaho, Southern Utah, and Northern Arizona.

SIDEWINDER, COLORADO. The sidewinder ranges from extreme Southwestern Utah and Southern Nevada to Southeastern California and South-Central Arizona into West-Central Sonora and to the Gulf Coast in Baja, Mexico.

RED CAROLINA PYGMY RATTLESNAKE

BLACKTAIL RATTLESNAKE, Arizona. The blacktail rattlesnake is almost always found in rocky areas, but it exists in a variety of habitats such as deciduous forests or pine woodlands, grassy hillsides, or cactus and agave groves. They sometimes climb into low-growing bushes. They are found in central Texas, west through New Mexico, much of Arizona, and Southern to Northern Mexico.

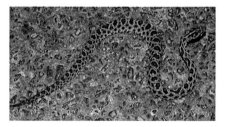

CAROLINA PYGMY RATTLESNAKE, South Carolina

TWIN SPOTTED RATTLESNAKE. The twin spotted rattlesnake is found in the pine and oak forests of Southeastern Arizona and South to Northwestern Mexico. It lives in relatively high altitudes of 6,000 to 9,500 feet. Photo from the American International Rattlesnake Museum.

GREAT BASIN RATTLESNAKE. The Great Basin rattlesnake can be found from the Rockies to the Sierra, including Southeastern Oregon, Northern California, Southern Idaho, Central Idaho, Central Nevada, and Western Utah. While suppressed under desert-like conditions, this snake is commonly found in the open and under ledges within canyons. Photo © by Jeremy Coates.

MIDGET FADED RATTLESNAKE. The midget faded rattlesnake mainly resides in the Southwestern states such as Eastern Utah, extreme Western Colorado, and extreme Southwestern Wyoming. Photo © Geoffrey A. Hammerson.

EASTERN MASSASAUGA. The eastern massagua ranges from western New York and Pennsylvania to Eastern Iowa throughout Michigan and south through Mid-Illinois, Indiana, and Ohio.

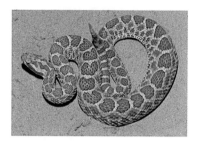

WESTERN MASSASAUGA, Oklahoma. The western massagua can be found from Southeastern Arizona, the Valley of the Rio Grande and the Gulf Coast of Texas, north through Southeastern Colorado and Central Oklahoma, to Eastern Kansas and Southeastern Nebraska.

DESERT MASSASAUGA, Texas

ARIZONA RIDGEDNOSED RATTLESNAKE. Photo by Tim Vickers.

SOUTH WESTERN SPECKLED RATTLESNAKE. Photo by Chris Brown.

ARIZONA CORAL SNAKE, Arizona

WESTERN CORAL SNAKE. The western coral snake can be found in the Sonoran Desert of Arizona and Northern Mexico and the southwest corner of New Mexico below 5800 feet.
www.desertusa.com

TEXAS ALBINO CORAL SNAKE,
Photo by Michael S. Price, Direcor of
the San Angelo Nature Center.

EASTERN CORAL SNAKE,
Florida

POISONOUS SPIDERS

Be alert to any potential encounter with poisonous spiders. Depending on where you hunt in North America, the widow spiders, recluse spiders, hobo spiders, and yellow sac spiders are the only spiders of medical importance. Although a red-legged widow spider lives in Florida, the black widow bites are much more common. There are about thirteen species of poisonous spiders in the United States, but the brown recluse causes the most severe bites. The hobo spider lives in the Northwestern states, and the yellow sac spider bites are very infrequent, and in most cases, fairly minor when they do occur. Spider bites in general usually are not fatal, and some cause no reaction at all. Any spider bite can get infected, but immediately seek medical attention for any reaction to a spider bite, especially bites from the brown recluse.

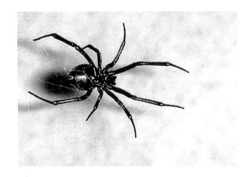

BLACK WIDOW, Wikipedia,
Black_Widow

BROWN RECLUSE, Courtesy
of Dr. Brenda Gilmore

HOBO SPIDER

YELLOW SAC SPIDER, Courtesy of Micha L. Rieser

During bow season or any time you are hunting in warm temperatures when the ticks will be active, be sure to wear enough clothing to cover your body, and spray your clothing with a good tick repellent such as Permanone. Certain tick bites can cause Lyme disease, which is an infection caused by the bacterium Borrelia burgdorferi. The disease often starts as a skin rash and can progress to more serious stages involving joint, nerve, or heart tissue. Antibiotics are usually effective,

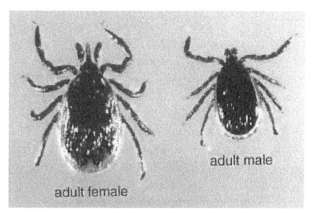

adult male

adult female

BLACK-LEGGED DEER TICKS

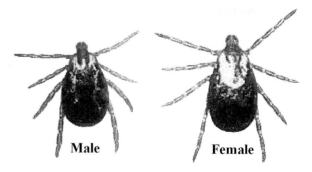

Male

Female

AMERICAN DOG TICKS

especially if treatment starts early in the disease process. Lyme disease has now been reported in at least forty-seven states in the United States and in many countries around the world.

Actual size (left to right) of larva, nymph, adult male, adult female, and engorged adult female ixodes (deer ticks) and adult male and female dermacentor (dog ticks).

In the United States, two closely related tick species have been identified as harboring and transmitting the disease, passing Borrelia bacterium to people and animals. The black-legged tick (deer tick) is found in the

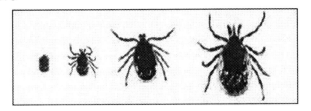

Four forms of the ixodes tick: larva, nymph, adult male, and adult female.

Eastern United States, and the western black-legged tick (deer tick) is on the West Coast. Keep in mind that these species are smaller than the common American dog tick, which does not transmit Lyme disease. It is believed that in some states (Nebraska, for example), imma-ture stages of the lone star tick may be responsible for most of the cases of Lyme disease since neither of the other two species are found there. The lone star tick is found primarily in the southeastern part of Nebraska, and this area has reported the majority of the Lyme disease cases for that state. Lone star ticks have been found on a large

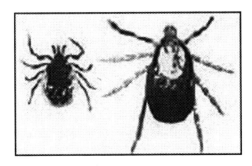

At left: adult female ticks ixodes (deer tick) left. At right: dermacentor (dog tick)

Lone star ticks. Amblyomma ameri-canum (lone star tick). Left to right: nymph, male, female.

number of whitetail deer in this part of Nebraska, too.

Often, a thorough examination of your deer will reveal him to be hosting a number of black-legged (deer) ticks. These photos will give you an idea of where and what to look for. These are Lyme disease-carrying ticks, so use caution.

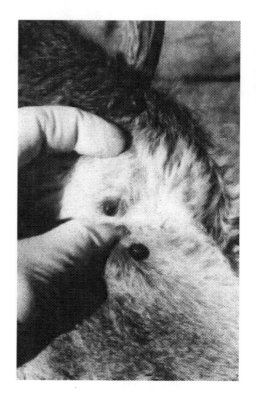

If you do get a tick bite, the sooner you remove the tick, the less chance for an infection. Use some type of fine-pointed tweezers and grasp the tick where its mouth parts enter the skin. Tug gently and repeatedly until the tick releases its hold by withdrawing its barbed mouth part from your skin. Be patient because proper tick removal may take time. Try to avoid pulling the body away and in the process severing the head, leaving it attached to your skin. This will almost certainly cause an infection. Clean the bite area with soap and water if possible and apply an antiseptic. Call or see a physician if an infection occurs.

*These photos and much of this information was derived from a pamphlet produced by Pfizer Global Research & Development as a public service, with the assistance of Drs. Louis A. Magnarelli and Kirby C. Stafford, III, Department of Entomology, Connecticut Agricultural Experiment Station, New Haven, CT; Dr. Robert T. Schoen, Department of Rheumatology, Yale School of Medicine, New Haven, CT; Dr. Joseph J. Gadbaw, Jr., Infectious Diseases Department, Lawrence & Memorial Hospital, New London, CT; and Dr. Steven A. Levy, Durham Veterinary Hospital, Durham, CT. PHOTO/ART CREDITS: M. Fergione, B. Tucker, L. Zernel, J. Stratton. Designed by: S. Badgett and J. Crandall, Pfizer Research Graphics. Website developed by Jeffrey Wheeler. (Website address: http://www.lyme.org/gallery/other_diseases.html)

POISONOUS PLANTS

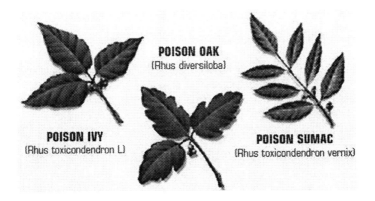

Poison ivy, poison oak, and poison sumac are the most common plants that cause a skin rash. The sap that comes from these plants causes the rash. The name of this sap, urushiol, causes an allergic reaction. It is not really a poison, and not everyone reacts to urushiol. If you are allergic to it, you can get a skin rash when you touch poison ivy, poison oak, or poison sumac. You could acquire a rash by touching clothing, shoes, and even pets that have the sap on them. If you come in contact with the smoke from these burning plants, you could develop a rash.

The rash comes a day or two after the initial contact. Some of the symptoms you should look for are itching, redness, a burning feeling, swelling, or blisters.

PREVENTION

Know what the three plants look like in order to avoid them:

Poison Oak and Poison Ivy both have three leaflets per stem. This is why you may have heard the saying "leaflets three, let them be."

Poison sumac has a row of six to ten leaflets. One leaflet is at the end of the stem. The other leaflets are in two rows opposite each other. If you know that you have come in contact with one of these three poisonous plants, do the following things within six hours to prevent an allergic reaction:

1. Remove all clothes and shoes that have touched the plant.
2. Wash your skin with soap and water.
3. Apply rubbing alcohol with cotton balls to the parts of the skin that are affected.
4. Rinse with water.

If problems such as swelling of the throat, tongue, or lips occur or if you have a hard time breathing or swallowing, seek medical help. If you feel weak or dizzy, acquire bluish lips and mouth, or become unconscious, you should receive medical attention.

Always try to be aware of weather conditions so that you may plan accordingly. The weather is always subject to change, so you should always be ready for these changes. Always pack for good and bad weather and you can't go wrong.

Be prepared for all types of weather, both good or bad. Photo courtesy of Troy Lilly, ForestWander.com

Know beyond a shadow of a doubt exactly what you are shooting at before you fire your weapon. There are too many stories of a hunter accidentally shooting another hunter. This is the most ridiculous type of accident I can imagine. When you consider the fact that a hunter is supposed to distinguish not only whether the deer is a buck or doe but also pick a vital area on the deer to aim for before shooting, this type of accident is inexcusable. When you add to this the fact that in most states all legal hunters during gun season are supposed to wear a certain percentage of blaze orange, this is inconceivable. In my state of Tennessee, we are required to wear a minimum of 500 square inches of daylight-fluorescent orange on our upper body or at least a blaze orange vest and cap, which normally fulfills this requirement. Try pretending that you have only one round in your weapon to dispense at your quarry and to bring him home: you must have perfect shot placement in a vital area. If you can get in the habit of doing this whenever you spot a deer or what you think to be a deer, it will become common practice to look for this vital area first before shooting.

Never shoot toward livestock or in any unsafe direction.

In addition to looking for the vital area, know what is on the other side of your target. Never shoot toward a busy highway, houses, or anywhere that people or livestock could accidentally be hit. Know that you are shooting in a safe direction; if a deer is lined up in an unsafe direction, you may have to wait for a safer shot.

Whenever you hunt with other hunting companions, you must always consider their locations when considering your direction of firing. You must also consider the possibility of them walking in your direction, even though this is something that should be resolved before the hunt. They should respect your hunting space and stay out, but they might not, so you should be prepared for this.

Always keep the safety on your weapon in the ON position unless you are ready to release a live round at your target. This is the only time you take the safety off, and once you make your shot, the safety goes right back on. Never maneuver around, climb, or even walk with the safety off. The only thing you should ever do with the safety off is prepare to fire your weapon or unload it after the hunt is over.

I cannot emphasize the importance of tree stand-safety enough. Every year there are reports of hunters falling from tree stands and injuring themselves or even being killed. Most if not all of these types of accidents could have been prevented if enough importance had been placed on safety. You should research the stand you purchase and then learn everything you can about the safest possible way to use it. Spend whatever amount

Know your stand and practice good safety techniques.

of money it takes to get a quality product, and pick the manufacturer's brain about it. Read all of the instructions, and keep it well maintained.

Be very careful to select a safe enough tree for your stand. You should be sure that the tree has no dead limbs that could blow down in a heavy wind and hit you and bark that will allow the stand to bite into it. Trees that have smooth bark may allow your stand to slip when you shift your weight a certain way and cause an accident. When you apply the stand to the tree, it may fit nice and snug and sit at the proper angle at ground level, but since the tree may get increasingly smaller as you climb, the stand may not sit properly on the tree at this height. Some stands come with features to allow for this so you can adjust your stand once you are at the proper height.

When stand hunting, always use a safety belt or safety harness. There are several different styles, so check several to be sure you are getting one that offers you the most unrestrictive but adequate safety possible. You want one that you can also use while climbing and when you are settled in your stand but will also allow you to sit or stand or

Always use a safety belt up around your chest or a safety harness.

both without having to readjust it. It should not restrict your movements in any way. The portion of the safety belt that goes around your body should be placed high up around your rib cage so as not to restrict your breathing should you happen to fall and end up hanging from it. If you place it around your waist, below your rib cage, it will greatly restrict your breathing if you fall. The tether between the safety belt or harness and the tree should be above you on the tree with the least amount of slack possible to still offer you total comfort and movement.

The safety belt or harness should allow you to be tied off as you climb since this is when falling is more likely to occur if you aren't totally careful.

Make sure that there is no snow or ice on the floor of your stand for you to slip on. If you use a ladder-type stand, make sure the ladder itself is free of any snow or ice.

Perhaps the most unsafe time when you are stand hunting is when you have made your climb to the proper height and it is now time to turn around and get situated in your seat. Be careful not to get tangled in the safety belt as you turn around, and turn around very slowly and carefully.

Practice using your new stand at ground level on a tree before you start climbing with it. Learn the best way to get into and out of it and how to maneuver in it safely.

Use a great deal of caution when attempting to use an unfamiliar permanent stand. The best choice is to not use it at all, but if you elect to, check it over thoroughly to be sure that it is safe.

Practice turning around to get situated in your stand.

Old, unfamiliar permanent stands can be unsafe.

Never carry your weapon up with you when you are climbing into your stand. Use a pull rope attached to your weapon, making sure the safety is on and no round is chambered, and attach the other end to your stand or to your belt loop so that once you climb up the tree and get settled, you can pull the weapon up safely. There have been too many accidents as a result of hunters taking their rifle or bow up with them. They could fall and discharge and actually hit you there on your stand, possibly even killing you, but at the very least damaging your weapon and ruining your hunt.

Pull up your weapon with a pull cord.

Always handle your weapon as though it was loaded, even if you are 99.99 percent sure that it is empty. There is always that 0.01 percent chance that there could be a live round in the chamber. Someone else may have handled the weapon and loaded it without your knowledge, or you might have been disturbed while unloading it and gotten careless. Don't rely totally on the safety because safeties have been known to fail, so just use common sense.

You should take special care of your equipment and your weapons, making sure that they are in safe, working order. Keep your equipment, and especially your weapons, well-lubricated and clean.

You should always wear the required amount of blaze orange to be safe from other hunters, regardless of your state requirements. You must wear at least what your state requires, but if you would feel safer wearing more, then do so. The more concealed you are from the deer, the better, but the more conspicuous you are to other hunters, the better, so you have to consider these factors, depending on when and where you are hunting.

Always wear the legal amount of blaze orange during gun season.

Always be extremely careful when walking up on a deer that you have shot and assume to be dead. Be sure that he is dead before you get too close since he could cause you some damage in a last ditch effort to get away if he has not expired.

Don't be careless with fire when you are in the woods or in any dry area. Many landowners may ask you not to build a fire if it has been extremely dry for the past few weeks. Never leave a campfire unattended, and douse it with water to be sure that it is totally out. Use your common sense regarding matches, smoking, campfires, and so on.

Be extremely safe with campfires.

When cutting firewood or kindling for a campfire, be extremely careful with axes, machetes, hatchets, saws, knives, and other cutting implements. Any of these tools can do serious harm to you if you are not absolutely careful.

Take extreme care when cutting firewood for camp.

Never use gasoline or any other comparable highly flammable, explosive chemical to start a fire. If you have trouble getting fires to start for you, there are several different types of fire starters available at your grocery stores and local hardware stores that are quite safe.

You should never smoke in your deer-hunting area, but if you do, never throw your lit cigarette butt down; it could start a fire. There have been numerous forest fires started this way.

When you are scouting or walking around in the field, realize that there are always dangers where you may least expect them, such as a rabid fox, skunk, coyote, or other animal, or hidden hornets nests, underground yellow jackets or honey bees nests, or maybe a wasp nest attached to your permanent tree stand. In the wild, all of these things as well as many others are possible and can occur at any time.

Hornet nests are one of the many dangers you must avoid.

KNOW YOUR WEAPON

Hunters have always put a great deal of effort and concern into the care and cleaning of their weapons. In the old days, the weapon was much more valuable to a hunter's survival than is typical in today's world. There are exceptions even today, though, and a weapon plays a much more important role than just hunting. For the purposes of this book, we won't go down that road. Our weapons should more or less be an extension of us when we are hunting. We should never go into the field without having given our weapon all the time and consideration necessary to be able to do what we want to do with it.

Never go into the field or woods without knowing how your weapon shoots. Spend whatever time is necessary out in the field or on the firing range to get totally familiar with exactly where your weapon is hitting the target at certain ranges. Check your weapon thoroughly for worn, cracked, or broken parts that could cause you problems in the field. Check for loose or missing screws or loose parts, such as your scope or sight. Be certain that your sling mounts are screwed in properly. You should do this in plenty of time before the start of hunting season to be able to get a part repaired or replaced if necessary. When you are hunting a whitetail buck, you want to have all the confidence you can, and that starts with your weapon.

The following rifles and their capabilities are more than adequate for whitetail hunting, no matter where you hunt. This is valuable information that you need to know in order to make an educated decision on a rifle selection. This is also necessary information for long- or short-range shooting accuracy. You need to know what your rifle is capable of doing with whatever projectile you choose to use in it. There is a wide variety of rifle types, styles, sizes, and manufacturers, as well as bullet sizes, styles, grain weight, and manufacturers. In this high tech world of today, it's truly amazing how much weapons and ammunition manufacturers have advanced. The new technological discoveries have made us hunters so much more capable than we used to be.

1. The .270 with its oversized case holds enough powder to push a 150-grain bullet in the 3,000 fps range, and the retained energy at 400 yards is nearly 1,200 ft/lbs.

2. The .308 Winchester has bullet speed and weight that closely matches the .30-06 at shorter ranges. In the .308 Winchester, a 180-grain bullet will retain over 1,200 ft/lbs of energy at 400 yards but will have dropped about 52 inches.

3. The .30-06 Springfield has a long history. It has been and still is among the favorite all-around big-game caliber firearms. For the hunter who will hunt everything from deer to moose or even prairie dogs, the .30-06 is a great choice. You get a range of bullet weights from the 110- to the 220-grain bullet. Loaded with the 180-grain bullet, the .30-06 will retain over 1,300 ft/lbs of energy at 400 yards. That is plenty to knock an elk off its feet, although the bullet drop at that range is nearly 50 inches. One advantage of the .30-06 is that finding a rifle action, model, and style you want is easy. The .30-06 is available in almost every action and almost every brand of firearm on the market. Also, because of its popularity, you will have no problem finding or borrowing ammunition no matter where you are.

4. The 7mm magnum has a slightly larger case and holds enough powder to push a 175-grain bullet faster than the .270 could move its lighter bullet. That means the 175-grain bullet from the 7mm magnum retains nearly 2,000 ft/lbs of energy at 400 yards. Bullet drop is about 42 inches at 400 yards, better than the .270 and with only a little more recoil. Minimal bullet drop and its knockdown power at extreme ranges are its credentials.

Depending on where you hunt, you should consider a good scope for your rifle or muzzleloader. If the area where you hunt is likely to provide you with as much as a fifty-yard or greater range shot, a scope will certainly help. Even if you hunt in a thick area that can open up into longer shots, as most areas do, I would still recommend a scope, but with open scope mounts to allow you that open sight shot should you need to use open sights. You want everything possible working in your favor to put that shot in the kill zone every time, and a scope makes you more capable of doing this. There are many types and sizes of scopes at a wide variety of prices and qualities. You don't have to purchase the most expensive one to get good quality, but you want the best quality that you can afford. It is extremely important to check the scopes out thoroughly to see what works best for you. There are several considerations, such as clarity of field, variable-range or fixed-range, wide field or symmetrical, and built-in range-finder or not, as well as others that you will discover as you begin looking at them. For a little more money, you can get a scope with a yardage adjustment. If your rifle is zeroed in at a certain yardage you can turn an adjustment on your scope to adjust it to a greater distance, and it will still be zeroed in at that distance. By checking out several brands and types, you will develop a good basis for comparison so you can choose what's best for you.

Don't go deer hunting with a shiny-finish weapon or one that will reflect sunlight. If your weapon was not factory-camouflaged or does not have a nonreflective finish, you should camouflage it yourself. For your rifle or muzzleloader, purchase a gun sock to slip over it when you go to the field, or use a camouflage wrap. There are also camouflage bow-limb sleeves if your bow is not camouflaged. However, unless you hunt with an old bow, most bows that you purchase for hunting nowadays are camouflaged. Your weapon must not call attention to you by reflecting your presence to a deer.

Take the necessary precautions to silence your weapon. Be sure that any movable parts are well lubricated to prevent any sound during operation. Camouflaged gun socks also help silence your weapon. When you flip off your safety to take a shot, do so carefully so as not to make any noise. If you just flip the safety off, a deer may be close enough to hear the sound.

Your bow has many movable parts that can make noise, so as you practice, note each sound and determine what to do to silence it. Take special care to silence your rest so that when you draw your arrow across the rest there is no sound, and be sure to keep your shafts waxed or oiled and your wheels or cams lubricated.

A sling on your weapon is extremely valuable. If you harvest a deer and have to drag him out of the woods to your vehicle, you have to be able to shoulder your weapon, which you can only do with a sling. If you are still-hunting for hours, sometimes you are going to want a break from carrying your weapon in your hands all day. After a few hours of carrying the weapon, it gets heavy, so use a sling, even on your bow.

The ammunition you use is extremely important, and some ammunition will be more compatible with your weapon than others. Certain brands of ammunition will be more accurate in your weapon than other brands. Certain grain ammunition may be more consistently accurate in your weapon. Using trial and error, make these determinations, and always use the same ammo for hunting that you use for zeroing in the weapon. Always practice with the same arrows or bolts and broadheads that you plan to hunt with—but be sure they are extremely sharp, because they are going to get dull due to practice. Always use razor-sharp broadheads since this maximizes their potential. When a dull broadhead penetrates a deer, it may actually rub past a vital organ but not cut it, preventing you from making the kill. If the blades of your broadhead are sharp, the broadhead will rip open everything it touches as it passes through the deer.

Before putting your weapon away, regardless of what the weather was like when you hunted, clean it to be sure that there is no residue on the weapon anywhere to affect its operation the next time out, its long-term operation, or its finish. If the weather was at all damp or wet, thoroughly clean your weapon. Break it down as far as you can, clean it, and coat it with a lightly saturated oil rag. Run a light coat of oil through the bore and place a few drops into all of the action parts to be sure any water will be displaced by the oil to prevent rust. You must keep all of the movable parts of your bow lubricated, especially after hunting in damp or wet weather. The limbs and bowstring should be consistently waxed to prevent wear. We should all keep in mind that there are many different elements that may affect the operation or finish of your weapon, such as light moisture from dew, fog, drizzling rain, humidity, dust, dirt, fingerprints, and many others.

Practice shooting your bow all year long to be tuned to your bow when deer season comes around. Practice shooting from heights to simulate actual hunting scenarios from a tree stand. Most of us can shoot off of a balcony, set our stand up in a tree in our yard, or even build a shooting platform. It is important to be comfortable shooting down at silhouette-type targets from fifteen to twenty feet up in a stand. Hitting a deer from these heights is different from shooting at a deer on a level plane with you. Practice is the best way to master your comfort zone at these heights. The more you shoot, the more confidence you will acquire, and the more accurate you will become.

You must keep your bow in perfect tune to be consistently accurate. If your arrow fishtails in flight, wavers from side to side, or porpoises in flight (bobs up and down), it needs to be tuned. The nocking point location on your string can cause porpoising, so by moving it up or down the string, you can correct this problem. If you are using properly matched arrow shafts, grain weight, wall thickness, length, and proper release technique, fishtailing should not be a problem. Some bows have a cushion button on the riser that may need to be adjusted in or out to correct a fishtailing problem. This problem may also be caused by using improperly installed fletching for the type of arrow rest you have on your bow: as you make your release, the fletching hits the rest, causing improper flight. Other arrow flight problems may result if the fletchings are mismatched, are not installed properly, or drag across the rest as the arrow passes over it. If the shaft size and weight is not matched to the grain weight of the broadhead, this can be a problem. This causes problems if the weight of the broadhead is too light or too heavy for the shafts. Your shafts should be matched to your draw length, and your bow should be set for your personal draw weight, the number of pounds of pull necessary to comfortably draw your bow to full draw. The spine of your arrows is how rigid they are based on the diameter of the shafts and how thick the shaft wall is. This spine or rigidity varies with the particular bow being used, and is the main reason it is so important to match your shafts to your bow. Once you have your arrow flight tuned to where the arrow flies true and straight, set your sight for whatever distance or distances you plan to take shots from. Some hunters use multiple pins set at various distances from twenty to twenty-five yards all the way up to sixty or sixty-five yards. Others, including myself, prefer a single pin set for a specific distance and then allow one way or the other for variations in relation to this distance. Once you have your sights set like you want, practice at that distance or distances over and over, and also from heights at these distances.

When installing the nocks on your shafts, be sure to position the nock so that when nocked on the string, the cock vane or fletching will lie on your rest properly to slide across the rest freely. A cock vane is basically a different-colored fletching from the other two on your shaft that will allow you to visually nock your arrow by mentally noting the position of this cock vane and knowing that your nock is lined up with the string. This can be quite valuable when attempting to nock an arrow in dim or poor light. Some hunters don't use cock vanes since they use four fletchings on each shaft and are able to nock their arrows either way. You will normally set the nock so that the cock vane is pointed down or off to the side; the type of rest you have on your bow determines this. There are a number of things you can learn about your bow and the proper care of it, so be sure to read any and all material you receive with your bow, and talk to other bowhunters or archery shop technicians. Learn all that you can; this will make you a better bowhunter. Some very good books and videotapes are also available on this subject.

Your draw weight should never be set higher than you can comfortably pull and hold for a full sixty seconds without getting too shaky—there will undoubtedly be times when you make your draw a little prematurely and have to hold the draw for a few seconds longer than you had anticipated. You should not have to strain to pull your bowstring back to full draw. If you come to full draw and have to hold it for very long, you will begin to weaken and shake and undoubtedly scare off the deer.

Don't practice for deer hunting with your field points, because they will definitely fly differently than your broadheads. You may as well not practice at all for accuracy if you do this.

Once you get your bow sighted where you want it, place a small dot of super glue on the pin threads to prevent it from moving, and also scratch or mark the pin support at these settings in case the pins do get knocked off their positions. This way, you will be able to reset your pins without too much trouble. If the pins do get knocked off, take a few practice shots after resetting them to fine-tune them if necessary.

I prefer to use brightly colored fletchings on my arrows, because they are easier to find and easier to see in the deer's body as he is running if the arrow failed to go all the way through, and because you can see where on the deer the arrow hit. Lighted nocks are also available, and are quite popular among bow hunters. The one disadvantage in using brightly colored fletchings is that if you move them around, they make you easier to detect. Keep the quiver camouflaged so that the only arrow noticeable is the one you have nocked in your bow. I prefer to detach my quiver from my bow once I am in my stand, and I also practice without it on my bow, as well as on my bow, in case I am still hunting or stalking.

Photo © by Mary Morris

SECTION II

◆

SCOUTING: WHAT TO LOOK FOR, WHEN, AND WHERE

Photo © by Mary Morris

SCOUTING: WHAT TO LOOK FOR, WHEN, AND WHERE

While I was writing this particular section of this book, I kept reflecting on the first time I took my son on a hunting trip for his first deer. I got off work on a Friday early in the afternoon so that I could take my son, Ronnie, scouting for a good location to hunt. We had a two-hour drive from home to our deer hunting property, which was a 235-acre tract of family-owned property surrounded by several thousand acres of corporate-owned woodland.

Once we arrived, we took care to camouflage ourselves and apply plenty of cover scent. We wanted to make sure that we didn't spread human scent around the area and defeat our purpose for being there in the first place. We were finally ready to head to the woods with a few basic essentials for preparing his hunting spot. We took a few reflective tacks, a little blaze orange ribbon, a sharp pair of pruning shears, a small tree saw, and our stands, which we dropped off along the way to save us some energy the next morning. This also helped keep us from getting sweaty with all of our hunting clothes on.

I had scouted the area the weekend before and had a good idea of where I wanted to take my son scouting. I had found several fresh rubs in a nucleus area with a great deal of fresh activity. The rut was well underway, and I felt that we should be able to locate a good primary scrape by the time I brought Ronnie back. As we approached this area, I saw three new rubs and a small secondary scrape only a day or two old.

We began following these rubs and found a couple more small scrapes. As my son and I stood discussing these types of deer sign, I looked over and saw a large, very fresh primary scrape with the licking branch almost chewed off but still hanging by a small piece of bark. He pointed out to me the buck track in the freshly pawed ground. It was obvious that the buck had freshened it sometime that morning. We were both excited; we could not have asked for a better location for the next morning's hunt. This was the exact type of spot you want to be hunting over if you can.

We began looking for the various trails into and out of this area and compared them to where the sign was located and the direction the buck appeared to be headed when he made them. We located a good double-trunk tree that would accommodate both our stands that was about fifty yards away from the scrape on what I figured would be the downwind side the next morning. (I did have a couple of other trees picked out just in case the wind was working against us.) We took the pruning shears and got rid of a couple of small saplings that might interfere with a potential shot. Using the reflective tacks at strategic points along the route to the stand, we felt quite confident about our chances for success the next morning. I remember thinking on our walk back to camp that night how wonderful this particular father–son day had been and how great it would be if I could get my wife and daughter more involved somehow.

Once we arrived back in camp, we relaxed awhile and discussed the early morning departure to the stand. After a good dinner of my wife's homemade chili, we turned in for the night with the clock set for 3:00 AM.

We dressed warmly, since the weather was quite cold, but took our time walking to the spot where we dropped off our stands. When we got to the stands, we took a short break, and then, with the stands on our backs, proceeded on to our hunting location, being careful to walk in on the downwind side to our tree. While trying to be as quiet as possible, we attached the stands to the tree. I told my son to go ahead and climb up and get situated while I laid down a good doe-in-estrous trail down the middle of an old logging road that ran past our stand location. The road was about thirty yards away and had at least two trails that crossed it. When I finished, I joined my son on my stand up in the tree. I climbed to a height just a little bit higher than his to be out of the line of fire in case the deer came from a different direction.

Just at daybreak, I noticed one lone deer on one of the trails leading to the logging road. I whispered to Ronnie to be alert and watch the logging road carefully. I figured there was a good chance that if it turned out to be a buck, he would very possibly pick up the scent of the lure I laid down and follow it up the middle of the road.

As circumstances turned out, this was exactly what happened, and a nice six-point buck walked right up broadside past my son, and Ronnie made a perfect shot on him. Words cannot express the excitement in his face at that moment. The buck ran off about fifty yards and disappeared into a dry creekbed. We waited a few moments before climbing down to find him.

After restraining Ronnie as long as I could, we began looking for his buck. There was a good blood trail as far as the creek bed, and then it disappeared. I sent Ronnie down the creek bed in one direction, looking for signs of blood where the buck possibly crossed to the other side, while I went the other direction. I hadn't gone far when I found more blood where the buck had crossed out of the creek bed up into the edge of an old, grown-up field. I walked to the edge of the tall grass and saw the buck where he had expired. I looked for Ronnie and told him to start working in my direction to look for his deer. I wanted him to find it, so I moved away from the carcass and more or less gave him suggestions as to where to look until he found it. The look on his face when he saw his first buck lying there before him and realizing that all of his scouting effort had paid off was priceless. Every parent should be able to draw from these types of wonderful memories with their children.

PRESEASON SCOUTING

In order to be a successful deer hunter every year, you absolutely must get out in the woods or field and do a sufficient amount of scouting. This should be done at various intervals throughout the year. There are several situations that can possibly change the habits of deer from year to year, even from the last time you scouted to the next. You may think they are doing a certain thing in a certain area, but since you last scouted the area, the adjoining property may have been logged, causing the deer to stop approaching your area from that direction. The weather may have caused a drastic change in deer movements. A forest fire may have consumed food sources and cover. The only way you will be able to stay on top of the current activities of the deer is to periodically check their activities through adequate scouting.

Scout several times throughout the year and document all of the different sign you find. Study these notes throughout the year and formulate your strategy based on what you perceive the deer to be doing by the time hunting season arrives. It's very important to determine their patterns in order to

Try to learn their current patterns. Photo courtesy of John Munt.

properly plan your hunting strategy.

Locating the deer sign is extremely important, but equally important is determining when, and during what part of the day or night, it was made. All sign other than sign found during the heavy rut should be related to the fact that normally the deer will feed at night, midday, and very

Figure out why deer are doing what they are doing at the time.

early in the morning or very late in the afternoon, and will bed down during the day with a few exceptions. This tells you what they are doing and when, so if you can add to this puzzle the "where" factor, you can formulate your strategy. Scout for the current bedding areas and current food sources and find their trails into and out of these areas.

If you notice that the deer are doing a certain thing in a particular area at a certain time of day, try to figure out why, because this could be a critical factor in getting a nice deer. If their pattern suddenly changes, try to determine why it changed. The more you question about the whitetail deer, the more you will learn.

These deer are about to enter a corn field from a heavily used trail.

If you hunt a particular spot this year and it proves to be very productive for you, don't plan on waiting until next year's opening morning hunt to go back there if you plan to hunt there. You must preseason scout this area; the fact that it was productive one year doesn't mean it will be the next. As I have mentioned before, there are many factors that may affect the travel patterns of deer.

Use topography maps, aerial photographs, CamTrakker night-vision cameras, stereoscopes and stereoscopic maps, and scouting notes and any other information you can compile to assist you in determining what the deer are doing in your area. You may also find that the local

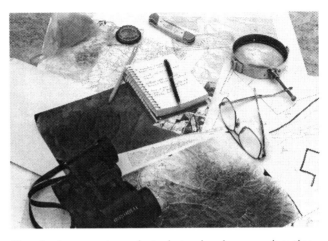

Scout, document, and study to develop your hunting strategy.

farmers store managers or owners are good sources of information. Check with the local state game and fish agency, wildlife resources agency, forestry service, and so on. Use all this information in conjunction with your scouting. Telephone linemen, propane gas deliverymen, mailmen, and any other such people who frequent the same areas over and over may also be helpful.

If you own your own property or have a lease on a certain piece of land, you might want to consider purchasing a twenty-four hour deer surveillance system such as CamTrakker. (Many of the photos in this book are the result of a CamTrakker.) This will make you aware of what some of the deer in your area are doing, especially at night, and also reveal the quality of deer and bucks you have in your area.

A positioned game camera.

Scouting close to and during hunting season is best done mid-morning or mid-afternoon in an effort to disrupt the least amount of deer activity. This does not apply to the rut because you may disrupt deer activity at any time during this period, so be ready at all times to see deer.

Scout during mid-morning or mid-afternoon hours so as to disrupt the fewest number of deer.

Remember that you are most likely to see deer in the early morning, midday, and late evening. These are the peak activity periods, so plan your hunting tactics or strategy accordingly.

Be prepared to see deer at any time, but especially during peak times.

I have found that if you check an area that you want to hunt a couple of weeks before opening day of the season and it looks good, then you should get out of the area and stay out until a couple of days before you plan to hunt it. You should make one last quick check, being careful not to leave any sign or scent in the area. If the area still looks good, stay out until your actual hunt. This way you should be

Check a good area briefly a couple of days before you plan to hunt it to be sure it still looks good.

able to slip into the area undetected and hunt and feel confident that you have not disrupted the activity of the deer.

One of the most exciting signs to come across when you are scouting is the sign of a big buck or one that might be a contender for trophy status. Depending on the area you hunt and the hunting pressure, many of these big, old bucks have become nocturnal and are active only at night, with a few possible exceptions. Peak rut will sometimes lure them a little further out of their bedding areas during the daylight hours. Hunting pressure sometimes can work to your advantage by forcing these old bucks out of their bedding areas as well. This peak rut period is when they are most vulnerable because of their preoccupation with servicing the does. In most cases, the most effective way to hunt them is to scout and hunt in relation to their bedding areas.

Buck bedded down on the fringes of a field. Photo courtesy of U.S. Fish and Wildlife Service.

A rub like this one was made by a quality buck.

This buck has been thrashing limbs, weeds, and so on.

Large rubs on large trees are normally a sign of a large buck. If you find a set of large tracks of a deer that is walking that are very deep, indicating that the deer is extremely heavy, this is probably a big buck also.

Often when a buck attempts to rub the velvet from his rack or when he is at his peak testosterone level, he will raise his rack and roll it around in the small tree limbs, ripping them apart. This is a very obvious sign, so when you're scouting, be sure to look for this.

A few weeks after the season ends is an excellent time to do some postseason scouting in an effort to determine the current activity of the deer as a result of the effects of hunting season.

If you were hunting a nice buck but failed to harvest him, scout between the bedding areas and the food sources for dropped horns or racks. The bucks normally begin to drop their racks shortly after hunting season ends, so if they survived the hunting pressure, there

Postseason scout to determine the effects of hunting season on the deer activity. Photo courtesy of Matt Grady with Batguys.

Photo © by Jack Izard.

Look for dropped horns between bedding area and food source.

should be some dropped horns somewhere. The most likely place to find them is on or near a trail between the bedding area and the food sources. If you find the dropped horns, this is a pretty good indication that the deer will be there next year.

Pay close attention to rubs, since they can tell you more than that a deer was there. Because the rubs are normally on the side of the tree that the deer is standing on when he makes them, rubs are a good indication that the deer came from that direction or from some direction on that side of the tree. As the buck rubs on the tree, he literally scrapes the bark off, and particles will fall to the base of the tree. Depending on the weather, you can determine approximately how recently the tree was rubbed by the freshness of these particles.

Bark that has been rubbed off the tree and fallen to its base can tell you approximately how recently the rub was made, depending on weather conditions.

Once you find the first rub, if you search this area thoroughly, you should be able to find another rub, which should give you an idea of the buck's line of travel. Follow this line and direction of travel and you can find more rubs and finally a scrape line. The size of the rub and the size of the tree can often tell you a little bit about the size of the deer. Large bucks

Large bucks will rub large and small trees to remove their velvet.

rub large and small trees, but small bucks seldom rub large trees. You can tell how recently the deer rubbed the tree by how fresh and crisp the shavings are that are located at the bottom of the tree. If it has been raining, this is not as easy to do as when it has been dry for a few days. If the weather is too hot, the shavings will dry up and make it harder to pinpoint a time when they were made. If you find a rub that is moist in dry weather, this rub was probably made during the previous night or within the last few hours.

Two examples of fresh rubs indicating recent activity in the area.

A scrape line is a string or nucleus of small secondary scrapes located in an area not far from a buck's primary scrape. These scrapes are located in what is considered the buck's core area.

Small scrapes in a series are secondary scrapes often leading to a primary scrape.

If you find a primary scrape, it will be quite large, perhaps three or four feet in diameter. The ground in this area will be pawed out down to the dirt, and the scrape will be located under a low limb, approximately four or five feet off the ground. This limb will be chewed on, and in some cases, bitten off, and is called a licking branch. The buck will rub his saliva and adrenal glands on this limb as a calling card to estrous does. Other bucks, both young and old, may also leave their scent on this licking branch. Other bucks may also freshen the scrape. The licking branch seems to be a communication link for estrous does and bucks. The buck will also urinate over his hocks into his scrape and leave his hoofprint in the middle of the scrape. These primary scrapes are described in more detail in the chapter on the rut.

Primary scrape less than a day old.

If you are seeing deer, at least you are where the deer are. Certain things force deer to move from one area to another or change their habits, so if you find very fresh sign, rest assured that you are where the deer are—or recently were—and, in all likelihood, will return to. Seek out a hunting site in this area along a good, used trail.

If you see deer, look for fresh sign in the same area. Photo courtesy of David Wagner.

If you are driving along and a nice buck crosses the road in front of you, make a mental note of where this happened. Consider going up to the nearest house around and inquiring about the possibility of hunting on their property. You might be pleasantly surprised at the response, especially if you are very courteous and sincere and offer to help them do something around the place.

Suddenly a buck crosses the road and jumps the fence. Photo © by Peter Eades.

Make a special note of deer crossings about the area, and relate these crossings to things you know or hear from people in the area about the deer activities. This is another way to gain information about the deer travel patterns to help you get an idea of where to try to acquire hunting permission slips.

Make a mental note of regular deer crossings on the highway.

Often when you are driving along and you spot a deer crossing sign, look around and see if it looks like a potentially good hunting prospect. If there are any homes in the area, you may be able to acquire permission to hunt the area. These crossings are sometimes used and sometimes not, but these signs are indications of deer having at one time crossed here on a regular basis.

Deer love acorns but will normally feed on acorns that are presently falling to the ground. You need to know that acorns begin to fall first from the

Don't underestimate the potential value of deer crossing signs to your hunting strategy.

Fresh deer droppings displaying a shiny appearance.

Older deer droppings beginning to lose their sheen.

oak trees that are highest up on the ridges, and then gradually begin to fall from the lower-lying trees, then finally from the trees at the bottom of the ridges. Deer are going to be feeding on the trees that are presently dropping acorns, because they are the freshest. Scout these areas thoroughly for current or extremely fresh deer sign. To locate these areas, first check the acorns on top of the ridges and listen for falling acorns hitting the forest floor. Notice if the squirrels are feeding on these acorns also; not only do they prefer them fresh as the deer do, but they also cause a large number of acorns to fall to the ground, making them available to the deer. You should also look for deer droppings in this stand of oaks. This indicates that the deer are frequenting the area, especially if there are various stages of age droppings. Depending on the freshness of the droppings, you should be able to determine if they are still feeding there. These droppings may be round or oblong like a bean, and if they are fresh, they will be shiny black and moist, and will appear this way for a few hours, depending on the weather. If they are older, they will have a duller appearance and be dry and more fibrous. It may be difficult to determine the number of deer in the area, since biologists say that a deer will deposit approximately one dozen piles of droppings per day.

Spend a great deal of time looking up into the treetops. Use field glasses to attempt to see what mast crop will soon be falling for the benefit of the deer.

Deer are browsers, and when other types of food sources are not available, they will browse on the tender tips of small saplings, buds, brush, tree tips low enough for them to reach, shrubs, and so on. Look for where the tips have been bitten off of small saplings, ironwood, honeysuckle, or many other food sources.

Deer are primarily browsers. Photo © by Kevin Lammi, Northland Images.

If you hunt around cropland, scout for trails into and out of these food sources. The trails leading into the crops such as cornfields, soybean fields, alfalfa, wheat, and so on will be prime late-evening hunting locations.

By fertilizing specific natural food trees such as red and white oak, persimmon, apple, cherry, and others, you can increase their production and the deer activity around them.

Heavily used trail revealing a good deal of deer activity on the route to a food source.

Fertilize natural food sources to increase their production for the deer.

If you have created your own food plots by planting small areas of clover, winter wheat, peas, or beans, keep close tabs on the activity around these areas. These are like magnets to the deer and will definitely draw them in if there is no other comparable food available.

Keep close tabs on your food plots, since they serve as magnets to the deer. Photo courtesy of John Munt.

Create salt licks and watch them closely, because this is one of the best ways to lure deer into your area from other areas. Keep tabs on how frequently they are using the salt, and in the summer months you can quickly determine if there are a large number of deer in your area.

Deer are primarily fringe-type animals. They prefer areas where the terrain changes from one type of cover to another. They like the fringe portion of

Wildlife resources agencies move entire herds of deer by creating salt licks.

power line clear-
ings or where a
woodline turns
into a brush or
briar thicket. These
fringe areas are
excellent potential
bedding areas.

Fringe type areas make excellent potential bedding areas.

If you seldom
get snow (as we
do here in middle
Tennessee), take
advantage of a
snowfall when
you do get one by
doing some serious scout-
ing to see what the deer are
actually doing. The fresh snow
will help you find where they
are bedding down, where
their trails are, and what food
sources they are working at
the time. You can also get an
idea of their numbers and, by
the size of some tracks, how
many large deer or possible
bucks there are. If the ground
is covered with a blanket of
snow, it will be much easier
to actually see deer. Do some
scouting on these days even if
you have to take some vacation time or a day off to do
it; doing so will pay off in the
long run.

Trails reveal more precise deer activity after a snow begins to expose them.

When a buck rises out of his bed, he will normally urinate in it or beside it before he departs from it. A doe, however, will move away from her bed to urinate. This should be easy sign to find in the snow, so if you find a bed in the snow that has been urinated in, the odds are it is a buck.

Deer normally defecate after they rise out of their bed, so bedding areas will tend to have a lot of various age

A buck having just risen from his bed.

An assortment of variously aged droppings, in addition to sheen and texture. Note the droppings partially covered by leaves, also a sign of age.

droppings around the area. A temporary bedding area will not have all of these various ages of droppings, because it was only used once to relax during a feeding or browsing period.

Bedding areas can be very helpful to you when you are scouting, depending on who is using the bed. Most of the time, hunting the bedding areas is the best way to hunt the old, mature bucks; for the most part, those bucks are nocturnal and only stir at night. For this reason, their bedding area is the

Temporary bed used during feeding.

only place you will find them during the day. Beds found in and around food sources are primarily relaxation beds used at night during the feeding process. During the day, deer tend to bed down on the fringes of terrain changes, on the edges of fields, in power line clearings, or on the sides of hills where they can cover great distances.

The old bucks will bed down in the thickest cover in the area, where no one is likely to disturb them. When you find a deer bed that you feel to be a buck's bedding area, avoid going too near it. You do not want to get any foreign scent in this area, since you will need to hunt this buck while he is comfortable and feeling unthreatened in this area. Knowing where this bed is located will help you prepare your hunting strategy. If the deer just left as you approached, don't revisit the area for a couple of days, in order to give the buck a chance to relax again. When you do go back, go back to actually hunt the buck.

This buck is well hidden in his bed. Photo by Bruce Macqueen.

It's difficult to spot bedded deer before they see you, but if you search the area in front of you as intently as is necessary to locate a bedded deer, you will definitely see more. There are many times that if you had just taken one last look around the area before taking the next step, you would have seen the deer before they saw you.

This doe was bedded down just below a ridge top.

Bedded deer are often difficult to see, so you must concentrate on looking for parts of deer.

Trail crossings are generally excellent areas to hunt, depending on how well and freshly used the trails are. Your chances of seeing deer are greatly increased by the many different directions of travel the deer may be using.

Pay close attention to heavily used trails. Study them. How heavily used are they, and where

Trail crossings can be excellent areas to hunt.

do they lead to and from? This will help you determine how to set up to hunt the area. The direction of the food source and the direction of the bedding area should tell you which direction the deer are traveling in the morning and in the evening. Scout these areas early in the season, and monitor them as the year progresses so that you know what the deer are doing just before the season opens in the fall.

A fellow Tennessee deer hunter, John Sloan, a freelance writer and lecturer on whitetail deer, offers an excellent analogy. When you are suddenly told that dinner is ready, normally you will stop what you are doing and head straight to the dinner table. After dinner you may go outside to have a smoke, go watch television, go to bed, or what have you. In other words, there is no certainty as to what you will do or where you may go after dinner. When you relate this type of behavior to deer hunting, you can understand why the trail leading from a bedding area to a food source should be considered a preferred area for success. A deer trail connecting these two areas will normally be well-worn due to heavy use, indicating a lot of deer activity. The majority of the deer heading in this direction are on their way to satisfy their hunger. Once they do this and are ready to leave the food source area, just like humans after dinner, they may go their separate ways in any number of differ-ent directions. Some of the deer may head back to their bedding area, some may go to another

Active trail leading from food source to bedding area.

food source, some may head for a temporary bed site, and so on. The lightly used trails around a food source area are light due to fewer deer using them. This is why these trails should not be considered optimal potential hunting sites.

Deer have some very basic needs such as food, cover, and varying terrain that also offers structure such as creek beds, fence rows, old logging roads, and so on. Deer receive most of their water require-ments through their food intake, but at times this is not enough, so water is certainly another basic need, as is their need to reproduce. When scouting, try to relate as many of these basic needs to your hunting area as possible. The more needs that are present, the better your odds for success.

Look for other types of crossings, such as a low place in a fence, or look for deer hair caught on the wire or barbs of barb wire, indicat-

ing that deer
are crossing
in that area.
Look for sign
or clues at the
end of a fence
row or the end
of some rocks
or boulders that
give way to a
trail they might
take. Look for
sign of where
they cross
creeks, rivers,
or streams, or

Look for regular crossings such as fences crossing runs and other types of structure. Photo courtesy of Philip K. White, U.S. Fish & Wildlife Service.

where they are drinking by the water's edge.

Look closely around any unique structure areas for sign, such as the old sawdust pile pictured, once part of a sawmill deep in the woods that was shut down many years ago. This sawdust pile was like a child's sandbox and was used almost like a play area by the deer. It was covered with deer tracks almost every year. Always investigate an area such as this thoroughly.

A unique structure area such as this old sawdust pile could reveal a great deal of deer activity.

Deer will often have a single rub in an isolated spot with no other rubs around it; in some cases, this is a type of signpost rub. Some of these rubs are located at strategic points to let the deer know when they are coming up to a specific crossing of some type. If there is a low place in a fence that they are using to cross from one side to the other, they will often have a signpost rub back on the trail to let them know this. These signpost rubs can be very helpful in determining activity. These rubs are not to be confused with those larger signpost rubs that are returned to year after year by several bucks during the rut period. We will discuss these later in the book.

One single signpost rub very near a low place in a fence where the deer cross the fence.

Don't ignore tracks simply because the deer are no longer present. Try to determine what the tracks indicate.

Tracks can tell you a great deal if you study them carefully. They let you know if the deer were calmly walking along, or running from or to something. You can determine if there are any heavy or large deer by how deep or large the tracks are, and thus if there are any potential bucks in the area. You can determine the direction of travel and approximately how recently the tracks were made. In many cases, you can also determine the number of deer that made the tracks.

There are certain trails that the deer seem to use over and over every year. Some years they are used more heavily than others, but they are still consistent paths of travel. If you hunt in an area that has certain trails like this, you are very fortunate, because trails like this open up many more opportunities for you.

Trails used heavily year after year.

Find where deer have to negotiate fallen trees, rockslides, washed out gullies, and so on. Deer tend to leave more sign in these areas because of having to put forth extra effort to negotiate the structure.

Check out areas where two or three hollows or ravines come together or where logging roads fork together, or any other type of funnel areas.

This buck must detour around this fallen tree and may leave more sign in the area than normal. Photo courtesy of U.S. Fish & Wildlife Service.

These areas offer more than one route for the deer to travel. If there are many deer in the area, these funnel-type locations should produce some obvious sign. Study these areas closely and determine the best way to set up to hunt the area.

This aerial photo reveals several draws or hollows that all funnel into one, offering a great hunting site.

Deer feces or pellets can help a great deal in determining what the deer are doing in your area. If the droppings are fresh, they tell you that the deer were there fairly recently. If they are plentiful and all basically at the same stage of freshness, this is an indication that there were several deer, and if the pellets are at various stages of freshness, this indicates that the deer are coming through this area often. If there are a lot of pellets at various stages of freshness, this is probably a feeding area, so examine what they are feeding on and begin looking for a good stand location; this is a good hunting site for late-evening hunting. The deer will be leaving their bedding areas and approaching this food source late in the evening, and you will already be on the stand waiting for them.

Deer droppings are very important sign for scouting purposes.

Try to locate escape routes from certain key areas such as food sources and bedding areas. If you know how a deer will escape to avoid you from a specific area, this gives you additional options to hunt him.

This doe was jumped out of a bed, so take note of how she escapes the area.

Do not overscout your area to the point of affecting the deer habits. Use good judgment about when to scout so as to disrupt the least amount of deer activity, and always use good cover-scent tactics, just as if you were actually hunting.

Do not overscout an area; this may cause the deer to change their habits. Photo courtesy of John Munt.

Don't underestimate the value of talking to the local farmers and the wildlife and forestry officers in your area. They have provided me with some very valuable tips over the years.

Talking with local farmers like my granddad or local residents like my dad have proven very beneficial over the years.

Photo courtesy of U.S. Fish & Wildlife Service.

FOOD SOURCES

Deer spend most of their lives feeding or in search of food. If you wish to become a successful deer hunter, you must focus a great deal of effort on this aspect of a deer's life. Become familiar with what food sources deer will eat, which ones they prefer to eat, which ones offer them the most nutrients and satisfy their health needs, which ones are present in your hunting area, and where these sources are located. Know what other sources of food are on surrounding tracts of land bordering your property because these food sources might be luring the deer away from your property. You need to know when these food sources are most desirable and when they are available to the deer. The food that deer eat and their feeding habits vary from one part of the country to another. For example, when are the hard- and soft-mast crops falling from trees? This is when they first become available to the deer. Learn to recognize as many of these food sources as possible, how to recognize the deer's effect on them, and when and where the deer are feeding at the time you plan to hunt. Remember the old adage that says "the way to a man's heart is through his stomach?" Well, to a great extent, the way to a deer's "heart" is through its stomach as well.

The whitetail is a ruminant. It has a four-chambered stomach that processes large quantities of low-nutrient foods. A deer can fill its stomach in one or two hours, depending on the abundance and type of vegetation or mast it eats. When a deer feeds, it tongues food to the back of its mouth and chews just enough to swallow. Food passes down the gullet and into the stomach. Food then goes into the rumen, which can store eight to nine quarts. The rumen acts as a fermentation vat, and most digestion occurs in this area. Billions of microorganisms break down fibers, cellulose, and other plant components and convert them into materials that can be used by the deer's digestive system. The lining of the rumen has small, spaghetti-like fringes called papillae. Over 40 percent of a deer's energy is derived from the acids absorbed through the papillae and the walls of the rumen. After a doe or buck fills its paunch, it lies down in a secluded place to chew its cud. After chewing its cud a while, the deer reswallows the food, and the food passes to the second portion of the stomach, the reticulum. The reticulum has a lining that looks like a honeycomb. It holds food in clumps that can grow to the size of softballs. The main function of the reticulum is to filter out any foreign material. After about sixteen hours, food passes to the third chamber, the omasum, where intensive digestion and absorption take place. The omasum's lining has forty flaps of varying heights, and they absorb most of the water from the food. The last compartment, the abomasum, has a smooth, slippery lining with about twelve elongated folds. The abomasum produces acid to break down food pieces for easier absorption of nutrients. Food eventually passes through a deer's intestines, where most of the liquid is absorbed and undigested particles are left behind. These particles are passed as excrement. A deer urinates and defecates an average of thirteen times a day.

Scout for food sources and map out where they are located. Find where the largest oak trees are located, and remember that oak trees begin dropping their acorns from the trees up on top of the ridges first and gradually work their way down to the lower elevations last. The

My cousin Rick, a forest ranger, stands beside an exceptionally large oak tree that not only is a good landmark, but also a food source.

deer prefer to feed from the oaks that are presently dropping their acorns. Where you hear acorns dropping and find other deer sign such as droppings, tracks, used trails, and so on, consider this a good potential hunting site.

Deer feed primarily at night, during early morning hours, in the late afternoon, in the evening hours, and occasionally during the middle of the day. When the hunting pressure is high, they may feed only at night in certain areas and bed down during the day.

During the spring and summer months, deer feed on a variety of stems, leaves, and plants. They do a great deal of heavy eating during this time of year.

This buck is calmly browsing. Photo by Heather Henkel, U.S. Geological Survey.

Three does on a browsing run.

Deer will be attracted to all types of food sources, such as red and white oak acorns, which are probably their best source of energy because they are so high in carbohydrates. These are also their favorite foods, and if you have a stand of oaks on your hunting land dropping acorns, the deer are going to be near them. They prefer the white oak acorns to the red oak acorns, and the white oaks drop their acorns before the red oaks, so keep an eye on both of these crops. About the time the deer consume the white oak acorns, the red oaks should be dropping if it is their year to do so. The red oaks only bear fruit every two years, while the white oak drops acorns every year, depending on weather conditions. These characteristics separate the white oak group from the red oak group. The members of the white oak group include the white oak, bur oak, post oak, chestnut oak, water oak, live oak, swamp white oak, English oak, and the overcup oak. The bark is very light gray and scaly, almost like a hickory. All of these oak leaves have rounded lobes or tips, and the acorns are sweeter tasting than the red oak acorns. The white oaks will normally bear fruit every year unless affected by abnormal weather conditions.

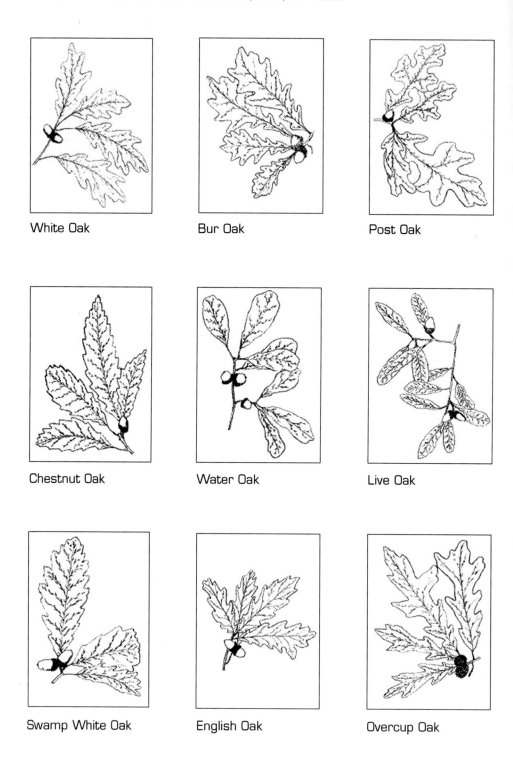

White Oak

Bur Oak

Post Oak

Chestnut Oak

Water Oak

Live Oak

Swamp White Oak

English Oak

Overcup Oak

The various members of the red oak group include the northern red oak, southern red oak, willow oak, chinkapin oak, scarlet oak, pin oak, black oak, and shingle oak. These oak leaves have pointed lobes and are very sharp tipped. The bark of the red oak group is darker in color and furrowed. The acorns mature every two years and have a bitter taste.

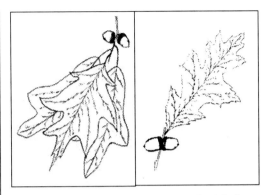

Southern Red Oak   Northern Red Oak

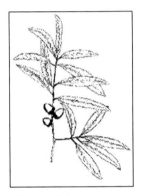

Willow Oak

Chinkapin Oak

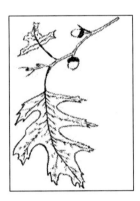

Scarlet Oak

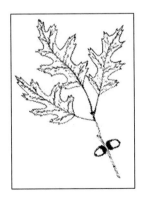

Pin Oak

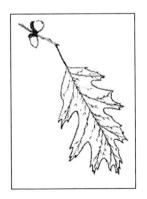

Black Oak

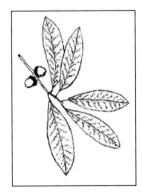

Shingle Oak

Soft mass or fruit trees in the area, like apple trees, pear trees, plum trees, and peach trees, and berries—like mulberries, blueberries, blackberries, strawberries, red raspberries, and others with ripe fruit available—will be a favorite hangout, especially if the fruit is falling to the ground. Other preferred food sources include beech nuts, soft-shelled hickory nuts, pecans, hawthorn, palmetto berries, dogwood berries, May hawthorn, dandelion, pokeweed, magnolia, wild persimmons, clover, wild grape, wild rose, wild cherry, creeping blueberry, wild hydrangea, sunflower, Black-eyed Susan, bearberry, and all types of domestic crops such as corn, alfalfa, soy beans, winter wheat, oats, peas, sweet potatoes, cantaloupe, pumpkins, and many others. Deer also eat mushrooms, including many that are deadly to humans. Mushrooms become very important to the deer in the winter. Some identification sketches to help you recognize these different food sources follow.

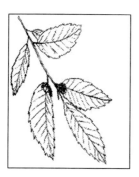

American Beech

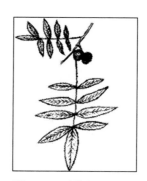

Bitternut Hickory

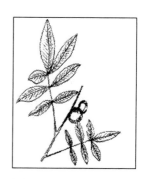

Mockernut Hickory

Pignut Hickory

Shagbark Hickory

Shellbark Hickory

Pecan

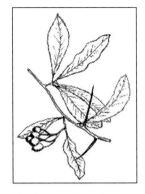

Cockspur Hawthorn

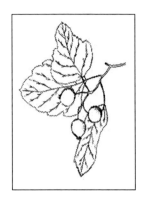

Downy Hawthorn

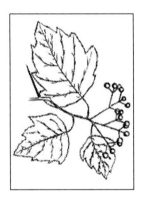

Washington Hawthorn

Flowering Dogwood

Cucumber Magnolia

Southern Magnolia

Saucer Magnolia

Umbrella Magnolia

Persimmon

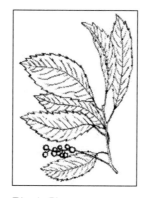

Black Cherry

Sour Cherry

When the leaves have fallen because the trees and plants have become dormant, offering little or no nutrition, the deer must browse. Look for where the tender tips or woody stems and twigs of small saplings, trees, and shrubs have been bitten off. The deer will probably have specific trails leading to and from these areas. Look for tender plants growing along roads, edges of fields, power-line clearings, the edges of wood lines, clear-cuts, and so on. If nothing else is available, deer will browse on dogwoods, honeysuckle, hemlock, maples, cockleburs, asters, teaberry, coralberry, holly, wheat grass, crabapple, sassafras, dewberries, honey locust, black-gum, aspen, greenbrier, sumac, poison ivy, wild plumb, poplar, witch hazel, willow, white pine, yellow birch, ash, wintergreen, fir, white cedar, oaks, lespedeza, snowberry, swamp ironwood, and a variety of other less desirable sources. Because deer are browsers during the winter, if there are no other quality food sources available, these will be their primary sources of food.

Eastern Hemlock

Ashleaf Maple

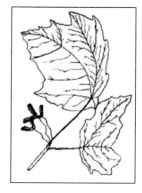

Black Maple

Norway Maple

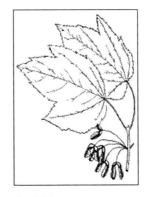

Red Maple

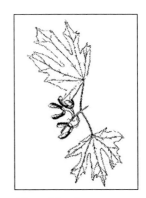

Silver Maple

Striped Maple

Sugar Maple

American Holly

Prairie Crabapple

Sassafras

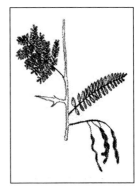

Honeylocust

Black Topulo Blackgum

Bigtooth Aspen

Quaking Aspen

White Poplar

Yellow Poplar

Black Willow

East White Pine

Loblolly Pine

Ponderosa Pine

Shoreleaf Pine

Scotch Pine / Scots Pine

Jack Pine/Scrub Pine

Red Pine

Austrian Pine

Pitch Pine

Longleaf Pine

Slash Pine

Paper Birch

Green Ash

River Birch

Blue Ash

White Ash

Balsam Fir/
Fraser Fur

Cocklebur

Poison Oak

Poison Ivy

Poison Sumac

Domestic crops are extremely important to deer, and a little extra effort on your part can prove very prosperous. Leave some of the corn standing for cover purposes to help the deer feel secure feeding there. Bushhog a few rows to make the corn kernels and ears available on the ground.

Corn food plot planted and modified for the deer.

Throughout the process of learning to recognize the various food sources that deer will eat, you will naturally become more woods wise. You will become more and more familiar with the various trees, plants, fruits, trunks, and bark that are present in the deer's habitat. Deer may use certain plants or shrubs for cover on a regular basis even if they don't use them as a food source. As a deer hunter, you'll do well to become as familiar as possible with the various plant life in your deer woods. Don't try to accomplish this overnight, but make a conscious effort to learn to recognize any plants or trees that are valuable to the deer. A few examples of tree bark to further help you recognize these trees follow.

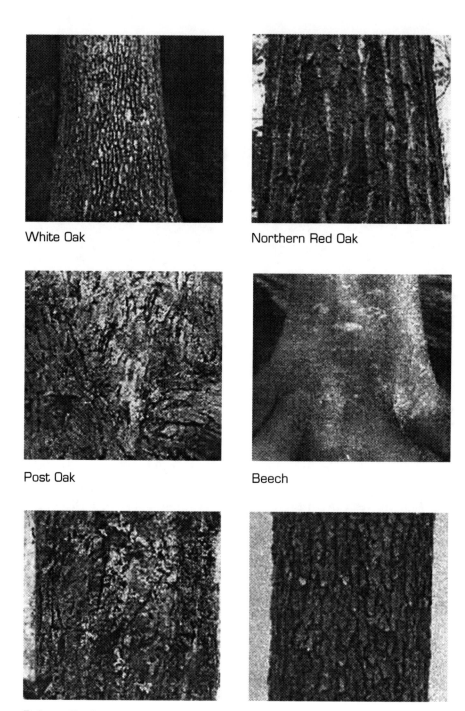

White Oak

Northern Red Oak

Post Oak

Beech

Balsam Poplar

Black Cherry

Sassafrass

Eastern White Pine

Eastern Cottonwood

Cherry Bark Oak

Overcup Oak

Green Ash

During the winter months, the nonwoody type of plants becomes very important to the deer. The deer will feed on grasses, sedges, and different types of legumes, asters, and ferns. Many of these plants emerge after a forest fire has consumed a section of woods. These tender plants draw many deer, almost like magnets.

Old bucks normally feed at night.

The deer normally use these food sources in the late afternoon and evening, so if you set up near these food sources and find that the deer are coming by too late for you to be able to get a shot, move farther away from the food source. Be sure and stay near their trail in order

The time of day the deer are frequenting the food sources will determine how to set up to hunt them.

to catch sight of them while you still have enough light to shoot. The deer are generally going from their bedding area to the food source, so you want to be somewhere between the two.

Food plots can be very useful in attracting deer to your area. A nice clover patch, winter wheat field, soybean field, or cornfield will begin drawing deer in as

My cousin Barry broadcasting fertilizer on a potential corn plot.

they supplement the deer's food sources. There are a variety of food plot options available through a number of companies, local feed stores, and the Internet. Refer to chapter 16 on deer management.

Mineral and salt licks are great for the deer's diet, but most of all, they lure deer into your area and help to keep them there. The deer will keep coming to the salt lick,

Resupplying a salt lick.

especially in hot weather. If you place twenty-five pounds of salt around an old, dead stump, the salt will melt into the ground, and the deer will literally dig the stump out of the ground over time to get to the salt.

Deer need water to survive. In the winter months, they need approximately one-and-a-half quarts for every one hundred pounds of body weight per day. In the spring and summer months, they require approximately twice this amount per day. The majority of the deer's required water intake comes from food, meaning the deer can get by without an actual water source for long periods of time.

Natural water source for the deer.

Photo © by Mary Morris.

10

SCRAPES AND RUBS

When hunting the whitetail deer, scouting is a definite prerequisite for a good successful hunt if you omit luck from the scenario. What part of the season you are in will determine what to look for when you are scouting. During the rut, you stand a better chance of getting a nice buck than at any other time. The primary reason is that the bucks have one thing and one thing only on their minds, and that is servicing those does. This makes them most vulnerable to us hunters. This is the time of year to focus most heavily on scrapes and rubs. Scrapes are especially pertinent only to the rut. There are certain types of rubs that you may find early on in the season, created as the bucks are rubbing the velvet from their racks, and also from the creation of signpost rubs. It always gets my adrenaline flowing when I find rubs and scrapes, especially in the same area.

A single rub can offer much if you analyze it.

Pay close attention to rubs when you find them since they can tell you a great deal more than simply the fact that the deer was there. These various clues are revealed in the chapter on preseason scouting. Learn how to really analyze each rub that you find, and make notes of your findings for future reference.

Shorter days seem to trigger rubbing activity and velvet removal.

The timing of the bucks shedding their velvet and rubbing activity is believed to be triggered by the days getting shorter as autumn approaches.

Scientists believe today that rubs have a direct bearing on stimulating the estrous cycles of the doe, and that the key is priming pheromones. This is discussed in more detail in the chapter "On The Rut" and is based on information acquired from the book *For Big Bucks Only*.[1]

Certain bucks might rub most anything when they are extremely hot in rut, such as a fence post or telephone pole, even though they

A preferred type of tree for rubbing.

normally prefer trees and shrubs with smooth bark and no lower limbs.

On northern ranges, bucks generally rub off their velvet during late August or early September, nearly two months before the first does breed. Some yearling bucks and unhealthy older bucks are delayed by several weeks. Here in Tennessee, we can expect our bucks to begin to strip their velvet around the early part of September.

The amount of rubbing a buck will do depends on his blood levels

This buck is almost ready to begin rubbing his velvet away. Photo © by Mary Morris.

of the male sex hormone testosterone, which in turn depends upon his age and dominance status. The prime-age bucks are normally the first to reach their threshold levels of testosterone, which causes them to shed their velvet. They also achieve higher concentrations of this hormone, which contribute to their higher aggressiveness. As a result, they achieve a higher social rank and tend to make more rubs.

This buck is checking out the scent left on this rub.

The number of rubs that you can expect to find in your hunting area may vary each year depending on the nutritional status of the herd. This is based on scientific research and directly correlates to the degree of breeding in your area.

The nutritional level determines both the amount of rubs and breeding activity. Photo by Tony Campbell.

Rub lines are among my favorite type of sign to find when I am scouting. Besides telling you all of the above information, they are in many cases a trail to a scrape line. Early season rubs in a nucleus area often indicate a larger buck's core area. These will commonly be found in a semicircle pattern or on trees that form this type of pattern and are often located in or near the bedding area. Sign like this can definitely put you on track for meat for the table and, in many cases, a nice trophy. If you find a scrape line linked to these rubs, there will be a series of small, approximately one-foot-diameter scrapes, commonly referred to as secondary scrapes. These scrapes are a buck's way of marking his territory and are in the vicinity of his primary scrape for the estrous does in the area.

Multiple rubs, including a large rub.

When you find or look for clusters of rubs in a nucleus area, they will normally be found in an area with a great deal of autumn food available. This may be heavily wooded cover near corn or alfalfa fields, oak trees with abundant acorns available, or artificial feeders or food plots. This makes a great deal of sense because this type of area would also attract

This buck's core area is not far from this food source.

many other deer to the buck's signpost area.

Early season rubs are more difficult to find and in many cases are made by smaller bucks. Since the smaller or younger bucks do not do as much rubbing as the older bucks, if you find a large number of rubs in your hunting area and in a wide variety of locations, it may represent a good younger buck population. If you find a large number of rubs but they are located in a fewer number of locations, you may have an older group of bucks. The older buck rubs are much more obvious, usually more plentiful, and tend to appear later in the season during the rut. It is very important to pay strict attention to the size and the timing of all the rubs you find.

Several rubs in a small nucleus area indicating an older buck.

Later in the season in the southeastern United States, when the more dominant bucks approach the rut, their rubs become much more massive. They are also made on larger, more aromatic trees such as cedar and sassafras, but the bucks readily rub alders, sumac, hemlock, eastern junipers, witch hazel, sourwood, striped maple, pines, or cherry trees.

The trembling aspen is the most highly preferred species for rubbing in the Northeast and upper Great Lakes region. In the smaller size classes, it

Large rubs on large trees are signs of a large buck.

has smooth, soft bark that is easily stripped, and the inner wood is light colored with long-lasting brilliance once exposed. Staghorn sumac, red maple, black cherry, balsam fir, pines, and willows are also frequently rubbed, whereas sugar maple, ironwood, beech, and paper birch are usually avoided.

Normally, young bucks do not rerub trees, so if you do find trees that have been rubbed several times, this normally suggests a dominant buck in the area.

A very large- or well-rubbed tree is usually the work of the area's dominant buck. It has only recently been concluded that certain of these large rubs will be revisited from year to year as well as during the season. Other bucks in the area may use the same tree will typically be found on a cedar tree, since it is one of the few trees that can withstand this type of treatment.[2]

A big, old, dominant trophy buck. Photo by Joe Kosack, U.S. Fish & Wildlife Service.

With the exception of signpost rubs, each rub or nucleus of rubs that you find will carry the distinctive glandular scent of the specific buck that made it and no other, so these also serve to count the bucks in your area.

Examples of other area rubs.

Examples of other area rubs.

The primary scrape will be located somewhere in a buck's core area and will be much larger and pawed down to the bare ground. As a result of this pawing of the ground, the buck has left scent from his interdigital glands. These scrapes are commonly three or four feet in diameter, and he will also urinate over his hocks—commonly known as the tarsal glands—into his scrape, further reinforcing his scent.

Very fresh, active scrape.

There will be a low-lying tree limb approximately four or five feet off the ground directly above the scrape. The end of the limb will be chewed on and normally broken, and may even be chewed off. This is the buck's licking branch, where he leaves scent from his saliva glands, nasal glands, and forehead and preorbital glands.

Licking branch hanging above primary scrape.

Other bucks will also visit this same scrape but in some cases may only be interested in marking the licking branch. This primary scrape is normally the nucleus or center of a buck's home-range rutting activity.

Scrapes are excellent locations to hunt anytime during the rut. A particularly good time to set up an ambush on the downwind side of these areas is just after a rain or snow. Bucks will normally return to refresh their scrapes after a weather change has reduced the effectiveness of their glandular secretions.

Buck refreshes the scent on his licking branch.

Nice buck checking for estrous doe scent while creating a scrape.

The older does in the area will come into estrous first, and then the younger does. The does will come into estrous for a period of twenty-four hours. If an estrous doe has not been visited by a buck, it is not uncommon for her to actually go in search of a buck. She will seek out these primary scrapes.

This doe seems to be in search of a buck.

Since the bucks in a given area may not be able to get around to all the does during the does' first period in estrous, some does may not get bred during their first estrous cycle. They will continue to come into estrous every twenty-eight days or until they are bred. In some cases, a doe may come into estrous four to five times a year if she hasn't been bred.[3] Once she is bred, her estrous period stops, and she begins her gestation period, which is normally about 200 to 215 days—about seven months. Depending on what part of the country you hunt in, the fawns are normally born during May, June, or July.

Newborn fawn waiting for its mother to return with dinner. Photo courtesy of U.S. Fish & Wildlife Service.

Bucks may go for three or four days without returning to their actual scrape, depending on their breeding activity, but they will check the scrape from downwind at least once a day. If the rut is at its peak, here again depending on a buck's actual breeding activity, he may visit his scrape several times a day to refresh it.

Buck returning to his scrape to freshen it up.

When hunting scrapes, don't place your stand too near the actual scrape. You must not contaminate the area with your scent. If the buck senses that his scrape area has been violated by a human, he will avoid it and not return. Try to determine where he would probably scent his scrape from downwind and focus on placing your stand in that area. Be sure that you can see the actual scrape site, but stay out of the immediate area. Try to pick a tree in the downwind direction from the scrape that is off to the left or right side of the true downwind direction. This will make it more difficult for the buck to detect your scent as he attempts to wind his scrape, especially if you hunt high, at least twenty to twenty-five feet up. Since wind has a habit of changing direction frequently, it is a good idea to have a backup tree in the area as an alternate in case the wind direction is not favorable to hunt your first choice. The area you are actually hunting will dictate just how much flexibility you have to do this. This may or may not work for you, but it is a good rule of thumb. If the buck is already on the scent of an estrous doe, the wind direction is not quite as critical. Bucks tend to have a one-track mind when it comes to their peak rut period. I once had a buck chase a doe right by me, and both the doe and the buck jumped the end of the log that I was sitting on. As they ran off, I had a nice broadside shot at the buck. On another occasion, I had a buck chase a doe right up to a tree where I was sitting on the other side. The doe was off to the side of the tree in full view, and the buck was no more than ten feet on the other side of the tree, just out of sight. After the doe ran off, the buck turned around and diagonally walked away, offering me the perfect shot. In both of these situations, I was in the buck's home range scrape area, and I also had the wind and peak rut period working for me.

Buck winding his scrape.

Expect rutting bucks to do the unexpected. Photo © by Mary Morris.

You might want to try creating a mock scrape. Sometimes a little push in the right direction will help to stimulate the rutting activity in your area. Since bucks quite often use other bucks' scrapes, it is not that uncommon to create a mock scrape and include all of the necessary ingredients and then have a buck use it. You must be sure to locate it in an area where the deer activity is quite heavy and near a well-used trail. Try to place it under a tree limb that is accessible and quite common to other licking branches you have found. Be sure to have your clothes and shoes perfectly cover-scented to guard against leaving any human odor in the area.

Use a stick or limb from the area scented with an appropriate buck or scrape urine, and scrape the leaves or grass away down to the bare earth. You can use a scrape-freshener drip bag hanging from the tree above the licking branch so that it will drip periodically into the scrape. This intermittent fresh scent will keep the scrape working for you when you're not around and hopefully convince a buck to start using it. Should a buck begin to use it, attempt to hunt it the same way you would hunt any other scrape. Go ahead and create two or three mock scrapes in your hunting area to give you the additional possibilities for success.

If you find a primary scrape, treat it with kid gloves, and never go looking for scrapes unless you use plenty of cover scent on your shoes and clothes. That way, when you find a primary scrape, you do not leave any human or foreign odor in the area. A good scenario would be if you were in Africa and accidentally stumbled into a big, man-eating cat's lair. If you leave scent in the lair, he will know you were there, and once he discovers it, he will track your scent back to you and kill you. In this case, you are going to do everything you can to be sure that he never knows you were there, since it is a matter of life or death. Treat a primary scrape the same way, as if it were made by that big, man-eating cat.

Look for scrapes on points of ridges; mouths of hollows; along routes between bedding areas and food sources; along old logging roads, fencerows, evergreen thickets, field edges, or fringes; and

This scrape has been inactive for a few days.

Bucks are where the does are. Photo courtsey of U.S. Fish & Wildlife Service.

anywhere there seems to be a heavy concentration of deer activity. If there are does in the area, there are going to be bucks as well.

Occasionally, you may find a single rub that was created as a type of signpost rub. This is a rub that serves as a sign to the deer that a particular crossing is ahead, such as a low place in a fence, a shallow

Signpost rub for a fence crossing to a food source.

creek or river crossing, or some other area where the crossing is more suitable to their travel route than the rest of the area.

When you suddenly find a large rub on a large tree, you know to begin looking for any sign of a large buck. Since larger, older bucks have, for the most part, become nocturnal, start looking for his bedding area. The buck's bedding area will become your focal point to hunt him.

Large rubs indicates large bucks.

Karen Alexy, a wildlife biologist, did a report on a scientific study conducted at the University of Georgia.[4] This study began in October of 1997 and revealed some very interesting findings that we white-tail deer enthusiasts and hunters need to be aware of. The study was conducted over a two-year period on a 3,460-acre study site in Madison and Oglethorpe counties in Northeast Georgia. These prop-erties had been under a strict whitetail deer management program for the past eleven years. The young bucks were protected, and the doe harvest had been somewhat liberal. The result was a large number of mature bucks and well-balanced sex ratio. The density of deer for these properties was about forty deer per square mile, and most of the breeding occurred during the first two weeks of November. Keep in mind that this study was a study of a wild population of whitetail deer. The scientists used motion-activated video cameras, allowing them to monitor scraping activity twenty-four hours a day. The setup consisted of an 8mm video camera, a passive motion-activated trig-ger, a seventy-five-watt floodlight (powered with a twelve-volt bat-tery) covered with a red lens and a waterproof enclosure (five-gallon bucket). When movement occurred in front of the unit, the camera recorded until the animal left the area. The light was programmed to turn on during evening hours, and the red light was used to mini-mize deer disturbance. In September of 1997, six traditional scrape sites were located that had been used in previous seasons. Four of these units were monitoring scrapes along field edges, and two were located in the woods over scrapes. The first year, the monitoring began on October 7, 1997, and lasted through February 21, 1998. The monitoring for the second year began on August 27, 1998, and ended on February 6, 1999. Antler and body characteristics were used to identify individual bucks and estimate their age. The follow-ing are the important points of the results of this study:

1. Of all scraping activity, 85 percent took place at night.
2. Overall scrape visitations were extremely low over the entire season, with very few opportunities to encounter bucks at scrapes during hunting hours.
3. Many different bucks worked the same scrapes, but overall scrape use was not very intensive.

4. Many of the bucks were yearling bucks and seemed to work the scrapes with the same intensity as the older bucks. This seemed to disprove the notion that the dominant bucks suppress the sexual behavior in younger bucks.

5. One interesting note is that almost none of the three-and-a-half-year-old and older bucks taken during these two seasons, although harvested within a couple hundred yards of a monitor, were ever caught on a video camera. There are several conclusions that can be drawn from this. The possibilities are that the deer were able to detect the monitoring equipment due to their additional experience cohabitating with man—or trying to avoid him, I should say. These more mature bucks may primarily refresh only their own scrapes and merely scent the other scrapes from the safety of downwind. Since these monitoring devices were checked every two weeks, the bucks could have sensed the people checking the monitors.

6. The most frequent marking behavior performed by bucks of all ages was overhead-branch marking. Nearly all marking activity included bucks marking overhanging branches with their forehead, antlers, or saliva.

7. Pawing the ground and urination occurred in less than half the visits that involved marking of any kind.

8. The peak of the rut in Georgia Piedmont typically occurred during the first three weeks of November. Marking by all ages of bucks monitored occurred almost exclusively during the months of October and November. Bucks visited these scrapes into December but performed no marking activity.

9. During this two year study, does were monitored in the process naturally, just as the bucks, but were not documented. Their marking activity, consistency, and so on seemed to parallel the bucks in many ways.

10. Based on this study, you should evaluate the area in the scrape vicinity to determine where you might best get a daylight shot at the buck. Since a great deal of the actual scrape markings take place just after dusk, moving back downwind far enough to catch him as he approaches in daylight hours or setting up

near the closest food source or his bedding area may provide the best opportunity.[5]

NOTES

1. *For Big Bucks Only*, by Jeff Murray, page 30, published by Mark LaBarbera of the North American Hunting Club.

2. The source of this information is *For Big Bucks Only*, by Jeff Murray, page 36, published by Mark LaBarbera of the North American Hunting Club.

3. *Hunting Whitetails Successfully*, by J. Wayne Fears, page 8, published by the North American Hunting Club.

4. Karen Alexy, a wildlife biology who received both her B.S. and M.S. from the University of Georgia. Alexy's two-year study on how bucks use scrapes was conducted from October 7, 1997, to February 21, 1998, and then from August 27, 1998, to February 6, 1999. The study was titled "Buck Use of Scrapes: What the Latest Research Reveals."

5. "Buck Use of Scrapes," by Karen Alexy.

This big buck in early morning fog offers an excellent opportunity for the hunter who can figure out his movements ahead of time.
Photo © by Matthew Choate.

Photo © by Mary Morris.

THE RUT

The most exciting time of the year for deer hunting is during the rut. This is the time of the year when does come into estrous and the bucks become obsessed with the right to service those does. During this time of year, there is much increased deer activity. With both sexes at their peak sexual cycles, there are more deer killed on the highways and more deer observed in general, because they tend not to concentrate as heavily on safety but more on their sexual drive. This condition makes them much more vulnerable to us hunters and offers us our best window of opportunity to successfully bag them. This period varies somewhat from the northern states to the southern, with our peak rut here in Tennessee falling around the second to third week of November, depending on certain conditions.

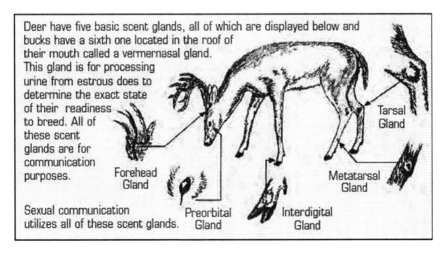

Deer have five basic scent glands, all of which are displayed below and bucks have a sixth one located in the roof of their mouth called a vermernasal gland. This gland is for processing urine from estrous does to determine the exact state of their readiness to breed. All of these scent glands are for communication purposes.

Sexual communication utilizes all of these scent glands.

Forehead Gland

Preorbital Gland

Interdigital Gland

Tarsal Gland

Metatarsal Gland

There is a great deal more vocalization, body language, and glandular scent communication between the bucks and the does during the rut. Whitetail deer have scent glands between their toes, called interdigital glands; on the outside of each hind leg, called metatarsal glands; on the inside of each hind leg, called tarsal glands; just below each eye, called preorbital glands; at the base of each antler, called forehead glands; and in the roof of their mouths, called vermonasal glands. Also located inside the mouth are their saliva glands, and in the nostrils, the nasal glands. All of these glands are used for communication purposes, especially sexual communication.

The period leading up to peak rut or pre-rut is an extremely good hunting period, too, because the bucks are still in bachelor groups, sparring and practicing on each other for the real fights to come. It is during this period when certain types of calling and some light rattling simulating sparring can be effec-

Two young bucks sparring.

tive. The younger bucks, due to their lack of experience, can be quite vulnerable during this period, since the hunting pressure is not very heavy yet.

During the actual peak rut period, the fighting escalates to a much more aggressive state. The bucks go at it with a vengeance to win the right to service the does in the area. During these matches, it is not uncommon for them to sustain serious injuries.

Two bucks fighting with extreme aggression.

During the peak rut period, since the bucks are so aggressive, plan to hunt all day whenever you can, because the deer will be on the move constantly. The bucks have one thing and one thing only on their mind, and that is chasing those does to service them. They do this with little regard to us hunters. They will be fighting other bucks for the right to do this, making them more vulnerable to us, and the hunting pressure itself will help keep them on the move, too. You may have some good luck with some very aggressive horn rattling during this period.

Do some serious and aggressive horn rattling during peak rut.

Use your horns to thrash around on the tree limbs, branches, and on the ground. Try to make yourself sound like an old, sexually frustrated buck out for blood. Keep in mind that during this peak rut period, anything goes—anything may work for you. The buck may do very foolish things during this time and present himself to you for a shot.

Aggressive rattling involves thrashing limbs, trees, and the ground and working the horns loudly.

Wouldn't this be a great buck to rattle in?

The best times to rattle are the two hours before dark and the two hours after daylight, but during the rut, it's worth a try any time if you haven't seen a buck. Try to be completely concealed so you don't expose any of your motion. When a buck responds to you, he will often come in cautiously and may see you unless you are well hidden. On the other hand, he may also come bolting in, enraged, to defend his territory, with little regard for caution.

As the rut begins, start to look for rub lines, scrape lines, primary scrapes, and very large rubs that appear as though more than one buck has rubbed them or as though a buck has rubbed them more than once. The primary scrapes are the nucleus of a buck's home range, but it is believed that these large, multirubbed trees may be equally important to a buck's rutting activity.

During pre-rut periods, begin look-ing for large trees that have been rubbed.

During peak rut periods, you will begin to find primary scrapes like this one.

You should set up in proximity to these areas to offer yourself the best opportunity at the buck. This will normally be somewhere on the downwind side of the scrape, and far enough away so you don't interfere with the buck's normal rutting activity. You want to still be able to observe the area, yet be in a position to harvest the buck if he approaches from the downwind side, as they commonly do. Bucks will often check their scrapes from the downwind direction without ever approaching the scrape itself.

Set up downwind and a safe distance away.

A buck will put forth a great deal of effort toward the creation and maintenance of these primary scrapes. They tend to create their scrapes on the edge of fields, near a woodline, down on the points of ridges, on the edges of old logging roads on top of the ridges, or in ravines. Where you find rub lines, begin to look for scrapes with the goal of locating a primary scrape. Bucks will paw the ground vigorously, exposing the bare earth for three or four feet in diameter. These primary scrapes will always be located under a tree limb that hangs approximately four or five feet above the scrape. The tip end of this limb, or the part that hangs closest to the scrape, will be chewed on, and sometimes bitten off. This occurs as the buck is attempting to leave a signature on his scrape. He will leave glandular scent and saliva on the tip of his licking branch. He will also stand over the bared earth, and with his hind legs together, he will rub his tarsal glands together as he urinates over the hocks and into the scrape.

Primary scrape located in the heart of a buck's core area.

Bucks will urinate over their hocks into their scrape. He will normally always leave a hoofprint in the center of the scrape as his final signature. He will tend this scrape, keeping it fresh for any estrous does in the area to find. An estrous doe

will come along and urinate into the scrape to let the buck know that she is ready for him.

You must avoid getting any human scent into the buck's primary scrape area. If he detects that you have been there, he will stop using this scrape, and you will be wasting your time. Scrapes may be used by different bucks, but not if they can smell human scent there.

Rutting bucks are constantly on the move, searching for estrous does.

As the rut continues, deer activity increases significantly. Deer may be on the move at any time during this period, and an adult buck may lose 20 to 30 percent of his body weight during the rut. This is largely due to his constantly being on the go; he may breed several does in a season.

As I previously mentioned, try creating mock scrapes to induce rutting activity where you want it. Since scrapes are often used by different bucks and some of the bucks are using a scrape that they did not create, they may as well use yours if you create it properly. The chapter on scrapes and rubs explains just how to create a mock scrape.

One of many typical breeding situations during the rut.

It is important to reiterate that when a doe comes into estrous, she remains in heat for twenty-four hours, and may actually go in search of a buck to be bred. If she is not bred during her first cycle, she will come into another estrous cycle every twenty-eight days until she is bred. Does do not all come into estrous at the same time in a specific area, and they are not all bred during their first cycle.

Scientists believe today that rubs do more than serve as signposts or territorial markers: they believe that the rubs have a direct bearing on stimulating the estrous cycles of the doe population. Since the timing of the rut is dependent upon when does first go into heat, it is very important to us hunters to know that by examining the rubs in a given area, we may be able to obtain an idea of whether the rut is going to be on time, early, or late. The key is priming pheromones—agents that do not necessarily cause a behavioral action or reaction (as do sex pheromones) but instead induce a biological change—that are deposited through antler-rubbing. In this case, these pheromones act as a biostimulant that induces early ovulation. The chemical signals stimulates females and helps synchronize breeding. As a result, the presence of the older bucks and their signposts helps to maintain social order.[1]

A very fresh signpost rub.

Scientists have also discovered that the whitetail buck has a sixth sense called vomolfaction. During the rut, when a buck comes across a doe's urine, he will lap it up and run it through his vemeronasal gland located in the roof of his mouth. In this way, he processes chemicals and more or less takes a doe's estrous temperature. Vomolfaction involves the buck's literally sucking the urine from the doe, and since the urine is never exposed to the air, he receives the benefit of being able to process certain chemicals that tell him things about the doe that he otherwise would not be able to know.

Whitetails have a vemeronasal gland in the roof of their mouth. Photo courtesy of John Stehn, U.S. Fish & Wildlife Service.

There are certain rut suppressants, such as weather, temperature, human pressure, and food sources. Weather patterns such as heavy rain, snow, or strong winds will bring the rut to a temporary halt in a specific area. Warmer weather will quickly shut down the rutting activity and in many cases cause certain bucks to become nocturnal. Strong hunting pressure will also

As hunting pressure increases, many older bucks become primarily nocturnal. You might tend to think that the rut occurred late or not at all, but the whole time it was occurring someplace else.

cause the rutting activity to dwindle or shut down. The bucks learn that darkness is much safer than daylight hours, so during the rut they become almost nocturnal. Often the deer will change food sources and move their rutting activity.

Small bucks pose no threat to larger bucks.

Bucks are more active in darkness.

Younger bucks normally pose no threat to the older, dominant bucks; as a result, very seldom will a younger buck lock horns with an older buck. During the rut, a second flurry of rubbing occurs as mature bucks prowl widely for the first estrous does (late October or early November in most regions, but later the further south you go). Look for extremely large tree rubbings, trashed limbs, and so on where a faint buck trail crosses a heavy doe trail. These large bucks will rub in these areas while scent-checking the does on the trail.

During the post-rut period, there tends to be a second flare-up of rut-ting activity due to the bucks' seeking out those few remaining does that have not yet been bred. There are normally a few does that fail to get bred until late in the season, so this is a second chance to har-vest a preoccupied buck.

Rub made by a larger buck.

Buck chewing on his licking branch. Photo by Tony Campbell.

You may come across a thicket with several gleaming rubs, indicat-ing one of probably two things: does may be bedding down in this area, and a buck is consistently coming into the thicket to check the does; or an old dominant buck may have moved his core area, which he has marked with all of these new rubs. A big buck will often thrash or rub eight or ten trees in a thicket like this out of sexual frustration, announcing his presence in the area to the does. Regardless of the reason for these rubs, this will be an excellent place to set up to hunt.

The best time to probably get a glimpse of this buck is either early morning or at dusk.

Violent rubs are indicative of the rut, so look for not only rubbed trees, but also thrashed vines, snapped saplings, ripped-up brush, and so on. These types of violent rubs are generally the work of sexually frustrated bucks heavy in rut. These will normally be in or near the buck's core area. Pick a strategic location to hang your tree stand, and you quite possibly will see this old buck on the prowl either very early in the morning or very late in the evening. Remember: the more violent the rub, the hotter the buck, and the more foolish and less nocturnal he is likely to be. Rattling may prove to be very good in this scenario.

Keep yourself alert to large (approximately three-and-a-half- to four-inch) tracks that make a deep impression, indicating a large buck.

A buck has made his presence known.

These small saplings were twisted off by a buck.

Scout for large, running, and looping tracks in muddy fields, creek crossings, or snowy woods, which indicate a rutting buck chasing does.

One tactic to use to find bucks during the rut is to hunt doe groups, since the bucks will normally be close by the does.

During the peak rut, a very good place to set up for bucks is on a trail from bedding areas to feeding areas. This should be a very active place to be from mid-afternoon until dark. You should determine how they are entering these food sources, and from where. In the afternoon, set up to hunt the area through which the deer are entering the food source.

A set of tracks made by a fairly large deer, probably a buck.

Buck entering a corn field after dark.

Often the old bucks will use the real brushy areas.

Often, the old bucks will use the real brushy areas, fence rows, or thicket fringes to woodlines to get from bedding areas to food sources to find the does.

A lightly used trail running beside a fence row is very possibly a buck trail.

Buck in route from a bedding area to food source.

NOTES

1. This information was originally presented by Larry Marchinton, W. Matt Knox, and Karl Miller, all three University of Georgia researchers, in a paper entitled *Whitetail Deer Signposts and Their Role as a Source of Priming Pheromones*, in which they also referenced a number of recent works they published in the *Journal of Wildlife Management* and in the *Journal of Mammalogy*. This information was obtained from *For Big Bucks Only*, page 30, written by Jeff Murray and published by Mark LaBarbera of the North American Hunting Club.

TRACKS EXPOSE DEER AND THEIR ACTIVITY

One of the most important tools we have as deer hunters is our ability to learn to read and understand whitetail deer tracks. Our forefathers did this so well that they could practically read the deer's minds. If you take the time to learn how to recognize and interpret what the deer are doing by their tracks, you will become a much more successful deer hunter.

You can determine if the deer are running or calmly walking by carefully analyzing the tracks. If the deer are on the run, the toes will be spread apart and will make a deeper impression in the ground. The tracks will appear to be larger than they actually are due to the sliding action caused by their forward motion while running as well as exposing their dewclaws.

If the deer is walking, the tips of the toes will be much closer

If the deer is running, the toes will be spread apart with a deeper impression and dewclaws will also be exposed in the track.

165

together and the track will not be impressed as deeply in the ground. These walking tracks also reflect more accurately the true size of the deer, because the tracks themselves are closer to the exact size of the actual hoof.

If the deer is walking, the tracks will display toes together with a shallower depression.

Generally you can determine if the deer are large, medium, or small by how large or small the tracks are and by how deep an impression they make in the ground. Soft, wet, or muddy ground can mislead you if you aren't careful. This type of surface will cause the animal to appear heavier than it actually is.

The larger tracks normally indicate a buck. Although

The size of the tracks normally directly relate to the size of the deer.

there are some extremely large does, they are rare compared to the bucks in the area. The whitetail deer are normally larger the further north, and smaller the further south, you find them.

WHITETAIL DEER HOOF MEASUREMENTS

TYPE OF DEER	Hoof Length	Width	Tip to Dewclaw
Fawn Buck	2-1/8"	1-3/4"	3-1/2"
Yearling Doe	2-3/4"	1-3/8"	4"
Yearling Buck	3-1/8"	1-1/2"	4-1/2"
2-1/2 + Year old Doe	3-1/8"	1-5/8"	4-1/2"
2-1/2 Year old Buck	3-1/2"	1-1/2"	5"
3-1/2 Year old Buck	3-3/4"	2"	5-1/2"

In many cases you can determine if a given set of tracks belongs to a buck or a doe. Although this is not necessarily the rule, some hunters believe that buck tracks on average are more rounded in the front than doe tracks, and that the older the buck, the more rounded or worn the toe tips appear to be. Doe tracks are believed to be more pointed in the front. The placement of the tracks in relation to each other can help you determine if a deer is a buck or a doe. Because a buck has a chest that is normally wider than his hindquarter, his rear hoofs will normally hit slightly inside of his front hoof tracks and slightly behind them. The doe, on the other hand, has a chest that is normally not as wide as her hindquarters, and therefore her rear hoofs normally hit slightly to the outside of her front hoofs and almost on top of them.[1]

These tracks indicate a doe.

You can quickly deter-
mine the direction of travel
simply by which way the
tracks are headed. I have
seen hunters that thought
the deer was traveling in
the opposite direction from
what it was actually going.
Imagine the hoof of one
of the deer that you have
harvested and taking that
actual hoof and pressing it
into the mud or sand. The
pointed tips of the hoofs
are on the leading edge of
the hoof, and indicate the
direction of travel.

How recently the tracks
were made is a valuable
piece of information to all
of us hunters and may be
obtained by determining
how fresh the tracks actually are. Sometimes it is

Tracks display a deer's direction of travel.

easier to age some tracks than others, depending on the weather conditions and the terrain. The weather may be fairly poor, or the terrain
may be rocky or grassy, making it very difficult to see precise tracks.
You may need to follow them as best you can to a different location
in an attempt to see them more clearly if you can follow them at all.
If the tracks have small particles of dirt, sand, or other debris hanging
from the sides that you figure can't hang there very long without falling into the track, they are probably pretty fresh. These tracks could
be as recent as a few minutes to a couple of hours old, depending on
the weather. If the weather is fairly poor, a track with sharp edges is
most likely only a few minutes old. You may have frightened the deer
away as you approached. On the other hand, if the tracks have less
sharp or even rounded edges and small debris in the bottom of the

track, this is probably several hours old. The less sharp or vivid the track, the older it probably is. If you come across tracks that have a lot of debris and are quite faded or worn, they are several days old, in most cases—again depending on the weather. Usually, the crisper or sharper the track, the fresher the track.

How sharp or precise the tracks are in conjunction with the present or recent weather conditions help to determine their age.

When the tracks were made, and the direction they were going, will help you determine where to hunt the deer. Since the whitetail deer feeds from late in the afternoon throughout the night until the early dawn hours and generally beds down throughout the day (with some exceptions), concentrate on where the tracks are going, and when. If the tracks are found in the morning hours and are determined to be fairly fresh (less than two or three hours old), consider what food source they may be leaving and follow them toward a bedding area. On the other hand, if the tracks are found in the afternoon or evening hours and are fresh, then they are probably leading from a bedding area toward a food source. These pieces of information will be extremely helpful in determining if you want to set up to hunt the deer going to a food source or to a bedding area, depending on whether it is a morning or afternoon hunt. The wind may dictate to a great extent whether you hunt the bedding area or the food source in the morning or in the afternoon.

When and where the tracks were made and their direction of travel will help determine when and where to hunt.

In many cases, you can determine how many deer passed through a particular area at the same time. If the deer are running, they are less likely to overlap each other's tracks and are therefore easier to count, depending on the type of terrain. The deer will often walk in single file on a single run or trail, and in this scenario, it may be difficult to count them. You may choose to follow them to a specific area where they cross a muddy or sandy area, making it easier to distinguish the different-sized tracks and estimate their number in this manner. The muddy or sandy surface allows the tracks to be more precise and distinguishable for the purpose of estimating numbers. The fewer there are, the easier it is to count them, because you have less overlapping.

Deer do leave some sign of their tracks, even on rocky surfaces. You may have to get down on your knees and observe very closely and carefully the rocky surface or other types of surfaces for scratches or small, chipped-off particles of rock. There are normally signs there if you look hard enough.

Soft surface areas are good places to check when doing your scouting.

Soft, muddy, or sandy surfaces make it much easier to examine the tracks.

When a buck is on the trail of an estrous doe and is trailing her down a deer runway, he will usually be traveling at a pretty good pace. When you are following his trail and suddenly notice that he is beginning to wander off from one side of the trail to the other, slow down and begin looking very carefully. You will probably notice that he has slowed down his pace in an attempt to either bed down or browse for a while. He may also be attempting to slow down in an effort to check the trail behind him or circle around and head back down to check the trail from downwind. Don't move without closely examining the entire area around you;

A buck cautiously walking down a trail.

Bucks tend to leave drag marks when walking in snow, but if the snow is deep enough, the doe will as well. Photo by Veikko Rihu.

when you feel it's okay to do so, move off the trail in the downwind direction and begin a wide circle in an attempt to get ahead of him.[2]

Normally a buck leaves drag marks as he walks if the ground is soft enough for his weight to penetrate the ground very deeply. The doe tends to pick her feet up in a daintier fashion than a buck, clearing the ground as she walks. Both bucks and does will leave drag marks in the snow if it is two or three inches deep or deeper.

NOTES

1. *The Deer of North America*, by Leonard Lee Rue III, page 36, published by Outdoor Life Crown Publishers, Inc.

2. A good tip from Noble Carlson in *For Big Bucks Only*, page 164, written by Jeff Murray and published by the North American Hunting Club.

Photo © by Mary Morris.

SECTION III

◆

DURING THE ACTUAL HUNTING PROCESS

Photo © by Mary Morris

DURING THE ACTUAL HUNTING PROCESS

There are many situations that take place during the actual hunting process: some good and some bad, some planned and some that just happen. If you do your homework and thoroughly plan each and every hunt, these things can—for the most part—be predetermined. Always keep in mind, however, that there will be setbacks occasionally, and Murphy's Law may apply from time to time.

I had leased a particular sixty-five-acre tract of timberland for the first time. There were several other properties that I could hunt, but I wanted a place near home where I could go after work. To get to this particular section of land, I had to cross the owner's home on my route. I would drive past his driveway to a stock gate to his pasture and then down a long dirt road to the far side and down into a dry creekbed. On the far side of this creek bed there was another stock gate that led to his sixty-five acres of timberland. He suggested that I drive through this gate to the edge of the woods and park there. He was a very friendly person and had been very helpful in informing me of where he often saw deer. He explained the lay of his land and had his son walk the property line with me. The day ended with me thanking them and letting them know that I would be driving the same truck each time I went in so they would know that it was me.

Over the next few days, I did some serious scouting and felt that I had a few good choices of hunting sites, depending on the wind. On opening morning, I drove in, crossed the creek, and parked the truck at the edge of the woods. There was rain in the forecast, but that didn't normally bother me, because I love to be in my stand just after a rain stops. I took my rain suit, set up my stand, and got situated. Before it even broke daylight, the rain came. It was just light showers at first, but very shortly afterward, the bottom fell out. I stood up and leaned over with my rifle under my rainsuit in an attempt to keep it as dry as possible. I thought that the rain would probably stop in a short while and the hunting should be good. It was one of those situations where I said to myself, "I'm going to stay just fifteen more minutes, and if the rain doesn't stop, I will head to the house." When that fifteen minutes was up, I would say, "Just fifteen more minutes," until before I knew it, the entire morning had gone by. I finally called it quits and headed for the truck.

I drove to the stock gate at the dry creekbed, or at least that's the way I remembered it being that morning. I couldn't believe my eyes when I saw that the creek was higher than the windows on my truck. Luckily, I had a cell phone and the telephone number of the landowner in my truck. I called him and asked him how I could get out with my truck and he told me of an old logging road that was semi-passable. Parts of it were washed out, and other parts of it had grown up. I had just purchased a new four-wheel drive truck, and now I was about to put it through its paces.

I spent the rest of the day working my way out, and I do mean working. I came to areas where I had to shore up holes with rock and logs, and other areas where I had to cut trees and find the shallowest part of creek crossings. I did finally get out and back home. It proved to be a hunt that I will never forget.

I didn't get a deer, but I did learn a valuable lesson: whatever you are doing in life, whether it's deer hunting or making some important decision, try to always have a contingency plan in case things don't work out as you expected them to. A good contingency plan is vital in many situations when you are deer hunting. The weather, hunting pressure, food sources, deer movements, and many other things may force you to change your plans, so be flexible. I hope that the chapters in this section will call attention to areas where you will need alternate plans.

Photo © by Mary Morris

Photo © by Mary Morris

SHOT PLACEMENT

One of the most responsible things you can learn about deer hunting—about any kind of hunting, for that matter—is good shot placement and selection. Knowing when and where to take the shot and where to focus your aim will make you a much more ethical and responsible hunter. We all want to do the right thing by our quarry and afford it the most humane and quick, clean kill possible, and we've heard too many stories of a hunter or someone else getting shot while in the woods hunting. This instances are unnecessary and preventable. Most of these cases take place because the hunter is shooting at merely what he or she thinks, rather than knows, to be the quarry. If we train our minds to focus on proper shot placement, we will accomplish more than just one goal, but most importantly we would prevent the senseless, accidental shootings of others. Proper shot placement forces us to concentrate instantly on the precise spot on a deer that we want to hit with our projectile, whether it is a bullet or an arrow. If we train our minds to look for this specific spot on our quarry, then we will take the time to identify with certainty that the target is a deer or some other animal and not another hunter. Then we focus on the shot placement. This keeps us from quickly shooting at a brief movement or a quick flash of white out of the corner of our eye. We are looking for a specific part of a deer's body. This attitude will become second nature to you before you know it, and will greatly improve your kill ratio and reduce the number of wounded deer every year. In general, it will make a better hunter out of you. Knowing when not to shoot will make you a more ethical hunter, too.

You should become familiar with a deer's anatomy and where the vitals are located. The vital areas of a whitetail deer include the heart, lungs, liver, spinal column, jugular vein (located in the deer's neck), and brain. You need to know how to place your shot to hit a vital area when deer are in various positions to you. Naturally, the heart-and-lung area offers you the largest target and, in most cases, your best kill shot. You need to learn when you have a potential kill shot and when you don't. Developing the ability to distinguish between a good shot and one that should not be taken is an ongoing process. We can train ourselves to consider this question each time we are presented with a shot. Will this shot offer you a clean kill, or is the outcome doubtful or marginal at best? Consider different hunting scenarios. For example, let's say you can partially see a very nice buck in some brush. The vitals are partially obscured by the brush, offering you a less than favorable shot. Do you take this shot or not? There are situations in which this could still be an acceptable shot. If the brush is not heavy or thick and is very close to the deer instead of you, such that a slight deflection would still allow the projectile to hit the kill zone, the buck may be worth the shot. This could be a difficult call; when in doubt, don't take the shot. This illustration shows the position of the vital organs within the deer.

You will notice the heart just above the elbow; the shaded area above the heart is the lung-and-liver area. The main arteries are running from the heart to critical parts of the anatomy. Notice the vertebrae running the length of the top of the deer's back.

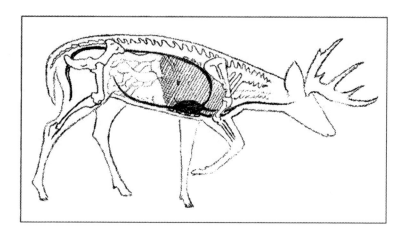

Always try to shoot from some type of gun rest or armrest when possible. This increases your chances for a clean kill. In most cases, you will have a tree limb, tree trunk, rock, or something to rest against to steady your aim. When you are still hunting or stalking a deer, always try to make a habit of stopping next to a tree or something to steady your aim should you get a shot. An armrest of some type should be an important part of your deer stand.

Try to become instantly aware of when a good shot is developing so you can prepare yourself to be ready to take the shot. It might be a lone deer walking down a run that has him angling toward a clearing, offering a perfect shot.

Suddenly, a good broadside shot has presented itself.

Try to think of the shot that you are about to make as being the only shot that you will get; in most cases, it will be. This type of attitude will promote good shot placement. Try to imagine that you only have one bullet or arrow to expend on the deer. If you don't get him with it, you don't get him at all. Here again, this is the type of attitude to enhance good shot placement for a definite kill. The lung area offers you the largest part of the deer to shoot at and has the greatest chance for a definite kill. If your shot penetrates the lung, you have made your kill.

Be alert; this may develop into a good shot, and it may be the only one you get.

When you are bowhunting and you release an arrow at a deer, the sound of your release generally causes a natural reaction in a deer, especially if the deer is the least bit attentive. A deer may drop his or her body eight to ten inches straight down in reaction to your release. This is normally a prelude to bolting away from the area. Dropping the body in this manner has caused many a hunter to overshoot the deer. Keeping in mind that in spite of the lung area being quite large, there are a couple of factors that might work against you when shooting down at a deer from a tree stand. The arrow will tend to rise somewhat as you shoot down, and the natural tendency of the deer will be to drop their body at the sound of the release. For these reasons, you should aim lower than normal. If possible, try to shoot when the deer is calm, with head down, feeding or grooming himself or otherwise letting you know that he is unaware of your presence.

This buck is fairly relaxed, unaware of a hunter's presence. Photo © by Eric Van Eck

When bowhunting, try not to make your draw too soon if you can help it; the deer may do something unexpected, and the longer you have to hold your draw, the less accurate you will be when you make your shot. If you have to hold the shot too long, you may begin to shake and move, possibly even making noise that could frighten the deer

Use a quick "Naaa!" or whistle to halt the deer for a quick shot.

away and ruin your shot. This can be a very tricky part of bow-hunting: being able to make your draw at the right time. While you don't want to make your draw too soon, neither do you want to make it when the deer can spot your movement or hear the draw. Experience is the best teacher here, as I am sure you will find out. The longer you bowhunt, the more capable you will become of reading the situation and knowing what to do.

It is never a good idea to try to hit a running target. Always try to bring your deer to a halt or stop for that still shot. Use a quick "Naaa!" or whistle or some type of call to bring the deer to a sudden halt as it attempts to determine where the sound came from. This momentary stop gives you a shot at a still target and a shot at the vitals area for a clean kill. Keep in mind that the deer will only stop for a few seconds, because he is already alarmed—so be ready to shoot.

It is never a good idea to shoot at a running deer, so always try to get a deer to stop.

There are locations on the Internet where you can go and research good shot placement. You will find pictures of deer in various positions and when you have a kill shot on these deer and when you don't.

Practice, practice, and more practice is your best strategy. Use either life-size 3D targets or life-size silhouettes in different hunting situations. Practice shooting down from a stand and from the ground, sitting, and standing. When you get a good opportunity to take your shot, you must be capable of making it a clean kill. I cannot emphasize the importance of practice enough—the more you practice, the more capable you will become at good shot placement and making a clean kill.

Poor shot placement will result in a deer wandering off to die a slow, painful death, never to be recovered, or will make it too weak to defend itself against its predators, ending up as another coyote or wolf statistic.

Poor shot placement will cause a deer to go off and die a slow, painful death or weaken him to the point of being unable to avoid his predators.

Here are examples of some deer positions that cause you to question where you do or don't have a shot.

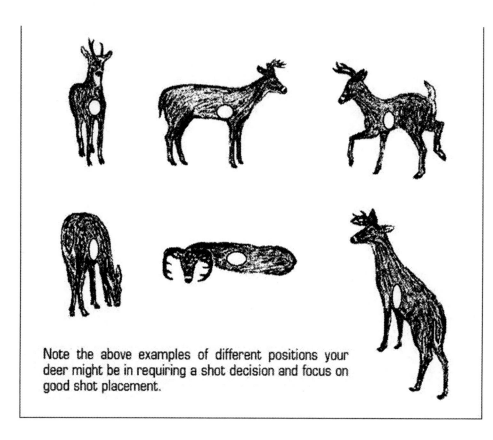

Note the above examples of different positions your deer might be in requiring a shot decision and focus on good shot placement.

DEER HABITS

In order to be a successful whitetail deer hunter, you must learn the deer's habits. You need to know what they are likely to do under certain circumstances and why they are doing it. The whitetail deer is one of the most challenging animals you can hunt, probably the most challenging in North America. He will constantly surprise you with his ability to evade you in the field or woods, and for this reason, it is here on his own home territory that you must study him. If you are a fairly new deer hunter, spend a lot of time in the woods just studying him and his habits. Take a camera, field glasses or a spotting scope, a note pad, and your stand into the woods, and set up and spend hours getting to know the whitetail deer. You will never completely get to know him, but you will learn much valuable information to help you when hunting season comes around. Read books, watch videos, talk to veteran hunters, and absorb all you can to qualify yourself for the whitetail deer hunt. Since repetition is one of the best ways to learn, I have reiterated many aspects of characteristics of the whitetail deer in these various chapters.

Deer have some habits that are instinctive, others that are strictly rut-related, some that are stimulated by hunger or thirst, and still others that are generated by their association with humans.

Deer communicate through their scent glands, body language and actions, and vocalizations. These are all very powerful means of communication among the whitetail deer. We can learn a great deal from them about their communication simply by observing them in their natural habitat. What you learn about their communication will greatly enhance your ability as a hunter.

Deer will often sharply bob or dip their heads up and down a few times until their curiosity is satisfied one way or another about suspected danger. If they detect danger, this action will also be accompanied by the stomping of a front foot. The whitetails will often go up in a flagged position; if you observe them doing this, they are already on the alert and in

These does seem to be discussing who should be boss.

most cases will move on out of the area. If they definitely detect your presence, they will vacate the area swiftly, but if they are merely suspicious, they may casually but nervously move out of the area.

If a deer's tail is twitching casually and down, this is a sign that the deer feels unthreatened, and as long as he remains this way, he should stay in the area a while longer or until his reason for being there is finished. If the tail is up

Flagging whitetail in a speedy retreat from the area. Photo © by Peter Eades.

with the white of the tail flashing, he is on the alert and suspects danger. Sometimes, if a deer has detected you but feels that you have not detected him, he may attempt to slip out of the area with his tail down to remain camouflaged from you. A common sight is the flashing white tail flagging in a speedy retreat from the area. This sight is commonly accompanied by the snorting or blowing sound they make when alarmed or frightened.

Tail up means deer on alert. Photo courtesy of U.S. Fish & Wildlife Service.

If you hear the blowing or snorting of deer in the distance, they have detected your presence and will be quickly gone. If you are walking through the woods, deer can spot you several hundred yards away, a great deal farther than you can spot them from. They can also hear and smell you from a much greater distance than you might think. Weather conditions play a big role in just how far away they are able to do this.

Deer can spot us long before we can spot them. Photo © by Kevin Lammi, Northland Images.

There are certain times when a deer suspects danger while feeding or going about any one of many other daily routines and will bob his head up and look in your direction, then put his head back down as if totally unaware of your presence. He will then quickly bob it back up again in an effort to catch you off guard. This is a way of attempting to outsmart us. If you are stalking this browsing deer, move toward him only when his head is down or in some other direction from yours. As you move toward the deer, do so slowly in as straight of a line as possible, since deer pick up side movement more easily than if you are moving straight toward them. If you are in motion toward the deer when he suddenly looks in your direction, be ready to freeze absolutely in place. You may have one foot up as if to take a step, but you must freeze on one foot if possible to keep from moving; if you have to put your foot down, do so extremely slowly. You should stay as low as you can to the ground and move from one point of concealment to the next toward the deer. Sometimes the deer will move unsuspectingly in your direction as he feeds. If you see the deer doing this, take advantage of his movements and let him do as much of the work as possible. The more he moves in your direction, the less you have to move in his.

Be ready for a deer to look in your direction at any time. Photo © by Beth Andrus.

Deer love to browse in a light rain or mist; this is one of the best times to hunt or stalk a deer.

Deer normally bed down and are inactive during a rain or snow-storm or heavy wind.

Buck bedding down.

Since deer are low-light animals and can see at night. Because they have learned that it is safer at night, they are naturally more active then. They will feed primarily at night and bed down during the day. Even though they can see at night, they can see better on clear nights with a full moon than they can on totally dark ones. It is for this reason that on totally dark nights, they spend more time looking for food than they do actually feeding. Deer tend to be less active on a day following a clear night with a full moon, because their stomachs are full.

Doe feeding at night. Photo © by Jack Izard.

The sun and moon have a definite effect on whitetail activity. The sun is more obvious in that it creates low-light conditions as it rises and sets. These seem to be the preferred conditions for most whitetail deer due to an increased feeling of security. The unique makeup of their light-gathering eyes and their four-part stomachs suggest that they're neither circadian nor nocturnal. Some biologists classify whitetail deer as crepuscular or low-light animals, but this is only partially true. Some nights, herds of deer can be seen feeding in fields at the same time, and yet other nights they are

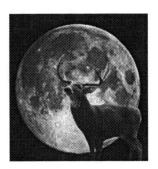

Moon phases have a direct bearing on whitetail activity.

nowhere to be found. Likewise, sometimes deer are active during the day, and sometimes they are not. In other cases, some older bucks have become strictly nocturnal. In general, most whitetail activity seems to occur when the moon phase coincides with the low-light periods. The more complete the moon phase during these periods, the stronger the activity. There are several websites available that greatly elaborate on hunting by the moon phases, and a very good reference book is *Hunting Whitetails by the Moon*, by Charles J. Alsheimer. You may also contact the U.S. Naval Observatory and find out when the sun will rise and set, and the moon transit for the days you plan to hunt.

Many hunters believe that the second full moon following the fall equinox, which is September 23, is the Hunter's Moon, and one of the best times to be in the woods. An equinox happens every year at two specific moments in time when there is a location on the earth's equator where the center of the sun can be seen to be vertically over-head. This occurs around March 20–21 and September 22–23 every year. It's a good idea to plan to hunt close to these times.

Deer are primarily brows-ers, and when other types of food sources are not available, they will feed on all types of browse.

Deer prefer red and white oak acorns to just about any other food source. Deer will normally be found feeding

Doe casually browsing. Photo © by Jack Izard.

on the acorns that are presently falling from the trees. Since acorns tend to fall from the oak trees on top of the ridges first and gradually work down the hills to the lower trees, the deer will be feeding on the acorns on top of the ridges first and then on down the hills to the lower oak trees. This is valuable hunting information, so you should take advantage of it.

You should anticipate more deer activity before and after a storm; for this reason try to defi-nitely be in the woods during or just after these periods.

As I mentioned in the chapter on preseason scouting, when a buck rises out of his bed, he has a habit of urinating in the bed before he leaves it, while a doe will normally walk away from the bed to urinate.

This doe walks away from its bed to urinate. Photo courtesy of John Munt.

Search for bedding areas on the fringes of where the terrain changes from one type to another, places where the deer can bed down and watch for danger, such as on the side of power line clearings, on the side of ridges or points, and in the thick brushy areas on the edges of fields.

Doe bedded on the edge of a field. Photo © by Peter Eades.

Buck heading out for his food source.

The old bucks are going to be bedded down in the thickest, least traversable cover they can find. Trails leading away from food sources will normally lead to bedding areas.

Deer are fringe-type animals that rely on these areas for close cover should danger approach. They prefer all types of fringes, such as woods that change to briar thickets, the edges of fields, a wood line that borders a clear cut, rough edges around a crop field or power line clearing, dry creek beds, and so on.

If you jump deer out of a bedding area, the chances are good that they will take the same escape route each time they are jumped. If

Bedding areas may be found anywhere that offers good visibility to spot predators, where the deer can feel secure.

you jump them more than once or twice, they will likely move to a different location.

When deer rise out of a bed, they will normally perform certain body functions, such as stretching, scratching, grooming, urinating, defecating, and browsing. If undisturbed, deer may linger in the bedding area after they get up before heading out to their preferred food source.

This doe is on the alert and ready to take flight..

A doe grooming herself before leaving her bedding area.

Deer seem to use certain trails over and over, year after year. Some trails are used more often some years than others, but they are consistent paths of travel. Outside forces such as weather may change these trails somewhat and force the deer to change part of their route, but the same basic trail is still used.

Trail used year after year by the deer.

Contrary to what you may have heard, deer do look up overhead, especially if there is anything that attracts their attention up there. Hunting pressure and tactics over the years have conditioned the whitetail deer to become even more suspicious of the treetops than they used to be. You must concentrate much more effort on concealment, camouflage, scent, and your hunting surroundings.

Normally, younger bucks will only rub smaller trees, while large bucks will rub small and large trees. Large rubs are very exciting to find when you are scouting.

This is a good, respectable-size rub, and it should be considered in any hunting strategy.

This buck is rubbing his forehead glands on a small tree. Photo by Larry Brown, http://www.flickr.com/photos/lwbrown/.

Bucks create what are called secondary and primary scrapes before and during the rut. These are created in the nucleus of their home range, and the primary scrapes are often used by other bucks. These primary scrapes are basically focal points of a deer's sexual activity. These scrapes are to alert does to his presence and his territory and lure them into the area by the scent he dispenses in and around the scrape.

Another good rub.

Typical secondary scrape.

Primary scrape apparently in need of refreshing after a windy day.

Bucks may be fooled into using mock scrapes (scrapes made by humans) since some bucks use other bucks' scrapes at times. If the mock scrapes are created properly, these bucks don't know the difference and may begin to use it, creating additional hunting possibilities.

Different bucks may tend the same scrape.

Bucks tend to band together in bachelor groups and begin sparring with each other just after they loose their velvet. This is done to more or less establish a pecking order. The younger bucks are learning the very basics for the fighting that will ensue later.

A bachelor group of four bucks. Photo © by Mary Morris.

When bowhunting, if you make a release on a buck, the sound of your release causes a reaction in the deer to drop his entire body eight to ten inches in an effort to avoid potential danger. This reaction as a result of his adrenal glands kicking in will often cause your arrow to fly over the top of the deer, or at least hit him high, and possibly miss a vital area. Many hunters have shot high on a deer because of this. To avoid this problem, try to make your release when the deer is definitely preoccupied, and aim a little lower if you are hunting from high up, anticipating this reaction in the deer.

When a buck is rubbing the velvet from his rack, he will often raise his head and roll his rack around in circles, more or less winding up tree limbs and pulling on them. He will twist up small saplings and rip them apart.

Examples of two small trees that were twisted off by a buck.

Deer will instinctively move to the downwind side of any suspected danger in an effort to identify the danger.

Deer will often freeze in a position when suddenly confronted by danger in an attempt to elude the danger by letting it pass. They will remain frozen until pressured further.

Large doe freezes in an effort to ascertain the degree of possible danger.

If a doe in estrous has not been bred during her twenty-four hours in heat, she will actually go looking for a buck to be bred. If she is not bred during this period, she will come into heat again every twenty-eight days until she is bred. This process can occur up to four or five times a year.

Does may actually seek out a buck to be bred.

When a buck senses danger in the wind, he will run across clearings or low-cut fields unless he decides to skirt around them, and will often slow down only when he reaches the other side. He will normally turn and observe his trail to determine if any type of predator is following him.

If a buck feels threatened and cornered, he may lie on his belly and crawl past you in an effort to elude you, or swim down the middle of a river in an effort to quietly slip out of the area.

This buck detects possible danger on the wind.

Bucks will sometimes use does as scouts or bait by sending them out in front of them on the trail to determine if danger lies ahead. There have probably been situations where you thought the buck was following the doe strictly for sexual reasons when actually the doe was merely making sure the coast was clear for the benefit of the buck's safety.

If a doe is scouting ahead of a buck, she will take long pauses with her nose in the

Does may sometimes scout ahead for the old buck.

air in all directions and will step off the trail in different directions in an attempt to draw out any potential danger. She will often look back in the buck's direction as if to reassure him, and sometimes she will backtrack a few steps occasionally as if to double-check the area she just passed through. She will certainly put herself in harm's way for the buck.

The doe will keep checking back for the buck's location.

Photo © by Mary Morris.

Photo © by Mary Morris

WHITETAIL BODY LANGUAGE

Agood whitetail deer hunter possesses many qualities and capabilities that have either been bred into him or that he has learned over the many years of deer hunting. A serious deer hunter has spent many, many hours in the woods or field doing nothing but studying the whitetail deer. If you enjoy something thoroughly, as most deer hunters enjoy hunting the whitetail deer, you can't help but become very knowledgeable on the deer. Sitting on a deer stand for hours and hours at a time, a hunter sees many deer—most of them are not the deer he will harvest—so a hunter has many subjects to study in their natural habitat, and nothing but time to do it. The whitetail deer communicate in various ways, and it is to the hunter's great advantage to learn all of them as early in his hunting career as possible. The deer use body language, scent glands, and vocal sounds to communicate with each other. All of these methods are very powerful means of talking to each other. We don't know all of their secrets and never will, but here are a few of their communication abilities.

When a deer suddenly sees something and isn't quite sure what it is, it becomes suspicious, and as a result, it will bob or dip its head up and down

This doe is suddenly alert.

205

sharply a few times. Once the deer has satisfied its curiosity as to what the object is, it will either relax and resume its original routine or, if it suspects danger, bolt and run away. As the deer bolts away, it will often stop a few yards away out of sight and have another look and snort a few times before leaving the area.

If a deer snorts or blows, this is a definite sign of alarm, and in most cases a prelude to a quick retreat from the area. Don't plan on seeing this deer again in the immediate future—he is out of there.

When a deer is suspicious of you in your stand, or suspicious of anything else, it may stomp its foot and bob its head in an attempt to get you to move to confirm its suspicion. This stomping of the foot is the whitetail's way of trying to force some

A quick retreat after a stout blow.

movement—even a hunter's blinking eye may be detected. Deer also make this gesture to alert other deer in the area of possible danger. Scientists claim that foot-stomping is also a method of leaving a warning scent from the interdigital glands on the ground for other deer that come into the area after the deer has left.

If you are watching a whitetail deer calmly browsing and he is secure and feels unthreatened, his tail will be down and slightly twitching. This is a good sign that the deer will probably be hanging around for your pleasure for a little while.

If you are the least bit careless on your stand, a whitetail may spot you the minute it comes into view of your stand. Courtesy of the U.S. Fish & Wildlife Service.

These deer are in a relaxed state and feeling unthreatened. Photos © by Kevin Lammi, Northland Images, and by Mary Morris

When deer have their tails up in the flagged position, they are already on the alert and normally making an exit from the area. The tail hair and rump hair beneath the tail flares out, lending the appearance of being much more pronounced, and all you notice is the white with the white tail flickering from side to side. Occasionally, the deer will flag their white tails and simply trot a few steps away as if they know there is danger but do not know how severe the danger is. When they flag their tail and run out of sight, they were aware of the degree of danger at hand. I'm sure that all deer hunters have seen this famous white tail bounding through the woods on numerous occasions.

This is a very common sight to deer hunters. We often see this white flag and nothing more. Photo courtesy of D. Gordon E. Robertson.

Occasionally a deer will slip away with his tail between his legs—in the down position—in an attempt to conceal himself. This is normally a buck, so watch closely where he goes, since you might be able to recall him. This will depend largely on just how frightened he was when he slipped away or what caused him to leave in the first place, as well as on how well you can use your call to lure him back.

A buck slipping out of the area, tail down.

When a buck is challenging his opponent, he will stomp and paw the ground and thrash his rack around in an attempt to psyche his opponent out as they approach each other. With his back slightly arched, the hair standing out on his back and neck, and with the ears pulled back, he is definitely a force to be reckoned with. His body language broadcasts to his opponent a readiness to fight.

Does will go through a kind of boxing process when they fight or become aggressive with each other. They will stand on their hind legs and attempt to kick each other with their front hooves. This is a way in which they establish a pecking order.

Two bucks squaring off somewhat aggressively. This photo by Kevin Lammi, Northland Images.

At times you will notice a deer with his head up into the wind. The deer has probably already caught a strange scent but has not pinpointed the source or

Does establishing a pecking order.

the degree of danger, or is merely intensively searching the area for any foreign scent. The deer will also probably have his tail held out parallel to the ground while sharply twitching it from side to side if he suspects danger. If it's during the rut, a buck could also be scenting an estrous doe.

Scenting for an estrous doe or sign of danger.

Whitetail deer pop their heads up and look in the direction of suspected danger and then put it down as if to act as though they intend to continue feeding. They then suddenly pop their heads back up again in an attempt to catch any suspected predator in motion.

A whitetail alerts other deer nearby to the presence of potential danger by sharply bringing his tail up to the horizontal to upright position, but in a stationary manner, and freezes while focusing on the area of suspected danger with both ears focused in that direction. He may stand perfectly still and move nothing but his eyes for several minutes. This alerted deer has suddenly become the focal point for all the other deer around him.

Whitetails pop their heads up and check for danger at random.

A doe in the presence of a buck may raise her tail and show her white backside, signifying to the buck that she is ready to breed.

Notice the alert deer with her tail in the horizontal position.

Notice the hocks: if they are very dark, the doe is probably in full estrous and ready to breed. There is a very good chance that a buck has picked up her scent and is on her trail to breed her, so watch her body language very carefully. If you notice her constantly looking in a certain direction, she may be aware of an approaching buck and give his position away to you.

If you happen to catch a buck doing the lip curl, he has probably scented an estrous doe in the wind and is attempting to pinpoint her location to go and breed her. He probably won't waste any time getting to her, so be alert. You may have to react fast in this situation in order to get a shot.

Be aware of does looking behind themselves.

In addition to the body language, deer also communicate vocally and use a variety of vocalizations. Try to learn as many of these as possible. There are various buck grunts, doe and fawn bleats, and bawls that you should become familiar with. The best way to do this in a relatively short period of time is to visit my website, www.awdhr. com, click on "Free Stuff for Hunters," and scroll down to "Whitetail Vocal Sounds." You can also purchase videos and audio tapes of vocal sounds from

This buck doing the lip curl has probably scented an estrous doe.

a variety of sources. You can learn the meaning behind these sounds and use your calls to duplicate them. You will need to practice these sounds over and over until you feel you have mastered them.

The whitetail deer has several different scent glands, most of them used for communication with other deer. The glands possessed by the whitetail are the tarsal glands, located on the inside of the hind legs, and the metatarsal glands, located on the lower outside portion of the hind legs. They also have interdigital glands located just above the hoof splits, preorbital glands located just in front of and slightly below each eye socket, and forehead glands, located near the base of each main beam. They possess a gland called the vemeronasal gland, located in the roof of their mouth, as well as their saliva glands, also located in the mouth, and their nasal glands, located inside their nostrils. Most of these glands are primarily used for sexual or breeding communication. Deer also leave scent to warn other deer of danger or let them know they are in the area and other general day-to-day communication. These different scent glands are illustrated in the chapter entitled "The Rut."

Bucks use their scent glands for all types of communication.

The chapters on scrapes and rubs and the rut goes into some detail explaining the use of the various glands for breeding communication.

Photo © by Mary Morris.

UNDERSTANDING GOOD DEER MANAGEMENT

We all would like to see the deer in our hunting area as healthy as possible and also see some Boone & Crockett or Pope & Young trophy-class bucks. This is possible for most of us to achieve given the right set of circumstances. It requires a great deal of consistent effort and knowledge of the whitetail and his nutritional needs. It also requires educated decisions for the benefit of your deer herd. Plan on a great deal of patience and a willingness to devote some time, sweat, and money to create a safe, healthy environment for the deer. Your overall goal should be to establish healthy, trophy-class bucks, which will strengthen the whole herd.

Bucks like this are possible within a well-managed deer herd program. Photo courtesy of Rick Stutts.

Most people who know anything about managing whitetails will tell you that there are some important basic factors in managing a deer herd. These are habitat, age, buck-to-doe ratios, genetics, nutrition, and geographical area. This last one certainly has an impact on the limit to the size of deer

213

that are produced. This is not something that you can do anything about unless you move. The further north you go, the larger the deer. The climate is harsher, and thus the deer have to adapt—they must have more body fat to survive. During the antler-growth season, the bucks are eating and storing fat for the winter to come, and this also aids antler development.

During a buck's first three years of life, body development takes priority over antler growth. A buck does not reach his full potential until age three and is in his prime from about age three to age five. Generally, a buck will start to decline after that, although depending on nutrition, availability, and competition for food, there are cases of seven-year-old bucks having antlers comparable to the antlers they had at five years of age.

The organic makeup of antlers during the growing stage is almost entirely protein. A substantial amount of protein remains in the antlers even after mineralization (hardening) is complete. A buck needs food containing at least 16 percent to 18 percent of digestible crude protein in order to grow the absolute best set of antlers his genetics and age will allow. The most important factor in growing trophy antlers is to provide the buck with nutrient-rich food during the growth period from April through October. Calcium is another element needed by the deer during and after the antler growth period. A deer can borrow calcium from bones in other parts of his body and utilize it for antler growth, but he still needs foods that contain a minimum of 0.45 percent calcium. Phosphorus is also needed for antler growth. The actual dietary phosphorus requirements are not completely

known; however, it is believed that the minimum level a buck requires for both antler growth and other body functions is 0.30 percent. Vitamin D is important in promoting calcium absorption and mineralization of the bone. A deer gets all the vitamin D he needs through the absorption of ultraviolet light through the skin and from eating vegetation that has been in direct sun light. Vitamin A is important to the antler development

Provide bucks nutrient rich food during the antler growth period. Photo courtesy of U.S. Fish & Wildlife Service.

once the bone hardening begins. Carotene in green leaves can be converted to vitamin A, but as you know, green leaves can become scarce during the winter months but still remain an important part of the deer's diet.

Luring or convincing the deer to come to where you plan to hunt is certainly a worthwhile endeavor and one that may pay big dividends. The other option is to hunt them where they happen to be, and this may or may not be a place where you can legally hunt. For example, they may be in your neighbor's corn field, where you do not have permission to hunt.

Deer will pass up a less desirable food plot for one they prefer more.

This is why it is so important to learn all you can about how to encourage the deer to come to your hunting property. You don't necessarily have to have the largest piece of property in the area as long as you make the most of what you do have. You want your property to draw the deer from the other surrounding properties like a magnet, and it is possible to do this. One key element is the amount of knowledge you have about good deer and habitat management and how much of that knowledge you put to use. This is not easy to do and requires a big commitment on your part as well as an ongoing conscientious effort toward this endeavor. Drawing deer away from other properties is not easy to do if that property offers one or more of their favorite food sources. If your neighbor has crop land or a good stand of red or white oak acorns presently falling, you may have a tough battle since one of their favorite foods is white oak acorns. If they are being drawn away from your property to fresh-falling persimmons in another area, you need to know this. Learn what food sources are on the other properties that might compete with your deer-management efforts. You must determine what efforts to make and when to make them based on what is happening around you.

The deer will be attracted to the most desirable food source available to them in their home range at the time. This choice is made from the standpoint of their nutritional needs at certain times of the year. Depending on what steps you take to draw the deer in, it is possible that you may cause the deer to either move their bedding areas closer to your food source or alter their home range a bit to include your property. Keep in mind that whatever food source is luring the deer away from your area will eventually play out, and you need to keep tabs on when this is about to occur because this is when they will be most vulnerable to your luring tactics. It is at this time they will be most susceptible to include your property into their home range and become comfortable there.

Deer relax within the security of their on home range, hopefully on your property.

One of the first concerns should be to identify the natural food sources that deer prefer in your area and take steps to enhance these for your deer population. Food sources that are available to the deer in the fall, winter, and early spring are the most critical to the deer for their body condition, ability to survive a hard winter, and their reproductive process. Deer browse on leaves, buds, stems, needles, and twigs of trees and shrubs. Deer do have preferences and will only eat the nonpreferred food sources if the preferred ones are unavailable. Some of the preferred natural food sources are white cedar, white pine, maple, yellow birch, dogwood, and sumac. A few of the medium-quality foods are aspen, jack pine, oak (acorns provide excellent-quality food), ash, white birch, and white hazel. Some of the starvation deer foods include spruce (deer will eat spruce only as a last resort), beech, red pine, balsam fir, tag alder, and leather Leaf. This group is the least preferred by the deer. Refer to chapter 9 on food sources for a much larger list of deer food sources. Ask yourself what can be done to improve or enhance the existing habitat for the deer. Begin by mapping out the entire existing habitat that is beneficial to the deer in any way. Document whether it is a food source or cover source and what it actually is. List also what needs to be done to make it more plentiful, more nutritional, easier to get to, or safer to use. There are certain things you can do to be effective in all of these areas. Selective bush hogging will do wonders in several ways. You can get rid of a great deal of unwanted weeds and small trees that are smothering out the more nutritional plants while at the same time open up safer, more desirable lanes of travel for the deer. These travel routes are still secluded so the deer will use them, but they are hopefully open enough to aid a deer in spotting a predator in time to avoid him and allow the deer a better chance of escape.

Be sure to bush hog existing deer runs or paths of travel to water sources, food sources, and so on. Stay away from known bedding areas, and consider these areas for a possible refuge when you find them. This would be an area that you do not hunt but instead allow the deer to always feel safe and secure in this area. If the deer can cross your hunting area to get to another refuge by taking the simplest or cleanest route that is still concealed, make it happen. Keep in mind that deer like to travel on easily accessible paths that still offer them safety and as much concealment as possible. Try forcing them to detour from their normal route by making it more difficult to traverse, and bush hog a new lane through concealment to strategic parts of your property.

Deer may travel your route instead of their own if you give them a little push.

Create desirable lanes or trails about your property to encourage the deer to use them. Kevin Lammi, Northland Image photo.

You cannot alter your neighbor's property in any way without his or her permission, but it never hurts to ask. Your neighbor may not be a deer hunter and might not mind. You should take steps to enhance any valuable natural food sources such as White Oaks, Red Oaks, Persimmons, and any other fruit or soft mast trees such as Apple, Pear, Plumb, Cherry, etc. Use a fertilizer specifically to grow nutritious, natural wildlife forage such as Scotts Native Plant Fertilizer 36-3-7. A time-release nitrogen formula maintains the food supply for several months. This type of fertilizer can increase the protein content of the plants by as much as 150 percent. Pick certain large, healthy oak trees or any other favorite food tree that you might have on your property and begin fertilizing them to enhance their production. As the deer find these high-producing food sources, they will begin returning to them over and over. Use fertilizer sticks or tablets such as Scotts Tree Tablets 20-10-5 around the drip line of these special trees in an effort to enhance the yield of fruits and nuts and thereby help to grow bigger deer. One feeding or application will last up to two years.

Notice the existing travel corridors to and from these existing food sources, and understand how they could play a vital role in your food-plot strategies as well as placing any mineral or salt licks in the area. Natural food sources are a definite plus to your overall food plot program, but some of these sources will no longer be available when the deer need them the most, especially depending on the existing deer density. Strip disc and bush hog certain portions of naturally occurring plants such as greenbriar, blackberry, and grasses in early spring. This will clear the way for the young, tender, more nutritious shouts and allow the deer more safety when feeding there. If you have this particular soil tested and follow the fertilization and liming recommendations, the nutritional value of the plants can be increased. These native plants will be better adapted to the area than agricultural plantings, and the fertilization will increase the productivity and utilization by the deer. Some other habitat-management procedures are prescribed burning, timber harvesting, mowing, and direct plantings.

One of the best ways to ensure that deer in a particular area receive the best nutritional value from the habitat or other food sources available is to make sure that there aren't too many deer competing for it and that the buck-to-doe ratios are well-balanced. If these numbers are out of balance, not only will you need a tractor and disc to attack the problem, but also a gun, muzzleloader, or bow in the hands of a well-prepared hunter. A buck-to-doe ratio of 1:1, 1:2, or even 1:3 is acceptable. If you find that the deer herd in your area is over 1:5, then you will also find that the hunting pressure on the bucks is heavy and that the average age is three years old or less. This average age may be more like one-and-a-half years, indicating that there obviously have been no harvest restrictions in the area at all. The use of a tractor and disc is to enhance the habitat or food sources and get the deer out into the open where a hunter can more easily look them over and make sure that he or she is not about to harvest a button buck instead of a doe. It allows you to make better decisions as to whether or not to take a particular deer from the herd. You never want to take a small button buck or small rack buck from the herd, and sometimes it's difficult to distinguish them from a doe at a distance. This is extremely important in areas that have too many does and too few bucks.

Deer populations often vary because of hunting pressure, habitat quality, disease, and poor deer-harvesting decisions. Never harvest the small bucks if you are trying to build a good herd of trophy-size bucks. Establish a rule that nothing less than an eight pointer may be taken, and if possible, no buck less than three years old may be taken, but preferably four or five years old depending on your deer densities and ratios.

You must harvest does in order to maintain the proper buck-to-doe ratio. Photo courtesy of Paul Frank.

You must harvest does in order to maintain a more even buck-to-doe ratio. Harvest only the older, sick, or wounded does, leaving the prime three- to five-year-old does to bear the fawns. Refer to chapter 35 for how to age deer, especially deer on the hoof.

A perfect example of a shooter buck and a nonshooter buck.

Try to cull out any injured or diseased animal that may infect or endanger the entire herd and any buck you feel is genetically inferior to the herd. You must have strict control over the access to your deer property and use good common sense when selecting where you will place a food plot. If you place it too near a public road or place no restrictions on the access to the area, before long, every poacher in the area will know about it.

Although this buck appeared to have had good genetics, he had a bad limp and needed to go.

Food plots have a very important place in the overall scheme of good deer management as long as good judgment and planning are used along with a good conscientious effort to maintain them from year to year. It is extremely important to realize when, where, and how to use a food plot for the best advantage to the deer. Food plots are more valuable to the deer during periods of high stress. There is a period around late March to early May when native browse is in what is referred to as "spring green-up," and nutrition levels are usually met without supplemental feeding. This only occurs in periods of good rainfall, and everyone knows you can't always count on the rain when you need it. It's best to be prepared for the native browse failing in case that's what ends up happening. These months are very important because this is when the does are carrying unborn fetuses and producing milk, fawns are weaning away from the mothers, and bucks are recovering from the very stressful rut and trying to grow their new racks. Food plots help to offset natural food shortages, like during the fall and winter months when the nutritional value of their natural food is low. They are even more important during a year with a poor acorn crop or in situations where the deer's natural food sources have been reduced or omitted completely, for some reason, by human encroachment. Your food plots need to be up and running far enough in advance of hunting season so the deer have time to get comfortable feeding there. There are numerous cases of individuals or hunting clubs that plant food plots and end up very disappointed in the results. In most of these cases, it was probably because someone failed to do his or her homework before proceeding with the plot plan. They first must make sure that they have in place standards for hunting that will maintain the deer populations at a level consistent with the carrying capacity of the habitat.

It's possible that an early morning trip or two to the local coffee shop to visit with the farmers and ranchers in your area could be a big help. These folk manage their land for wildlife, livestock, and crops for their livelihood. Most of these people are very knowledgeable and can offer valuable tips on planting times, fertilizer and lime requirements, and maybe even a new place to hunt if you "buy the doughnuts." They may also be willing to provide some necessary equipment for a small fee or barter it out for a little help on their farm or ranch.

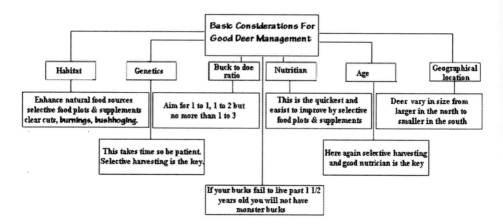

As hunters, we realize the importance of planting food plots to attract and hold deer in our hunting areas, especially considering that the average deer spends most of its life within a quarter of a mile of its preferred food source. It seems pretty clear that in order to improve the hunting in my area, I need to improve the food sources.

Food plots and agriculture become extremely important to the deer in the fall and winter when most of the natural food sources are gone in many areas. Due to all of the rutting activity, they are much more active during these months and less focused on food. This is when they are the most stressed and lose most of their body fat. The months of February and March are very critical months for deer to have to play

Forage oats, a good late-season food plot choice in a secluded plot location.

catch up and replace a lot of the calories and body fat they burned off during the hunting season. Most of the does are bred now, and the bucks are beginning to grow new antlers. Bucks store phosphorous and calcium in their skeletal system to later utilize for new antler growth. They need to regain these nutrients and carbohydrates in as short a period of time as possible to keep from starting out in the negative when their body needs them the most. In most areas, they will need supplemental food sources from food plots or agriculture in order for this to be possible.

You need to develop your own feeding program for your deer herd based on several criteria. Consider your geographical location and type of terrain as well as your average climate. Ask yourself if your property is hilly, flat, rocky, strictly woods or fields, or a combination of any. Would your plots be created on hills or in bottom land?

Food plots should be located near dense cover or escape routes, such as tree and shrub thickets or briar thickets. Consider small fields, logging roads, power-line cuts, clearcut fringes, an interior farm road, or right-of-way as a good place to start your plot. Your plot should have cover on three sides in order for the deer to feel safe while feeding there.

Keep a food plot as secluded as possible so the deer will feel secure using it.

While certain strategic aspects such as these are important to the actual hunting process, an even more important aspect is the soil content for your plot. You should prioritize your plot locations and then study a soil map, which can be obtained from your local soil conservation office. Once you select your plot locations, you should now take soil samples from different portions from the planned plot for testing. A bulb planter works well for this and pulls out four- to five-inch core samples each time. Mix all of these core samples together in a plastic bucket. The plastic bucket helps you avoid any possible contamination. Place a small amount of the mixed soil in a plastic bag for transport to your local cooperative extension office for testing. Kits for testing are also available at many of your lawn and garden centers. Soil composition is probably the most important and the most overlooked component of food plots. An accurate soil test is the most crucial step in the planting process. Even with great soil preparation and adequate rainfall, the plot can struggle to survive due to unbalanced pH or fertility levels. A soil test is inexpensive, easy to do, and is the most important preparation step in creating a healthy food plot. The pH level determines the acidity of the soil. On the pH scale of 1 to 14, 1 is extremely acidic while 14 is extremely alkaline. Most soils throughout North America are acidic, and high levels of acidity prevent plants from absorbing nutrients. A soil test will determine the pH of the soil and determine the appropriate amount of lime to disperse. Lime neutralizes the acidic elements in the soil. A variety of soil conditions can exist on one farm. Upland sites tend to be drier and less fertile, while bottomland sites tend to be more fertile and workable. Generally speaking, corn, soybeans, cowpeas, alfalfa, and some clovers are better suited in bottomland sites, while lespedeza and sometimes clover and alfalfa are better suited for upland sites. In either case, a soil test should be taken to determine soil fertility and pH value. A soil test will allow you to better choose a crop for each site. You can contact your local county extension office for soil testing, or you can use a soil analysis kit and price sheet. If you don't test your soil, you run the risk of planting something that just won't grow where you want it to. By testing your soil, you will learn what inoculate to use, what fertilizer is best, and the total protein content of your future food plot. The proper pH for most crops is between 6 and 7.5. You can adjust your soil's pH by adding lime. To adjust your pH one point—for example, from 5.5 to 6.5—you would add 75 to 100 pounds of lime for 1,000 square feet, or 2 tons per acre. Your local co-op should be able to offer advice and suggest a lab for analyzing the samples. Be sure to follow the recommendations that come back with the soil analysis. You should also consider the approximate size of your deer herd and what other agriculture is available to them already from your neighbors. Your deer density will play a role in what you plant and what size plot you should create. You might get by with a smaller size food plot if your neighbor has a large agricultural crop nearby that would be a major draw. In this case, plant something that would be available to the deer at the same time as the neighbor's large crop, and if possible, in a close proximity to their route to the larger agricultural field. If you have a large number of deer, the large agricultural crop will take some of the pressure off of your smaller food plot. If your neighbor has a large corn field, plant soybeans in your food plot. Soybeans are a very good, several-month–long food source and would provide a nice contrast to the very desirable corn field destination.

There is no magical size of a food plot, but forages produced in plots less than a half-acre may be overutilized early in their growth and produce little forage later in the season. Ideally, corn, soybeans, and cowpeas should not be planted in long narrow plots smaller than two acres since they may be over utilized early in the summer but instead in larger, three- to five-acre plots to provide grain and forage throughout the year.

This corn plot has been overutilized due to high deer density in the area relative to the size of the plot.

Experience has shown that a half acre of soybeans can be completely defoliated by deer within the first nine days of planting, depending on the deer densities. Plots smaller than one acre can successfully be maintained with the proper land preparation and forages, but these plots should really be planted in a clover mix to provide forage throughout the year. In areas of high deer densities, large clover plots might be more practical. Deer are primarily edge- or fringe-type feeders. This means that they feed along the edges of cover where they feel more safe and secure. Never make your food plot larger than 100 yards across its widest point. By doing this, the deer will feed all over the entire food plot and not just on the edges. Generally speaking, food plots of one acre in size or less are normally adequate so that they are not overutilized, and the deer move on to the other areas, as well. If you have 100 acres of habitat, you want to plant about three acres in some type of food plots. Your deer densities will have a direct bearing on this. If your property is overpopulated, you may need to plant more or larger food plots to keep them from being overutilized. For summer planting in the southeast, a good agricultural food-plot mix of grain, sorghum, brown-top millet, Loredo soybeans, and black oil sunflower can be used to plant the area. The seed should be mixed in proportion to the recommended broadcast rate per acre for that seed as compared to the other seeds. The seeds should be planted between May 15 and July 1 on a well-prepared seed bed at a rate of about fifty pounds per acre. Some people prefer to plant the outside edges of the plot with the black oil sunflower instead of including it in the mix. This provides for additional cover and an increased sense of security while feeding. It's best to include highly nutritional mineral supplement licks in conjunction with these types of food plots.

Your choice in food plot crops should be based on four criteria. Productivity is very important because you want your plot to yield as much as possible for all of your efforts and be available to the deer as long as possible. It should be palatable so the deer will desire it or even prefer it. It should most definitely be high in nutritional value for the deer as well as being tasty. The last criteria is the digestibility factor, or how much of the food source contributes to the deer as it passes through the body.

Let's consider clover as a food-plot selection. During the summer, clover is at its peak and grows thick. It is utilized very heavily by deer because it is a desirable food source and nutritious. It grows rapidly and comes back quickly when clipped and remains a good food source throughout the warm season. It's very high in protein, which is great since bucks need protein to grow their antlers and the does need it to produce good quality milk for their fawns.

The best protein producer of the clover family is Ladino clover. When it is properly fertilized and at its peak, it can produce up to 24 percent crude protein. One way to sustain this peak point for most of the summer is to mow it every four to six weeks. Ladino clover rates very high in protein compared to such other crops as corn (7 percent); oats (8 percent), soybeans (16 percent), and red clover (15 percent). Ladino clover does not do well in dry weather. While this is a great warm-season choice, its growth slows down in the fall and into the hunting season. Deer will still feed on it but not as much as they did in the warmer months.

When clover stops growing, it begins to lay down, making it less available to the deer. Later into the season, it will lay down flat, turn brown, and begin losing its protein value. Deer will still use it but not if other food sources are available. At this time of year, deer need high-carbohydrate foods that produce energy and heat. Since the clover now is low in protein, it has become a poor energy source for the winter. Remember, an important fact about clover is that it is primarily a warm-weather food source.

Legumes, such as beans, peas, and peanuts, seem to do great in the summer and can be some of your best summer food choices because they are very good at producing protein and drawing important minerals out of the soil. Deer love to feed on the nutritious leaves of soybeans in the summer, and later on, the pods themselves once they ripen. Since soybeans are fairly easy to establish, they

This soybean field provides nice green vegetation for the deer in the warm season.

are a good year-round food source. Be sure to get RoundUp-ready soybeans to ensure weed control.

Alfalfa is one of the few crops that rates higher than Ladino clover in protein, but it has some serious drawbacks. One of the main problems is that it doesn't green up in the spring as early as some other grains and turns brown quickly after the first frost, making it less desirable to the deer and not a good source during the stress period. Alfalfa can be difficult to establish and maintain and is pretty expensive as well.

Clovers other than Ladino can also be good choices depending on your situation. A mix of Ladino, Red, and Alsike is a classic clover blend to use. Red clover is inexpensive to establish and normally is better suited to a wider range of soil and climate conditions, but it's not as high in protein. Alsike clover also does well in many areas and types of conditions, including damp bottomland areas. All of these above-mentioned legumes will do well in the north or the south, but there are a few that seem to do better in the southern states. Some of these include cowpeas, alyce clover, peanuts, and lablab.

Lablab is a very good summer food plot choice that is high in protein, and deer love to feed on the large green leaves. It does very well when planted with sorghum, millet, corn, and other tall plants. Since it grows as a climbing vine, it will attach itself to the taller plants. Lablab is extremely drought tolerant, and the leaves will stay green through extremely dry periods, making them attractive to the deer. This is a food source that will have a high yield right on up until the first frost.

Forage oats can be an excellent food-plot choice to attract and hold deer. They are quick and relatively easy to establish. Oats will tend to grow back sufficiently for an additional harvest or grazing if planted in early spring and grazed or chopped early. Normally they can be grazed five to seven weeks after planting. Late summer planting can provide some grazing during September and October. Oats grow well during periods of cool temperatures (60–75 degrees is ideal).

Plant oats at a rate of sixty to eighty pounds per acre. Plant in October through November in southern regions or February through May in the South, Midwest and Northeast.

In order for the plants to properly germinate, these legumes need to be planted when the wet season is just around the corner. In the south, the best time to plant your summer food plots is from March through May or early June. In the north, you can plant in the spring, but you can also plant in September to take advantage of the wet season during October through November.

This forage oat plot extends out in four directions from the tower stand with each leg being approximately 40 feet wide by 75 to 100 yards long.

Corn is one food source that deer seem to love a great deal and seek out when the weather turns cold. Corn is high in carbohydrates, which provide them with badly needed heat when the temperature drops. Corn can do well in the north or the south, but it's not as drought tolerant as some other food sources. This is an excellent food source but requires a great deal of nitrogen to grow properly. One negative aspect to corn is that if it is the only readily available food source in the area and if you have a high-density deer population, they may begin to eat the stalks and leaves, rendering them incapable of producing an ear of corn. Corn goes through a stage, just prior to producing silk, when the stalks and leaves are very sweet to deer. At this stage, corn is low in nutrients and protein and not a good food source for the deer.

Just prior to producing silk, corn stalks and leaves are very sweet to deer.

It's only later in the year when the kernels become hard and the stalks and leaves dry up that the corn is high in nutrients and carbohydrates. This will probably not be a problem if your area has a moderate to low density of deer and there are other food sources in the area. Make sure that corn is just one of the food sources you use. It

Corn is high in carbohydrates which provide deer with badly needed heat when the temperature drops.

can be a great late-season attraction and greatly increase your hunting options.

Sorghum, although expensive to establish since it requires so much nitrogen, can be a good late-season food source, and it is more drought tolerant than corn. Deer will converge on the sorghum around September in most areas when the seeds reach the dough or milk stage. In areas with high deer densities, it is probably best to plant grain sorghum and the taller forage sorghum in separate rows. The taller forage sorghum will tend to break over, dropping the heads to an available height for the deer by late fall.

Winter wheat is also a very good food choice because it is available to the deer from fall all the way through spring. Wheat offers a respectable amount of carbohydrates and protein and can withstand fairly high–deer-density grazing. Another plus with wheat is that it is easy to establish and inexpensive.

Dwarf essex rape is a fairly new winter food source for most deer managers. Those who have used this highly attractive food source say that in late fall and winter, deer will eat it right down to the ground. They seem to really love it. Much like winter wheat, rape is easy to grow and inexpensive. There are those who claim that it is like a weed: just throw it out on a damp place and it will grow.

In addition to domestic crop food plots such as those mentioned before, you may also wish to include some blended mixtures. Deer will be attracted to all of these food sources depending on what else is available at the time. This is why when you plant any food plot, you must evaluate it in relation to what else is available to the deer at the time and where the plot is located in relation to the deer's present activity. If the deer are not active in a certain plot where

Deer will be attracted to all of these food sources depending on what else is available at the time.

you felt they should be, it may be because they are more attracted to another food source available to them at the same time. There may be some nearby persimmon trees dropping their fruit; deer love fresh-fallen persimmons. If you are lucky enough to have persimmon trees in your hunting area, nurture them so they will stay healthy and bear lots of fruit every year. There may be a stand of white oaks dropping fresh acorns nearby, and fresh falling acorns are like ice cream to deer.

Combination seed mixtures for your food plots can be very important, but should meet certain criteria: (1) The food plot has to produce enough forage to justify the cost, (2) it has to be readily eaten by the deer, (3) the protein content and nutritional value of the forage are suitable for digesting by the deer, (4) it has to be available when native forage is lacking in quality and the bucks and does are going through their most stressful months of the year, and (5) the food plot has to withstand heavy grazing. There are a wide variety of plants available, and the following lists are just examples of a few. Good warm-season plants are lablab, cowpeas, red ripper peas, black-eyed peas, purple hull peas, catjang, iron peas, claypeas, Alyce clover, American Jointvetch, and other summer clovers. Good cool-season plants are arrow leaf clover, Yuchi clover, Meechee clover, Amclo variety clover, corn, ryegrass, white clovers, and cool-weather oats and rye.

Unless you are using a food-plot mixture that guarantees a high nutritional value for the deer all year long, you should supplement your food plots with highly nutritional mineral licks to pick up the slack. These can be acquired from your local co-op, tractor supply, or feed and seed company.

There are a large number of companies offering food plot seed mixtures. These mixtures are available through local feed stores, wildlife feed companies, hunting clubs and associations, outdoor hunting and fishing shows, the Internet, and even word of mouth. Check out which ones are the most advantageous to you and your deer. They should be reasonably priced and offer a well-balanced, nutritional diet for the deer.

Check your food sources regularly to determine which ones the deer are most active in. One way to do this is to set up a utilization cage to determine how much forage is being consumed. Without a utilization cage, it is often very difficult to determine the quantity of forage deer actually consume from a plot. With the biologic cultivars, deer will consume an entire leaf. Since the deer cannot browse inside the utilization cage, you will be able to

This is a typical utilization cage application to monitor a clover field.

compare the density of leaves inside versus outside to determine how much forage is being consumed.

The three primary factors that affect antler growth are age, genetics, and nutrition. When you determine which food plots do best for you in your area at various times of the year, repeat the same process if possible next year. Depending on the circumstances, you may need to alternate certain crops to replenish nitrogen in the soil. It's better to plant several small plots throughout your property than to plant one or two large ones. A couple advantages of planting several small food plots instead of a couple of large ones are more hunting stand locations and reduced deer density. The deer also keep the plots in their youngest vegetative state, thus providing increased protein levels. Average food plot sizes range from one-half acre to an acre. Many people create larger plots for different reasons, but they are more expensive and therefore not as common, depending on circumstances. The more secluded the spot for your plot the better, keeping in mind that the plot will need three or four hours of sunlight per day for best results. You might want to consider selecting an edge type of food plot mixture to plant around the open edges of your less secluded food plots. This provides additional nutritional value, an added sense of security while feeding, and greater daytime usage. Try to have approximately three acres of food plots per one hundred acres of habitat, but consider the deer population density, too.

If you send your previously tested soil samples off to a company such as Tecomate or the Whitetail Institute of North America, they will make recommendations to you as to what will grow best for you. They will also instruct you on when and how to plant for the best results.

If you are in an area with fairly high deer densities and are planting only one food plot, consider planting soybeans in the spring and then come back in mid-September with a mixture of winter wheat and rape. Most of your soybeans will still produce pods, which deer love, and the wheat will benefit from the nitrogen the beans have added back to the soil. The rape will make a great late season attractant.

In areas with low deer densities, you might consider planting a one-acre plot, half in clover for summer utilization and the other half in corn for a late-season food source.

Keep in mind that corn and wheat require a large amount of nitrogen for proper growth, and soybeans replenish nitrogen in the soil. You might want to consider a rotation process for one or more of your plots. For example, plant corn in one of your plots one year, which will draw a lot of nitrogen out of the soil, and for the next two years, plant soybeans to replenish the nitrogen. You could then plant corn again the fourth year, and so on.

Consider rotating corn with soybeans. One year corn then two years soybeans to replace the nitrogen.

When the time comes to do the actual planting, you should decide whether you will use a no-till or complete-till process or broadcast the seed. Each has advantages. The no-till and complete-till method allows the seed to be underground and less susceptible to weather, birds, and other hazards, plus the seed tends to germinate sooner. The broadcasting method allows for planting in some areas where you can't get machines, which might be more favorable to the deer, and requires less work. With the no-till process, you will need a no-till planter, which is expensive. A cheaper way to go for this method might be the use of a local farmer. You could always try to barter for his services by offering to help him out around the farm or offer him some venison. If you elect to go the complete-till route, you should do a complete burn-down the year before. This will allow you to disc or plow the ground and plant into it easily using a conventional planter. This would be the cheaper way to go compared to the no-till method. Before either method, you need to prepare the plot for planting. You should first get rid of the weeds. The ground should be mowed or bushwhacked so that the seeds will reach the soil and receive the most advantageous amount of sunlight and rainfall; alternately, a good application of RoundUp consisting of three ounces to one gallon of water. One acre would require an application of approximately fourteen to fifteen gallons. If you use the no-till or complete-till method, you will need to use a spreader to spread the fertilizer and lime prior to planting the seed. If broadcasting, apply Roundup to get rid of the weeds about ten days in advance of seeding to reduce weed competition. You should also broadcast the fertilizer and lime about four to seven days prior to planting. This allows them time to react with the soil prior to you actually planting the seed. It's important that you do not overplant an area since the plants may become choked with vegetation and die from not receiving an adequate amount of sunlight or rainfall. Be sure to create a firm seedbed before planting; a firm seedbed is necessary for maximum germination. Leaving the soil somewhat loose may look good, but seeds can fall into deep cracks and not grow enough after germination to reach the soil surface. You should attempt to plant just prior to a rain. This is an ideal situation because the rain ensures that there will be adequate soil moisture for germination and growth. In addition, the impact of the raindrops will bury the seed and compact the soil.

Rough up the top of the soil. You may not need to disk up the soil depending on its condition. If this is the first planting on the site, you should disk the soil . If you don't have to disk, you should still loosen up the top two or three inches of soil to allow the seed to contact the soil and germinate. A four-wheeler and harrow drag works great for this. You can even drag an old set of bed springs or something like that around to help rough up the top soil.

For small plots, the use of a four wheeler can accomplish the task.

Based on the results of your soil test, it is now time to fertilize and lime your plot. The testing step is very important. If you are going through all of the time, troubles, and expense necessary to create a quality food plot, then do it correctly. You can use a seed spreader for this process and then again for the actual seeding process.

The actual seeding process is next. If possible, do this step just before a light rain. The rain will aid the germination process.

Now that you have spread the seed, drag the seed bed with the drag harrow turned upside down in an effort to make the seed contact the soil. By dragging the harrow flipped over, you are actually smoothing the soil rather than loosening it.

If you choose to plant certain seeds such as soybeans, rape, clover, wheat, and so on, you need only to work the seed into the top half-inch of the soil. For this, you can simply use a harrow or cultipacker.

Spread seed just before a light rain.

MAINTENANCE OF YOUR FOOD PLOT:

Mowing certain plots will stimulate new growth, which delivers the high levels of protein necessary for maximum antler and body development for your deer. It also keeps the deer coming back to your plots. In addition, mowing helps to reduce competition from annual weeds since they don't mature and go to seed.

Lime and fertilizer should be applied as indicated by your soil test results. Supplemental applications of fertilizer should continue as your budget allows, but do so at least twice a year in the spring and again in late summer. Spring or fall applications of lime depending on soil tests should be considered over the lifetime of the plot.

WHEN SHOULD I PLANT MY FOOD PLOTS?

It's time to plant when the soil temperature in your area reaches 55 degrees. Waiting for this temperature ensures the best germination rates.

You can start plot selection and preparation anytime, and then you'll be ready when the soil warms to 55 degrees. If you are ever in doubt as to when to plant a certain crop, simply check with the source of your seed. You will find that the seed company itself, your local co-op, or any of the other feed and seed companies are very knowledgeable and more than willing to assist you.

In the northern states, you can plant most crops any time after the threat of frost in the spring up until three to four weeks prior to the first average frost in the fall.

SOME DOMESTIC FOOD PLOT INFORMATION:

Corn

An excellent energetic food. Provides bedding and escape cover throughout the winter. Plant matures in 150 to 180 days depending on the variety. In agricultural fields, the outside, less productive rows can be left. Several varieties are available.

Site: Does best in fertile, well-drained soils. Best suited for bottomland sites. Should not be planted in plots under two acres. Avoid planting long, narrow plots.

Date: Mid-April through May, or as soon as the threat of frost has passed.

Rate: Twelve to fifteen pounds per acre in thirty-six- to forty-inch rows.

Maintenance: Herbicides and cultivating should be used to deter weeds. Insects can be a problem.

Cowpea

An easy-to-grow annual, viny, summer legume similar to soybean. Will continue to grow until frost. Seasonal forage production from May until frost. May not be practical in areas with high deer densities, but would be a better choice than soybeans. Excellent varieties include Combine and Redclay .

Site: Does best in fertile, well-drained soils. Tolerates lower soil fertility and pHs.

Preparation: Plant in a well-prepared seedbed or no-till drill. Follow soil test results for fertilization and liming. Usually 200–300 pounds per acre of 0-20-20 is sufficient.

Date: Mid-May through July

Rate: Broadcast at fifty pounds per acre. Harrow to a depth of one inch or drill seed in twenty-four-inch rows at about fifteen pounds per acre. Inoculate seed.

Maintenance: Weeds should be controlled with an herbicide. Annual grasses may be your biggest problem. If planted in rows, cultivation can be used.

Soybean

Annual, warm-season legume. Not practical in areas with high deer densities. Forage production from planting until October. Seeds are also important. Very adaptable to a variety of conditions. Excellent varieties include quail haven or any forage variety.

Site: Adaptable, but does best in most well-drained soils. Better adapted than cowpeas.

Preparation: Plant in a well-prepared seedbed or no-till drill. Follow soil test results for fertilization and liming.

Date: May through early July

Rate: Broadcast one bushel per acre. Harrow to a depth of one inch. Plant in rows at twenty to thirty pounds per acre. Inoculate seed maintenance. Weeds should be controlled with an herbicide, or cultivate between rows. Annual grasses may be a problem. New variety by Monsanto called RoundUp-Ready Soybean is resistant to RoundUp herbicide.

Annual Lespedeza

Good reseeding, low-growing, annual legume. Forage production peaks in July and August when other forages may not be available or are in poor quality. Good choice for draught upland sites. Good choice for no-till methods. Seeds cherished by quail.
Varieties include common, Korean, Kobe, and Marion. Avoid Serecia or shrub varieties.

Site: Adaptable to a variety of conditions, except for wet or fertile soils.

Preparation: A clean seedbed can be used, or broadcasting on established sites. Sodseeding can give adequate results. Follow soil test results for fertilization and liming. 200 lbs. of 0-20-2 per acre should be sufficient. Do not fertilize with nitrogen.

Date: February through April

Rate: Broadcast forty pounds per acre cover with 1/4-inch soil or allow frost to work the seed in. Inoculate seed.

One very productive way to lure deer to your area that will work most of the time, especially in warm weather is to create salt and/or mineral licks on your property. Find an old dead stump or log in a fairly close proximity to a travel corridor and pour about fifty pounds of salt around it, or place a salt or mineral block there.

The salt or mineral will seep into the ground and the deer will dig it out as they need it. I have seen them literally dig

Put out about twenty-five pounds of salt.

a large stump out of the ground to get at the salt. This is how the wildlife resources agency moves entire herds of deer. If there are no salt licks on the surrounding property, the deer will find your salt licks and begin using them. You should create one lick for every fifty to sixty acres. This tactic should get the deer to start coming on to your property on a fairly regular basis, so now you need to convince them to stay awhile each time they visit.

Create a mineral or salt lick approximately every fifty to sixty acres.

If you own or hunt on a farm, you will have plenty of deer if you have domestic crops available for the deer to feed on such as corn, soybeans, alfalfa, or wheat. When you harvest the crops, leave a certain portion of it standing for the deer, and bush hog a little down each year before harvesting. Keep certain areas of the property bush hogged around these food sources for the benefit of the deer.

During the warm season, the deer spend a great deal of time around this salt lick.

Throughout the year, automatic feeders can provide a healthy supplement to the deer's diet. Set them to disburse food at a precise time, and before long the deer will gather nearby and wait to hear the sound of the food being dispensed on the ground, at which time they will come in to feed.

Deer must have water, so if you have a ready supply of water available for the deer, you can expect this to be an active area. If your property has no water supply, you can possibly dig yourself a pond or get permission to rechannel part of a stream onto your property. Fresh water would greatly enhance your chances of luring deer to your area.

Maintain these feeders throughout the stressful time in a deer's life.

All deer require a dependable water supply.

Keep track of your deer herd and monitor their movements by using a night vision camera, such as one or more CamTrakker night cameras installed at different strategic locations. Since these cameras are not inexpensive, start out with one or two and see how they perform for you. You must remember that the key will be to locate them at the best possible activity sites

Keep track of the deer movements by using a night-vision camera.

or specific areas of interest to you. These cameras will also help you determine your approximate buck-to-doe ratio.

Now that you have gone to all the time and effort to create your food plots, you want to be sure that they are not overutilized. The only way to do this is to maintain the proper carrying capacity of your land. You do not want more deer on your property than your land will support. Contact your area wildlife biologist and ask them to come out for a deer-herd–dynamics evaluation. What this means is that after performing surveys (visual surveys, scat surveys, sign surveys, etc.), the biologist will be able to suggest what you need to

do to get your deer herd in line. If one of your goals is to bring your buck-to-doe ratio in line, the biologist will be able to tell you how many does or bucks to harvest to meet that goal. He or she can also recommend what type of bucks to eliminate from your herd so that the genetic characteristics you are looking for will be passed on during the rut. The biologist can also tell you how many deer per acre

Two young fawns anxiously receive their dinner, caught on a CamTrakker night-vision camera.

your land can handle. It is definitely a good idea to get to know your local wildlife biologist and establish a close working relationship with him or her.

When you take into consideration the changing needs of deer throughout the year and the various stages of the different food sources throughout the year, there is no perfect crop for all of your food plot requirements. You want to acquire as much knowledge as you can to make the best educated guess you can for the benefit of your deer herd. You never know what curves Mother Nature might throw you. Do the best you can to provide the most nutritious and attractive food sources to help your herd reach its full potential while at the same time drawing and retaining the deer in your area.

http://www.foodplots.com/articles/four-season-food plot-plan

Photo © by Mary Morris

HUNTING TACTICS AND STRATEGIES

How successful you are at taking a nice deer depends largely on how well you know and understand good hunting tactics and how often you apply the correct tactics at the right time. This ability only comes with experience gained from studying the whitetail deer in its native habitat. You must know and understand its feeding and bedding habits and what it is likely to do in different types of weather conditions. You need to understand the rut and how it affects both bucks and does. You must understand that deer will react differently depending on the hunting pressure, their varied types of home ranges, food sources, and so on. Different hunters use different tactics for the same situations at times, but it's how well they assess the situations and apply a particular tactic that determines their success. The following are some tactics that I use at certain times that have allowed me to be successful a respectable percentage of the time.

Always be aware of the fact that deer may approach you from the most unlikely directions. You may be focusing your attention in the direction of the most active sign or the area where you would most likely expect the deer to come from, but they may appear from the exact opposite direction. One sure thing is that in

Deer may stroll into your area from any direction, so be alert at all times. Photo courtesy of John Munt.

245

deer hunting, nothing is sure. Concentrate your attention on the area where you strongly expect the deer to be, but always be aware of the entire area around you, and don't underestimate or prejudge any sound or movement. Take this advice and I guarantee you'll see more deer and be more successful.

Don't wear out a potentially good spot or hunting area. Don't hunt it over and over, morning and evening, day after day. After the first time you hunt a particular area, the deer know you were there. The absolute best opportunity you will have in a particular stand location is the very first time you hunt it each year. You slip in with the element of surprise on your side, and if you're lucky, you take your deer. If you aren't successful the first time you hunt this area, hunt it once more at the most before you try another area, and give this area a chance to relax again. Give this area a few days so that all sign and scent of your having been there is gone. You want to try to keep the deer guessing so that they can't anticipate your next move, and this is not easy to do. This old buck apparently knew the best day to come by this stand.

You should have been in the stand.

You may have a couple of different areas close together that you like to hunt. Decide which of the two areas you will hunt this particular outing, and stroll into the area you don't plan to hunt in from a direction to drive the deer from this area to the area that you do plan to hunt. Once you feel that you have the deer up and moving— hopefully in the direction of the area that you do plan to hunt—turn around and slip quietly out of this area and head for the other area. Move into the other area from the downwind direction, and be as quiet and cautious as possible, and just maybe, the deer you previously spooked will move toward you. This has worked for me on several occasions. You should already have your stand set up prior to initiating this tactic so that you can get into your stand as quietly and

Buck slipping out of the area.

Attempt to get the deer on the move in the direction of where you plan to hunt. This technique has worked for me on several occasions.

quickly as possible. Hopefully you will catch the deer calmly and quietly strolling away from your presence in the previous hunting area.

In the event that you don't have a range finder with you, tie bright-colored ribbons to various trees whose distance from your stand you have measured. If you are bow hunting, use the distances that you normally practice from and are committed to shoot from. Do this at strategic points about your stand so that if a deer approaches from any direction and is about the same distance as one of your ribbons, you can more readily judge his distance and hopefully be more accurate with your shot. Even if you are rifle hunting, as you approach or leave your stand, step off the distance to various distant points from your stand. This will help you on the next hunt from this stand.

There are certain areas commonly referred to as funnel areas. These are areas where two or more ravines, ridges, or other types of structures come together into just one and offer deer coming from more than one direction to this one point. You should set up your stand in such a way as to take advantage of the deer funneling to this point.

Buck walking down a funnel area.

If you are hunting in an area or at a particular time when the hunting pressure is significant, stay in your stand for longer periods of time. Most hunters will leave their stand around 10:30 or 11:00 AM on a morning hunt, especially if they aren't seeing deer. As they exit the areas to return to their vehicle or go back to camp, they will likely stir up deer and get them moving, and these deer may move past you in the process.

Stay on your stand for longer periods of time than other hunters do so that their leaving may force deer past you.

Another hunter's departure may force deer into your area.

Early morning, midday, and late evening are the most active times for deer to be moving unless they have become nocturnal, like some of the big, old bucks. With this knowledge, it would stand to reason that these are the times that you certainly would want to be on your stand. This big fellow is a perfect example of why you should stay in your stand.

This is a fine, prime-time buck. Photo courtesy of D. Gordon E. Robertson.

If the area that you want to hunt is a particularly good-looking area and you anticipate a lot of activity, you may want to consider placing two stands in the area to have a second option to counter a wind problem. If your presence would be detected at one stand location because of the wind, the other should offer you a concealed hunting option.

Deer will always remember and avoid an area where they encountered danger. For example, if you shoot at and miss a nice deer, you may as well forget trying to hunt that deer in that specific area again because he or she will probably not be back. You may get another deer from this location, but that specific deer, in most cases is gone.

Deer are quick to escape danger.

An area that is extremely thick, such as a clear-cut or briar thicket (or just a heavily grown-up area), offers the deer excellent cover when the hunting pressure is intense, and you can bet that they are using these areas during these times. These areas can be well-worth your effort and produce nice deer. Try to locate where the deer are entering and leaving these areas and set up strategically to hunt them. Most likely they have more than one source of entry and escape routes. Sometimes you may be able to find a high point to locate your stand that allows you to see over into the thick area. Most hunters will avoid hunting these areas because you must go to some effort or trouble to get set up just right to have a significant chance at the deer. You just might get a shot at a really nice, big, old trophy buck in these types of areas because this is where they like to hang out during the day.

During the months of hunting season, where there are doe, there are probably going to be bucks, depending on the buck-to-doe ratio in the area. This is much more likely during the rut. If you are seeing doe, at least you are where the deer are, and this is a good place to be. It is important to be where the deer are and not so much where they have been. Sometimes it is difficult to distin-

Nice buck about to leave a clear-cut. Photo by Kevin Lammi, Northland Images.

guish the difference between where the deer are active and where they were recently active. This is when you must determine why the deer are there in the first place. Is this a prominent food source area, a bedding area, or what, and whatever is luring them through this area, is it

still as alluring to them? If the sign is still fresh and you are seeing deer in this area, consider it a worthwhile hunting site.

Always try to be situated in your stand at least thirty minutes before daylight. This allows the entire

If you are seeing does, there will probably be a buck in the area.

Does in the area mean bucks are not far away.

area to calm back down and all that you disrupted in the process of getting in your stand a chance to get back to normal. Believe it or not, you will disrupt a lot of wildlife in most cases during the process of getting to your stand.

You need to give the surrounding wildlife a chance to settle down and regain a sense of feeling unthreatened so it won't frighten an approaching deer. Any deer you may or may not have jumped or alarmed on your way to your stand may relax and even stay in the area if given long enough to settle down, depending on the hunting pressure.

When you are searching the area from your stand, move only your eyes, and when you must move your head or another part

You will often jump deer on the way to your stand.

These does have been alerted to your presence but may settle back down if you get situated quickly and make no more disturbances.

of your body, do so very slowly. Deer are quick to pick up distinct movement, but if the movement is very slow, you are much more likely to go undetected.

Move as little as possible when you are on your stand.

Deer are quick to detect movement. Photo © by Kevin Lammi, Northland Images.

When you are on your stand and you spot a deer, watch the deer carefully and make no movement when the deer is looking in your direction. Whitetail deer can detect the slightest movement, so move only when the deer is focused elsewhere.

Move only when the deer are not looking in your direction. Photo © by Kevin Lammi, Northland Images.

This deer just spotted me but doesn't know what I am. Her ears tell it all.

When you are bow hunting and you happen to shoot and miss your deer, don't give your location away. Just because he heard your release and the arrow hit the ground does not mean that he knows where you are. He is now very alarmed and is sure to vacate the area, but may do so cautiously, and if he does not know where you are, he may come by you on his escape

Startled buck sensing the degree of danger. Photo © by Kevin Lammi, Northland Images.

route, offering you another shot. Try to nock another arrow as quietly and cautiously as possible so you will be ready.

If an alarmed deer approaches your area on the run, don't just throw up your weapon and shoot. It's difficult to get a good shot placement on a running deer. You can make a "Naaa" sound in an attempt to stop him. Sometimes, when a deer is running from one type of area (such as a field) toward

Deer often slowdown for a terrain change.

the woods, as he approaches the woods, he will slow down and walk into the woods. He will quickly check out the entrance he is taking into the woods to assure himself that his route is safe, but this change in his stride offers the opportunity a hunter needs to get off an accurate shot.

Always try to be higher than the highest point that you expect the deer to come from. If you place your stand halfway up on a hill side, expecting the deer to approach from the top toward you, this will place them higher than you, and you are more likely to be seen as they approach. In this case, they will probably see you before you see them because they are looking down at you. If you must hunt this type of situation, be well-camouflaged and as inconspicuous as possible, and be very cautious of the wind direction. If the wind

Try to be higher than the deer's anticipated approach. Photo © by Peter Eades.

is wrong in this situation, you may as well not hunt there.

When hunting scrapes, don't place your stand too near the actual scrape. Bucks tend to check their scrapes from the downwind direction in many cases without actually coming to the scrape. If you are too close to the scrape on the downwind side, the deer will probably wind you in the process. Try to set up in the downwind direction but pref- erably diagonally off to the side and as far away as you feel you can get and still get a good shot.

This nice buck will check his scrape safely from down- wind. Photo © by Kevin Lammi, North- land Images.

The terrain and wind shifts will determine just how successful you will be at this, but this is all the more reason to be as far away from the actual scrape as you can be and still cover the area. You may apply this same tactic to bedding areas and food sources, and always pay close attention to the wind direction.

Give any scrape a wide berth when setting up to hunt it.

When choosing a tree for your stand setup, try to choose a tree with multiple trunks. This offers you additional concealment and less likelihood of being detected. In many cases, such trees provide additional safety and additional shooting stability by offering a better opportunity for an armrest.

Multiple-trunk trees offer many advantages.

During the peak rut period in your area, stay on the stand all day if necessary since you are likely to see deer at any time. The bucks are running does at all varied times, and you are likely to get a shot at any given time of the day. It is during this time of the year that you, the deer hunter, have the greatest advantage over the whitetail deer. The bucks are chasing the does with no regard for their safety. The only thing on their mind is that estrous doe and servicing her. If they are not chasing a doe, then they are more alert.

There may be a buck chasing this running doe, so be alert.

Try to position yourself so that you have to move around as little as possible. If you have your back to an area that is naturally going to give away the presence of a deer coming up behind you, this is a big advantage. A good bed of dry leaves, brush, a briar thicket, fairly still water, rocky ground, or anything else that would let you know that a deer is approaching will allow you to concentrate more on other areas.

If you locate an area where there are a substantial number of droppings, you have probably found either a bedding area or a food source. Try to determine how fresh the droppings, whether the location is a food source or a bedding area, and how the deer are approaching and leaving the area. If it is determined that the area is a bedding area and you plan to hunt it in the morning, check out how the deer are entering the area to determine your stand location. If you are hunting it in the evening, then check out how they are leaving the area, and set up in such a way as to hunt their exit route. If you determine the area to be a food source, your strategy should be just the opposite. In the morning, set up to hunt the exit route, remembering that these exit routes from food sources might be difficult to select. In the evening, set up on the entrance side of the area.

Generally speaking, deer will exit their bedding areas in late evening and enter them in early morning.

Deer enter food sources in late evening hours and exit them in early morning as a rule. There are several factors that may influence this behavior, however, such as weather, hunting pressure, and the rut.

Fresh droppings like this indicate current activity in the area and various stages-of-age droppings indicate recurring activity. This would most likely be a current food source or bedding area.

Deer have been conditioned over the years due to increased hunting pressure to look up more than they used to. They are not as likely to notice you up in your stand as they would be if they noticed movement or something conspicuously out of the ordinary up there. Strategically locate your stand and take advantage of existing cover as long as it doesn't hinder the actual shooting process. Pay close attention to the background so that it will aid your concealment rather than highlight you or cause you to stand out, and use good camouflage and cover scent strategy while remaining aware of prevailing winds.

Use old 35mm film canisters with cotton balls saturated with your preferred scents. When you arrive at your stand, place these about your stand and remove the caps. The scent is totally sealed and stays fresh until you remove the cap. You may also refresh them and use them over and over. There are wick-type dispensers available that are also good to use.

Tie a drag rag saturated with your favorite scent to your boot for whatever period of the season it happens to be. If it's during the rut, you will probably want to use a buck-in-rut or a doe-in-estrous lure. Once you arrive at your stand area, refresh the drag rag with your lure and circle your stand location approximately thirty or forty yards out from your stand. Now turn and walk in toward your stand to a shooting lane and hang the drag rag on a small tree before finally entering your stand. If it is not during the rut, you may want to use a common food-source scent or a masking scent.

During the early weeks of bow season or the legal hunting period prior to the rut, deer are primarily concerned with feeding. This should dictate how you hunt them during this period. Find the food sources in your area and determine which ones they are actively working, and focus your strategy on these. Once you locate the food sources, look for multiple droppings in the food source area that are fresh, indicating that the deer are presently using this food source.

When walking to and from your stand, be aware of any new sign or fresh rubs, scrapes, and so on, especially just prior to, during, and after the rut, that may have been made during the last few hours. If you come up on an area of extremely fresh sign, locate a good stand site, taking into account the wind direction, the deer's direc-

This herd of deer has been feeding in a clover plot.

tion of travel, and when he probably made the sign, and once set up, sit tight. I have some of my best luck in these spontaneous hunting sights when I just happen to find them by accident. Your chances in this area are the very best that they will ever be, so you should seize the moment.

Many deer become nocturnal or feed strictly at night when hunting pressure becomes intense, especially older bucks. You should attempt to locate their bedding areas and focus your strategy in these areas. They will commonly bed down all day, only

Nocturnal bucks are active primarily at night.

Pay special attention to any fresh rubs or scrapes.

occasionally rising out of their beds to feed a little, but only in the immediate area. They will not leave their bedding area at all during the day unless frightened by something or someone; they normally leave only after dark to travel to a food source. The rut is the only time to gain a better advantage over these nocturnal bucks.

Try to concentrate more during the peak activity periods. These are early morning, midday, and late evening. These periods apply during periods other than the prepeak rut, peak rut, and postpeak rut. During peak rut periods, you are likely to see deer at any time, so be alert at all times. During these periods, the deer are not concentrating on danger as heavily, offering you a greater advantage.

Look for deer at anytime in peak rut. Photo © by Kevin Lammi, Northland Images.

If you are on an either-sex hunt and you begin to see does, don't be impatient because the longer the does hang around in the area, the more likely you are to see bucks. If you are strictly meat hunting, you may want to go ahead and take a doe, but then again, you may want to use the doe to try and lure a buck into range.

Unless you are meat hunting, try to use does to lure in bucks. Using calls, try to keep the does in the area as long as possible.

If you jump a deer out of a bedding area, note which escape route is chosen. This could be valuable information for a future hunt.

When you are walking to your deer stand, don't walk too fast or you are sure to start perspiring, and this will make for a very uncomfortable hunt, not to mention the increased human odor. Leave early enough to walk slow, and take breaks along the way. If this is an afternoon hunt, take advantage of still-hunting your way to the stand; this way you won't get overheated in the process.

If you jump deer out of a bedding area, take note of how they exit the area. Most likely, if you approach this area from the same direction again, they will probably vacate the area in the same direction the next time if they are still there. Use this information to your advantage, and the next time, have a hunting buddy set up on the escape route; when you approach this area again, you force the deer toward your buddy.

Try to locate escape routes in other areas so that you will have an idea how to use a buddy, and hunt these areas, too. Knowing the escape route or how a deer will exit when he sees you, tells you just where your buddy should set up. You and your buddy may alternate responsibilities, and with one of you doing the walking and the other doing the hunting on different occasions.

A startled buck making an exit.

In most cases, you should anticipate more deer activity before and after a good rainstorm, especially during a steady, light rain. These are good times to be in the woods for deer hunting. I prefer to still-hunt on days like this or on light, rainy days. It is easier to walk quietly in the area if the ground is wet and your scent is not as distinct. (The damp air lessens their sense of smell.)

Be attentive to the alarm sounds of other animals since they might have just been startled by a passing deer headed in your direction. Squirrels, in particular, will sound the alarm at just about anything. These animals have let me know on several occasions that other game was approaching, and in many cases it was a deer. Just be alert to the alarm sounds of other animals and see what happens.

If you suddenly see a deer, before you move to take a shot, be sure there are no other deer in a position to see your movement and sound the alarm. Sometimes deer will approach simultaneously from different directions. If you aren't careful, you may miss seeing some deer because you are concentrating too heavily on an obvi-

Deer may simultaneously appear from different directions.

ous deer that happens to be in view. Movement could alert some deer that you do not see because they are looking straight at you, and they in turn may sound the alarm and frighten the one in view away.

When you are still-hunting or walking in the woods, you cannot avoid making some noise, but the noise a lone hunter makes walking in the leaves sounds much like a wild turkey walking in the leaves. Use a turkey call occasionally, and try to convince a deer that you are a turkey and not a threat. If you are successful, the deer hopefully will not feel threatened since they are used to the sounds of a turkey walking in the woods.

A walking hunter can sound like a lone turkey.

One of the most exciting signs to come across when you are scouting is the sign of a large buck that just might be a contender for trophy status. Depending on the area you hunt and the hunting pressure, most of these old bucks have become nocturnal and are active only at night with a few exceptions. Peak rut will

This nice buck seems quite content. Photo by Matthew Isanki.

sometimes lure them out of their bedding areas, and hunting pressure can sometimes work to your advantage by forcing them to move.

This is when they are most vulnerable. Normally, the most effective way to hunt them is to hunt for their bedding areas, and this can prove to be a great deal of work. Search for bedding areas. Deer like to bed down on the fringes of areas where they can watch for danger. Examples of this would be the fringe portion of power-line clearings or the brushy area around the edge of fields. They can be found bedded down on the side of a hill where they can cover a large area for danger. The old bucks will be found in the roughest, thickest cover in the area.

These bucks bedded down in the middle of fields. Photo © by Peter Eades

There are certain trails that the deer seem to use over and over, year after year. Some years they are used more than others, but basically they are consistent paths of travel. If you have certain trails in your area like this as I do, you are fortunate because this offers you more hunting options.

Some trails are used year after year.

If you were hunting a nice buck but failed to get him, or if you just want to know if there is a large buck that survived the season, look for dropped tines. The best place to find them is between the bedding areas and the food sources they were using toward the end of the season. Bucks begin to drop their racks shortly after the end of hunting season. This varies from north to the south, with the bucks dropping their racks last in the southern states. Here in Tennessee, the bucks begin dropping their racks around the latter part of February and into March. If you search hard around early March, you might get lucky and find them.

Dropped tines may reveal if a certain buck survived hunting season.

Deer are primarily fringe-type of animals. They prefer the edges or fringes of terrain where fields change to thickets, woods change to brushy areas, woods change to thick power-line clearings, and so on. I have always found power-line clearings to be good hunting spots.

If you see deer, try to remain as perfectly still and calm as possible so they remain in the area as long as possible. The longer they are there, the more likely you will see others come into the area. If you can keep a few does hanging around with an occasional call or a doe bleat when they start to leave, you just might have a nice buck

Deer prefer the fringes of fields and wood lines.

come in and present himself. Even if a buck doesn't come into the area, watching those does is one of the most enjoyable aspects of deer hunting.

When you locate a spot where a deer has bedded down, if you lay your hand in it, you may find that the deer just left as you approached because it is still warm. It's difficult to spot a bed-ded deer before he sees you, but if you search the area around you

Once you see does, try to keep them in the area as long as possible in the hopes of luring in a buck. Photo © by Peter Eades.

when you are in the woods thoroughly and intently enough to spot a bedded deer, you'll probably see more deer.

Look for parts of deer that might be bedded down.

Be aware of any developing patterns that the deer seem to be following. They may all seem to converge to one certain point to feed before going their separate ways, they may be using the same bottleneck at about the same time every day, or they may be coming to the same food source each day at approximately the same time. Keep in mind that any consistencies that you discover will help you plan your strategy and determine just which tactic to use to hunt them.

Deer are primarily browsers, especially when other types of food sources are not available. They like to browse on tender tips of small saplings, buds, brush, tree tips low enough for them to reach, shrubs, and so on. They love to browse in a light rain, so this would be an excellent time to hunt them.

This doe is calmly browsing.

If you choose to hunt from the ground for one reason or another, remove any leaves or other debris from around the base of the tree. This will allow you the freedom to move your feet without stepping on dry leaves or twigs and making noise.

Another good tactic to use from the ground is to find an area that will allow you to completely blend in. Use good cover scent, and only use the site if the wind is right for it.

Use attractant or luring-type scents from where the deer are to where you want them to be. If you know the deer are using this one trail, place enough of a lure-type scent near the trail to arouse their curiosity but not so much as to make them nervous. You don't need to use much because of a whitetail's keen sense of smell. Place a drop or two of the scent strategically on leaves or saplings back to where you want the deer to end up for

An excellent ground hunting position on the side of a hill that offers concealment.

your shot. It is critical not to leave any other human scent along the way as you do this. Be sure the bottoms of your hunting boots are clean of human or foreign odor and masked with a good cover scent. Do not use a different lure on the bottom of your boots since this is likely to confuse them and make them suspicious.

Creating mock scrapes will sometimes lend a little push in the right direction and help stimulate the rutting activity in your area. Since bucks use other bucks scrapes quite often, it is not uncommon to create a scrape and have bucks start using it. You must be sure to include the proper ingredients, however. Begin by wearing rubber gloves and rubber boots totally free of any foreign odors. Locate a limb hanging about four or five feet off the ground near an active trail or on a ridge point near a trail. This limb will become the deer's licking branch. If a buck decides to make your scrape his primary scrape, he will chew on this limb and rub his forehead and preorbital glands and saliva on this limb to leave his calling card. Take a limb or stick of some type from the area and scuff up the ground under this limb approximately two feet in diameter. Rake the leaves and grass away down to the bare ground. Place a few drops of buck or doe in estrous urine or a scrape scent in the middle of the scrape. Hang a scent drip bag filled with doe-in-estrous scent or buck urine up in the tree above the scrape and higher than your licking branch, The drip bag will periodically refresh the scrape scent, and the buck will remain interested in it long enough to take it over as his own. You may want to try to create a couple of these mock scrapes in your area, giving yourself more chances for success. Remember to keep all human odor out of these areas, or the scrapes will not work.

Deer calls are valuable hunting tools if used properly. If you understand when, where, and how to use your call, you will achieve more opportuni-

The use of deer calls can be very helpful.

ties at deer than you would otherwise. You must remember that there are different types of calls, and you need to be able to read the situation to determine which type of call to initiate. If you are hunting a dominant buck, an aggressive buck call or doe bleat would be fine. If you are hunting a subdominant buck, you would not want to use an aggressive buck call because the subdominant buck would probably feel threatened and not come in. You would either want to use a nonaggressive buck call or a doe call of some type. I highly recommend that a young hunter these days learn as much

Certain times of the year, such as just before, during, and just after the peak rut, are good times to aggressively rattle.

as possible about calling deer. There are many tapes and videos available for that purpose.

Rattling bucks is another method of luring bucks into range for a shot. Since deer are curious, this gives you

When the real aggressive fighting is occurring, do some aggressive rattling.

additional opportunities to get that shot. Here again you must know what you are doing and use the proper type of rattling at the proper time. During the prerut period, when the bucks are hanging together in bachelor groups and sparring with each other, a light tickling of the horns or loose clattering is a common sound to deer, and this type of rattling will tend to lure them. During this period, you would not want to do any real aggressive rattling since the peak rut has not begun. Immediately prior to the peak, during the peak, and immediately after the peak rut is the time to really get aggressive with your rattling and let the bucks know that this is where the action is for the does. Rattling is the best way to lure a chasing buck off of a hot doe. Again, there are tapes and videos on the subject of rattling bucks, and I recommend that you learn the proper way to rattle.

When you are still-hunting, the distance you travel is not as important as how slow you move to get there. The terrain and weather conditions will dictate how fast or slow you may walk and still be quiet, but take no more than six or seven steps a minute. You not only have to be quiet, but you also have to move without being seen, so this means moving very slowly. Continually look ahead and pick a spot where you will stop for a short observation period, and try to always stop next to a tree, rock, or some type of arm rest that offers concealment. Naturally, if you have a shooting stick or tripod mounted to your rifle, the arm rest isn't as important as the concealment. Once you stop, take the time to look the area over thoroughly before you move on.

When stalking a sighted deer that is merely browsing, pay close attention to his body language. Move toward him only when he has his head down or is looking in another direction from where you are. As you are stalking closer, do so in as straight of a line toward the deer as possible since any sideways movement is much easier

When stalking a deer, pay close attention to his or her body language.

for the deer to detect, and then be ready to freeze in position if the deer's head pops up. Sometimes a deer will pop his head up for a few seconds, then put it down, then pop it right back up if he suspects danger. Study your route to a shooting position, and then try to inch your way from one cover source to the next. If the deer looks as though he might begin to feed in your direction, take advantage of this and let him close the gap as much as possible. Don't move any

When still-hunting, look for deer only partially exposed. By doing this, you will most likely see more deer before they see you. Photo by Kevin Lammi, Northland Images.

closer to the deer than you absolutely have to for the shot.

If you enjoy still-hunting like I do, scout for still-hunting routes. Search for routes that will allow you to be as quiet as possible, such as dry, flat, rock creek beds, old logging roads, or edges of fields with grassy areas that would allow you to walk quietly. Remember: a little extra effort here and the rewards could be greatly enhanced later.

When you are still-hunting, only look for parts of a deer. If you look for deer in their entirety, since you are moving, they will prob-

Photos by Kevin Lammi, Northland Images.

ably see you much sooner than you see them. Look for part of his rack, a flash of white, or a horizontal straight line that could be the outline of a deer's back. Occasionally get down on your knees to get the same perspective the deer has. You would be surprised how different things can look from this perspective.

Always still-hunt or stalk deer into the wind, either in a straight line or at a slight angle to the wind. This tactic will offer you the best advantage in dealing with their sense of smell.

Use topography maps, aerial photographs, stereoscopic maps, scouting notes, and any other information you can compile to clue yourself into what the deer are doing in your area. Many times local farmers, storekeepers, and others who live in the area can be good sources of information. Check with your local game and fish, forestry service, wildlife management sources, and so on. Use all of this information to try to get

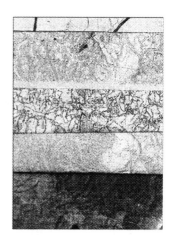

Aerial photos, topo maps, road maps, plats, and so on.

the best understanding that you can on the whitetail deer herd in your area.

Having a clear understanding of prevailing winds and air currents or drafts is vital. Thermal air currents tend to travel uphill in the morning and downhill in the evening. Be aware that wind direction can and often does change very quickly, so keep your options open in case you have to change your hunting strategy in midstream. Here in Tennessee, most of our threatening weather comes out of the western portion of the country.

Rub-lines are one of my favorite types of sign to come across when I am in the woods because they definitely get my attention. These rub lines are often accompanied by a series of small secondary scrapes that quite often lead to a much larger primary scrape. If you find these secondary scrapes, search the area thoroughly because there will more than likely be a primary scrape in the area somewhere. It will normally be located under a tree limb that has been recently chewed on by the buck in an attempt to rub his adrenal glands on the limb to attract does. This primary scrape will be the nucleus of the buck's rutting activity and an excellent area to hunt. Keep any human odor out of the area as much as possible and concentrate on the routes into

A secondary scrape is normally one of several in a buck's core area.

A primary scrape is much larger and much more obvious than a secondary scrape.

and out of this area. In most cases, the buck will check his scrape for doe activity from a point downwind from his scrape. Be particularly careful not to do anything to disrupt his normal pattern.

Locating deer sign is extremely important, but when the sign was made is equally important. If the sign was made when the deer left his bedding area, this tells you that he probably made it late in the evening, and this might be a better evening hunt location. On the other hand, if the sign was made as the deer was leaving his food source, it would probably be a better morning spot to hunt.

Look for signs of where the deer have been browsing by looking for plants, saplings, and other vegetation that have the tips bitten off. The tips of

Look for signs of where the deer have been browsing.

various tree limbs, leaves, and other vegetation are also signs of deer

These rubs are both on fairly large trees in excess of three-and-a-half to four inches thick.

browsing. There should be obvious droppings in the area as well.

Large rubs on large trees are normally signs of large bucks since smaller bucks seldom rub large trees.

If you find a set of tracks of a deer walking that are large and deep, indicating that the deer is an exceptionally heavy one, it is probably a large buck. However, it could be an exceptionally large doe, even though they are few and far between in the south. Larger does are more common up north, but then again, the does are not that large compared to the even larger bucks of the north.

Large tracks normally suggest a buck but could be a large doe.

There are some very productive ways to lure deer into your hunting area. One of these is to create salt licks with the help of the deer. Deer must have salt for their system just as we do when we lose a lot of body water in hot weather. Creating salt licks is one of the primary ways that wildlife management teams move herds of deer

Salt licks are a productive method of luring deer into your area. Photo by Rick Stutts.

from one area to another. The procedure is to find an old, dead stump or log near an active deer run and pour a twenty-five-pound bag of salt in and around it or use a salt or mineral block. The deer will find

it and begin using it and then redefine their home range around the area.

Another way to lure deer into your area is to establish food plots or agricultural crops that they prefer. There are many different types of crops that deer prefer available through a variety of companies, local feed stores, and on the Internet. Deer love

High-protein food plots will draw deer into your area. Photo © by Mary Morris.

clover, winter wheat, alfalfa, soybeans, corn, pumpkins, and various other crops. Deer will be attracted to all types of food sources such as acorns (probably their favorite), apples, beechnuts, persimmons, honeysuckle, dogwood, sumac, hemlock, wild grapes, wild roses, and others. Refer to the chapters on food sources and deer management.

We all have our own preferences. Some hunters prefer only bow hunting all season long, while others prefer muzzleloader or black powder hunting. Many hunters prefer rifle hunting because of the extended range capability. I love all three. However, I personally would rather be deer hunting on opening day of muzzleloader season than any other time of the season. This is when the deer are still calm and in their regular routine, unlike how they will be once the shots begin to ring out. Once they start hearing all the shots from muzzleloaders and rifles, they get harder and harder to find. Opening morning of muzzleloader season has always proven to be one of my most productive hunts. Opening

This buck is still following his same relaxed routine. Photo courtesy of U.S. Fish & Wildlife Services.

week of muzzleloader season begins about the same time as our rut here in Tennessee begins to kick in, which is another reason I am so partial to it.

Although it's not the safest way to hunt, if you hunt alone, you may tend to be more consistently successful than when you hunt with a partner or group. One hunter slips in and using discretion does not upset the deer movements nearly as much as a group does. When you get more than one hunter in an area, you distribute more human scent and disrupt the deer activity more. The lone hunter now has to focus on other hunters in the area as well as himself and his own hunting. His hunting is not as streamlined as it would otherwise be. There are times when I prefer to hunt with a friend, but there are definitely times when I specifically want to hunt alone for the sake of the hunt.

If you seldom get snow as we do here in Tennessee, take advantage of the ones you do have by doing some serious scouting to see what the deer are doing. The freshly fallen snow will tell you where they are bedding down, how they are traveling, when they are traveling where, and so on. You can get a better idea of how many there are in the area and whether there are any very large deer in the area, possibly indicating a large buck. You also stand a better chance of actually seeing deer due to them standing out against the white background and appearing more conspicuous.

Snow can reveal a great deal about the current activity of the deer.

You should definitely do some scouting on rare snow days, and if you have to take a vacation day or whatever to be able to get to the woods, do your best to do so.

Buck feeding beneath the snow.

If you hunt on your own land, set up an automatic feeder with corn. Locate it in an area with a good deal of sign apparent. Replenish the source as needed, up until it is time to stop based on your state hunting laws. If it is illegal to hunt over bait, you must be sure the source is gone prior to hunting there. This feeding process will help the deer become comfortable in the area whether you can hunt over it or not. This should help you to see more deer when the season opens.

Buck exerting his authority at a food source.

Note this obvious sign of deer feeding activity in this cornfield.

When you bag your deer and have finished the process of field dressing him, cut open the stomach and try to determine what the deer has been feeding on recently. This will help you decide how best to hunt the next one. I recommend waiting until you have completed the field-dressing process before cutting the stomach open because of the odor.

Photo © by Mary Morris

Photo © by Mary Morris

DEALING WITH THE SCENT PROBLEM

The whitetail deer has one of the keenest senses of smell of all the North American game animals. This is the greatest problem that you must overcome when matching wits with it. Of all the deer's senses, its sense of smell is by far its keenest, and is the most difficult one for humans to compete against. For this reason, it is imperative for today's deer hunter to become as knowledgeable as possible about luring and cover scents and to know when, where, and how to use each one. The hunter must know what tactics to use when applying certain types of lures or cover scents and what methods to employ to keep his or her entire body scent undetectable by the deer. The whitetail deer works very closely with Mother Nature (the wind) to evade us, so for this reason we have to let the wind dictate to us just when, where, and how to use our scent capabilities against it. There are many different tactics and strategies that will sometimes work to combat the whitetail's scent capabilities, but nothing will work every time. New and young hunters must realize up front that in whitetail deer hunting, there are no definites, absolutes, or guarantees. The most you can hope for is to fool the deer some of the time, and hopefully when it will net a big trophy buck. The more you know about how to try to fool the whitetail, the more often you will be successful at doing so.

Scent problems are ongoing and constantly changing, so you must be flexible and cunning. There are many different luring and cover scents available on the market from a wide variety of sources. What works best for some hunters may not work best for you. Do your homework and check with various sources to determine what would be best for you based on where you hunt and what period of the season you will be hunting in. You must determine by trial and error what works best for you in each hunting scenario. Talk to other deer hunters that you know and trust who are familiar with your general hunting area, and also check out what the manufacturers say about their products on the Internet or in magazines. Talk to the sporting goods stores in your area, and find out what scent products they are having problems keeping on the shelves. This is a good indication of what seems to be working for a large number of hunters and what just might work for you. Good luring and cover scents are not cheap—and you usually get what you pay for. There are scent-free soaps for bathing, and others for washing your hunting clothes. You may also use Scent-Loc clothing, a type of clothing that traps your scent within when used in conjunction with normal scent precautions.

There are a large number of devices for dispensing these various types of luring and cover scents available on the market. You must become knowledgeable of wind currents, up- and down-drafts, and the effects of other weather conditions that play into the whitetail's scent capability. The bottom line is that there are many ways to combat a whitetail's scent capability, many places to learn these different ways to do it, and many tools available with which to do it. You just have to take the initiative to learn everything you can about a potential scent problem and how best to deal with it.

Try to be as totally void of human or unnatural odor as possible. You should always try to take a good shower or bath in a nonodorous soap before you go hunting. Your hunting clothes should be washed in an unscented detergent. If possible, hang your clothes outside on a clothesline to dry, and then place them in a plastic bag with some type of masking scent or items full of masking scent, such as earth scent, pine needles or cones, hickory or cedar chips, acorns and oak leaves, or anything from the area where you will be hunting. The main objective is for your clothes and your body to smell as much like the area you will be hunting in as possible, with no human odor being exposed.

Depending on how much you want to spend, Scent-Loc clothing is available on the market that does a pretty good job when used in conjunction with other good masking scent tactics. A more economical choice would certainly be a good unscented detergent—and there is now a Scent-Loc detergent that releases carbon particles into your clothes that fight odor, as well as other good detergents available at your local sporting goods stores.

Be sure to wash your hunting boots with an unscented detergent or soap, and apply a heavy cover scent to them as well. Place these boots in a bag with cover scents, just as you do your clothes. You should also apply a good buck-lure scent to your boots as you get to the general area where you will set up prior to walking to your stand. An alternative to this would be to tie a drag rag saturated with a good lure scent to your boot and, after walking to your stand, tying the drag rag to a tree limb a few yards out from the base of your tree stand.

Wash your caps thoroughly, since humans perspire greatly through the head. This is an often overlooked item of clothing that should require some of the most dedicated effort. You should take more than one cap with you on a hunting trip so that you can switch off, since washing clothing is seldom practical while you are on a hunting trip.

Only wear your boots in the woods or field, and never out in public places or in your vehicle—the floorboard of your vehicle naturally collects odors from everywhere you go.

Pull your hunting boots off when you get back to camp to avoid walking in the typical camp odors such as kerosene, Coleman fuel, or anything that may have been spilled that would contaminate your boots with odor.

Do not carry anything with you to your stand that would have a foreign odor to a deer, such as any type of food, tobacco, lighter fluid, or any other such items unless they are in airtight containers.

When you climb into your stand, after you get completely situated and have pulled your weapon up, go ahead and pull up your pull rope and leave it rolled up on your stand or in your pack. This rope will collect odor and can betray your presence to a deer.

If you walk to your stand by the same route every time you hunt there, you begin to lay down a human scent trail that the deer will detect and avoid. Always use a good cover scent, and try to travel to your stand area by as many different routes as possible. This method of traveling to your stand allows your scent a chance to dissipate before you come along again to leave more scent. You should also avoid hunting the same stand over and over, for this same reason.

Fill a drip bag with a buck lure, such as doe-in-estrous, and tie it to your belt. Set it to drip about every four or five steps as you walk to your stand, and try to cross as many deer runs or paths of travel as possible along the way. When you arrive at your stand, reset it to drip much more slowly and hang it on a tree at a good shooting location. If you are lucky, a deer will pick up the scent and follow it to your stand area or to this spot.

As a rule, you will be more successful if you slip into an area alone and hunt than if there are more than one of you applying human scent to the area. This is the biggest disadvantage to hunting with hunting buddies and can be avoided by hunting alone. You must always be aware, however, that it's safer to hunt with a partner.

A lone hunter can often have better success than with hunting partners, depending on the type of hunt.

If you use an animal cover scent, be sure to use the proper cover scent for the hunting application. If you are hunting from a tree stand, then a good raccoon scent might be good; raccoons climb trees like you do, and this scent in a tree would be quite a common smell to a deer. A skunk or a fox, on the other hand, does not climb trees as a rule, even though I did once see a photograph of a fox up in a tree—he didn't look too comfortable up there, though, since he had a pack of dogs at the base of the tree. The point is, animals that normally do not climb trees would be out of place to a deer if their scent were detected up in a tree. Try to use a cover scent that will not alarm a deer but simply mask your odor. These are the types of things to consider when you are selecting what scents to use.

There are other natural cover scents that do a good job such as cedar, pine, apple, and earth, depending on where you are hunting. A good cedar, pine, or earth scent can be used almost anywhere with good success.

Use a drag rag saturated with a good luring-type scent tied to your boot from a heavily used trail to your stand area. You should have a cover scent on your boots along with this lure, and circle your stand about thirty or forty yards out from your stand. This provides you with an additional opportunity for deer to pick up this scent and follow it to your stand area. This is a good way to lure deer from a distant trail into your area that would otherwise pass you by.

If you are hunting during the rut, walk into your stand area and saturate a drag rag with a good doe-in-estrous or buck lure, and walk away from your stand thirty or forty yards. Do this in three or four directions, and each time take the drag rag up and drop it on the ground at your stand, each time resaturating it and dragging it away from your stand. This way, as the deer approaches and picks up the scent, the scent gets stronger the closer he gets to your stand area; the scent is strongest where you leave your stand and gradually declines as you walk away from the stand. Do this from your stand to any nearby trail in the area. At the point on the trail where you terminate the scent trail, place a couple of extra drops of the lure to enhance it in order to get the deer's attention. This is an enticement to get them to follow the scent trail back to your stand.

When you use a lure- or attractant-type scent, you should place it in such a position to offer you a good shot in case the deer tracks the scent to the canister and stops there.

Try experimenting with attractant-type scents such as vanilla-flavor scent. This was a suggestion from a couple of good hunting buddies of mine. I tried it and have had some luck with it. Put down a scent trail of this vanilla flavor into your stand area from a nearby trail and see if it works for you. This is a better tactic during bow season, when the rut is not on yet. Experiment with other scents and see if you can come up with an entirely new lure.

Use old 35mm film canisters with cotton balls saturated with attractant- type scents such as doe-in-estrous or a good rutting buck lure. Keep the lids on until you get to your stand, and then take the lids off and place these in strategic locations around your stand area. These can be tied to small trees in the area in order for the scent to be carried around by the wind. After the hunt is over, you can place the lids back on the canisters and reuse these over and over; you need only refresh them a little each time you use them. Be sure to keep the canisters in a plastic bag to keep the outside of the canister scent-free.

In the area around your stand, apply a luring scent at different heights to deal with the changing air currents that may be in the area. Place it on the ground, on the trunk of the tree your stand is in, and on the low-lying limbs or leaves of a few surrounding trees.

When you are hunting from any type of stand position and are there for any length of time, your scent begins to mushroom out from your location. You should apply your masking or cover scent to your location and to your clothes periodically to keep them refreshed and to keep your odor concealed from the deer. If you have hunted in your stand, it is best not to leave your stand on the tree in the area, even if you plan to go back there again on the next hunt. If you must leave it there, apply a good cover scent to it and hope for the best.

The wind direction plays a substantial role in combating a deer's sense of smell. If you can correlate your hunting strategy to the wind direction so that the deer cannot use the wind against you, you may be successful. Always try to keep your hunting efforts or the majority of your attention in the upwind direction. If you like a specific area, approach from the downwind side and set up somewhere in this area relative to what the deer sign dictates.

Learn as much as you can about air currents, up- and downdrafts, and prevailing winds, and the effects these will have on your hunting strategy. For example, in the morning, the air currents tend to travel uphill, and in the afternoon and evening, they tend to travel downhill. If deer sense danger on the wind, they will tend to travel with their noses in the wind as much as possible to pinpoint the source of the problem. Because of this, since deer tend to travel with their noses into the wind when they are uneasy or being cautious, they are more likely to smell you from uphill in the morning and from downhill in the afternoon. These are rules of thumb rather than hard-and-fast facts. Normally, prevailing winds here in Tennessee tend to come out of a westerly direction. Realize that wind direction is constantly changing, and that many times you must have alternate hunting strategies to compensate in case the wind begins to work against you.

Try to hunt as high as you feel comfortable hunting, since the higher you are, the less chance you have of the deer getting your scent. You can get away with a little more movement as well if you hunt higher up. Keep in mind, however, that the higher you place your stand, the more versatile you must be at shooting your bow from those heights. Generally the higher you are, the more difficult your shot with the bow will be.

Hunting high increases your advantage.

When you finish hunting for the day and plan to come back the next morning to the same stand, apply a good cover scent to your stand if it isn't feasible to take the stand with you (which is the best option).

Photo © by Mary Morris

WIND DIRECTION

Any good deer hunter worth his or her salt will tell you that learning as much as you can about the wind direction, air currents, up- and downdrafts, and air turbulence—even calm breezes—is extremely important. You must learn how they affect your hunting tactics and strategies, and what steps to take to deal with them. To go into the woods and set up to hunt even the best sign possible would be a futile effort without basing your strategy of just how to hunt this sign on the wind direction. The wind is probably the best friend the deer has, and a deer will take every advantage of it that it can to survive. In order for you to be any kind of challenge to the deer at all, you must focus your hunting strategies on the wind and just how it is reacting in your hunting area. Here are a few tips that I hope will help you along these lines.

Having a thorough understanding of prevailing winds, air currents, and up- and downdrafts is vital to good hunting success and must be factored into any deer hunt.

Try to always listen to the local weather and have a good idea of the forecast in your area. I'm sure we all know that the weather seldom cooperates with what we plan to do and seldom does what the weather folks say it will do. With this in mind, be prepared for the weather to do anything, and have an alternate hunting strategy ready.

In most parts of the country, the prevailing winds come from the western portion of the United States. They can, however, come from any direction, depending on what the surrounding atmospheric conditions happen to be at the time. Most of the time, these prevailing winds come out of the northwest or southwest, so you need to relate this information to how your hunting land lies and where you plan to hunt on it.

Thermal air currents normally travel uphill or in an upward direction in the morning and downhill or downward in the afternoon or evening. If you think about it, it relates back to something we learned in high school science class: warm air rises and cold air drops. In the early morning hours, as the sun begins to warm the air, the air travels upward, while in the late-afternoon and evening hours as the sun sets, the air cools down and travels downward.

Always hunt in accordance with what the air currents are doing at the time. You might not be able to hunt a particular stand when you wanted to because the wind is all wrong relative to how the deer are using that particular area. You may have to hunt the area you were planning to hunt from an entirely different stand location, so have another tree or two picked out just in case.

When you are hunting, focus most of your attention on the area in front of and beside you in an upwind direction, since most of the deer you see will be upwind. Depending on the precautions you take to mask your scent and conceal yourself, anything downwind of you will detect you before you ever see it, anyway. It is for this reason that you want to position your stand on the downwind side of the anticipated activity and hunt as high as you feel safe and practical doing.

Be aware of possible activity on the downwind side of you, especially if you have taken great pains to mask your scent and are well camouflaged. Deer will normally try to work their way around to the downwind side of you if they suspect danger in order to wind you from this side.

Periodically check behind you on the downwind side.

If the rut is in full swing and during its peak, a buck may approach you from any direction regardless of wind direction, especially if he is on the scent of a hot doe. You should still take the same precautions and focus primarily upwind, but expect the unexpected.

This early morning buck offers a nice potential shot.

Always stalk or still-hunt in the upwind direction or in a forward angle to the upwind direction. When you can't feel the wind in your face, periodically check it with an odorless powder. This offers you the best advantage for dealing with the deer's great sense of smell.

Use a reliable method for determining the wind direction. Some hunters use a down feather or string tied to their stand or to their weapon, and others use an odorless powder that you can purchase in your local sporting goods store. Regardless of what method you choose, use something other than your natural sense of feel. Sometimes it feels like there is no breeze or wind at all, while in actuality there is always a slight wind drift that will carry your scent with it. Wind constantly changes, and in some cases, it will force you to change your hunting strategy.

Depending on the wind direction and the force of the wind, you may have to make a slight adjustment to your point of aim for a good shot placement prior to taking the actual shot. The further away the deer is and the type of weapon you are using determine just how severe this problem might be.

The wind may be a factor in your point of aim.

If you don't take proper care to conceal your scent, the wind direction could suddenly change and give your position away to a deer. You must constantly be aware of the current wind conditions.

There are many good products on the market today to help combat a deer's sense of smell and their other senses. Place a great deal of importance on concealing your odor from the deer. Regardless of whether you use Scent-Loc clothing, masking scents, luring scents, or any other method, you must keep your odor away from the deer to be successful as a deer hunter.

Use a cover scent periodically while you are on your stand since your odor mushrooms out from your position. With the wind working against you, you must maintain as high a degree of cover scent as possible to combat these shifts in the wind.

Photo courtesy of U.S. Fish & Wildlife Service.

Photo courtesy of Dave Bishop.

YOUR TREE STAND AND SETUP

When selecting a tree stand, there are several things to consider first. There are so many styles and manufacturers out there that it can be confusing at times just which stand is best for you. The stand should meet specific criteria to justify the amount of money you are about to spend on it. You normally get what pay for. Your deer stand represents a considerable investment, so take your time and examine several to determine which one will best suit your needs. Here are a few things that I would look for when examining different deer stands.

You should look for simplicity when considering a stand, keeping in mind that you will be setting up or taking it down in the dark in many cases; you don't want a lot of parts you have to connect and disconnect.

Your stand should be extremely well built in order to be as safe as possible. The better it is built, the safer it usually is.

The stand should be safe when climbing, sitting, or standing. The most dangerous time is when you are actually climbing into the stand, getting situated in it, or climbing out of it.

Examine any new stand thoroughly for good welds. The welds should appear to penetrate both pieces of metal thoroughly wherever they are located, and should be free of any hairline cracks.

Wherever the stand utilizes bolts, nuts, and washers, these should be well tightened with either lock nuts, lock washers, or some other locking device.

Any part of the stand that must be unlatched or unbolted to fit to the tree is an area that will get a lot of wear over the years and should be examined thoroughly for long life. This should be considered one of the potentially weakest areas of the stand because of all the opening and closing of this particular part you will do over the years.

The stand should be as quiet as possible when you are setting it up or taking it off the tree, when you are climbing into it, or when you are sitting or standing in it. It should fit snugly to the tree so that it will not squeak or make any cracking noise when you shift your weight from side to side. The stand should have some type of rubber, nylon, or other type or noise-reduction bushings on all of the movable parts. If there is any part that still makes noise when you are setting up the stand, you should use Velcro, felt, cloth tape, or some other material to quiet these areas.

Be sure the retainer bar that goes around the tree does not damage the tree. There are laws in some states against this, and some landowners do not appreciate it.

There are several stands out there with all the bells and whistles—seemingly everything but the kitchen sink. Be sure to remember that you will have to carry this stand on your back in the field with whatever else you will have on your person at the time. You may be like me and prefer to go where the best sign is and end up walking a good distance, in many cases, to get to where you need to be—some landowners will not allow four-wheelers on their property. The bottom line is that you should keep your stand as lightweight as possible.

Your stand must be totally comfortable to allow you to sit on the stand for several hours at a time. The more comfortable you are, the better and more successful a hunter you will be. You won't be fidgeting or squirming around, frightening off the deer. There will be several days each hunting season when you will want to sit on your stand all day to increase your chances for a nice buck.

I could sit on this stand all day and night and sleep half the time and not worry about falling out.

Try to select a stand that you cannot fall out of if you fall asleep. There are several with this quality, and since we are all likely to do this from time to time (especially if we stay on the stand all day), we don't need this worry.

If you accidentally fall asleep in this stand, you'd better have on a good safety harness.

I highly recommend an armrest, both for safety and for an aiming rest to aid good shot placement. If you are unable to use an armrest on your stand, try to set up your stand to take advantage of a limb or part of the tree trunk for an aiming rest.

A good camouflage pattern is extremely important to keep your stand as inconspicuous as possible.

A weapon holder is another item that is very important. These are fairly inexpensive and allow you to have your hands free to call or rattle while keeping your weapon readily available.

One of the most important parts of whatever stand you purchase is a good safety belt or harness. You should get one that allows you total movement in all directions that will prevent you from falling to the ground.

Now that you have selected and become familiar with your tree stand, you need to apply other related information. You need to know as much as possible about the proper way to set up your stand. There are several factors that will determine just how you should set up. The deer habits, where you will be hunting, the weather, the time of year you are hunting, and the direction the sun rises or sets are all considerations for stand placement. Whether you are hunting food sources or bedding areas or hunting in the morning or in the afternoon, these are all factors that you need to consider when placing your stand on any tree. There are times when you may need to hang two or more stands, depending on the area and the wind, and other times when, because of the area, a tree stand won't work at all and you have to resort to other means.

Here are some other tips that you should be aware of related to tree stand hunting.

After you have done all of your scouting and research and determined exactly where you want to hunt, you now need to select an appropriate tree. Whenever possible, try to select a tree with more than one trunk. The more trunks, the better as long as you can set up to where you have good shooting lanes. These additional trunks offer you a great deal of additional concealment, allowing you more necessary movement without detection. They also, in many cases, offer you a good shooting rest.

Multi-trunk trees offer better camouflage, additional safety, steadier shot capability, and other benefits.

I personally like to hunt twenty to twenty-five feet high. This extra height offers me the ability to get away with a little more movement and also keeps my scent further away from the deer for a longer period of time, depending on what the wind is doing. Sometimes you may have to hunt lower than this because of the leaves' on other trees being in your way or blocking your view to the forest floor. In other cases, you may need to go a little higher to see over them.

Always try to be higher than the highest elevation you expect the deer to approach from. This way the deer won't be able to come over a hill looking straight at you. If you must locate your stand at eye level with the deer, be as inconspicuous as possible, and be very cautious of the wind direction. If your stand location or your scent is going to give you away to the deer, why waste your time hunting there?

Deer seldom look up unless movement, something conspicuous, scent detection, or something else out of the ordinary compels them to do so. Strategically locate your stand, taking advantage of existing cover and paying close attention to just how obvious your silhouette will be to the deer. Be sure that any existing cover that you take advantage of does not interfere with your view or your shooting capability. Pay close attention to the background and to what advantage it will offer your concealment. It should offer concealment rather than highlight your silhouette. Once you have your stand set up, place an article of camouflage clothing in the stand. Climb down and try to observe the stand from approximately three or four feet off the ground, much as a deer would be doing, to get an idea of how conspicuous you will be.

Whenever possible, depending on the type of stand you are using, try to set up on the opposite side of the tree from where you anticipate the most deer activity. This offers you a great deal more concealment, with that much more natural cover between you and the deer. Of course, this might be more of a disadvantage from the standpoint of shooting, and is pretty much a judgment call based on the situation. The type of stand you use might also dictate whether or not this is feasible.

When the forecast calls for a mostly sunny day, try to set up on the opposite side of the tree from where the sun comes up or goes down so that it is not shining in your eyes or highlighting your silhouette. The sun rises in the southeast and sets in the southwest, so place your stand on the northwest side of the tree in the morning and the northeast side of the tree in the afternoon if you can do so and still maintain good concealment for the particular application. All of these factors won't work together all of the time, so sometimes you have to make tradeoffs. Good concealment is the foremost thing to strive for, both from the sight and scent standpoint.

Try to position yourself so that you have to move around as little as possible in order to properly cover the area you are hunting. Try to keep your back to an area like a good bed of dry leaves, a brush or briar thicket, fairly still water, or any type of terrain that would betray a deer's presence behind you. By doing this, you can concentrate more intensely in front of you by sight and depend more on hearing for what's in the rear. This helps you cover what's in front of you and what's behind you at the same time. You still want to periodically turn and physically check the area behind you, but just not as often; this lack of movement allows you a better chance of going undetected.

I cannot emphasize the importance of being totally comfortable when you are deer hunting, whether you are on a tree stand, sitting or standing on the ground, sitting on a limb, or positioned any other way. If you are uncomfortable, you will fidget and move around. Figure out when you're setting up what you should concentrate on to be able to hunt comfortably.

This limb was going to be in the way of my descent back down the tree in my stand.

When you are getting situated in position to hunt, think through your comfort. Do you need to cut off a limb that will cause you discomfort, dig a rock away from your backside that would dig into you, or get rid of a thorny limb? Get rid of these before you settle down to hunt; otherwise, you will need a lot of luck to see a deer.

There can be a disadvantage to being too comfortable on your stand, and that is the danger of falling asleep and falling out of your stand or missing the sight of a big twelve-point buck walking by. Be

Try not to fall asleep in your stand, but if you do, be sure you can't fall out.

sure to get a good night's sleep the night before the hunt, and wear your safety belt on the stand. Doing so will make you more alert to any approaching deer and give you better reflexes.

If you are hunting in unfamiliar territory for some reason, whether you are someone's guest for the first time or just had no chance to do any scouting in the area, take some precautions. Be sure to use a GPS unit, but if you don't have one, use reflective tacks, ribbon, or some type of marking technique to help you get and stay oriented to the area until you learn the natural landmarks. These help you find your way to and from the stand and also help when you are walking out from your stand at night. The area can look entirely different at night from how it does in daylight. These markings are also a big help when you are tracking a wounded deer. As you are following a blood trail, place these along various blood spots to keep from losing the blood that you previously found in case the blood suddenly stops and you have to start a new search from the last spot found. These marks also give you a trail to follow out when you are ready to leave.

If you don't have a range finder, you can tie a piece of colored ribbon to specific trees located at specific distances from your stand. This is a valuable tool to use during bow season to help you judge distances. I set about three around the twenty-yard distance from my stand, and the same amount out at thirty-five yards. In this manner, if a deer comes up into this area, you can readily guess his distance. It's a good idea to set these distances at the same distances you normally practice at. It's also a good idea to learn the distance to certain points at 100 yards from your stand during gun or muzzleloader season.

Make a mental note of where you may wish to put scent canisters or lay a scent trail based on how you plan to approach your stand using a drag rag. I firmly believe in using a drag rag as you walk into your stand to help cover your scent. Have more than one route in mind to approach your stand in case the wind is wrong. Always try to approach your stand in an upwind direction.

Always strive to set up your stand on the down-wind side of bedding areas, food sources, actively used trails, scrapes, and any type of anticipated activity. Since deer will normally always approach these areas from the downwind side, try to set up slightly off-center or at an angle to the downwind side.

By properly covering your scent as you walk to your stand, this doe could walk in your same tracks and fail to detect you.

When hunting scrapes, bedding areas, food sources, or trails, don't place your stand so close to the actual activity that the deer could pick you up on its approach. You must pay special attention to wind direction at all times.

I use a variety of different types of stands depending on the hunting situation. You may need to hunt on a tree that will not allow the use of a climbing stand, so you would need to use a lock-on type. This type of stand allows you to climb up the tree and pull the stand up with a rope and attach it to the tree. In other situations, I may use a ladder stand while hunting over a large food plot, or I may hunt from a permanent stand that we previously built in a particular funnel area. Keep your options open, and use a great deal of discretion as to what might work best for the particular hunting situation.

Photo © by Mary Morris.

Photo © by Mary Morris.

STILL-HUNTING WHITETAILS

There are different techniques and methods for hunting the white-tail, but there are also different situations that sometimes dictate the best method to choose. The weather conditions may dictate whether it would be wiser to hunt from a stand or still-hunt by slowly walking through the woods, searching ever so carefully for the slightest movement or sign of a deer. When still-hunting, you will take slow steps while constantly searching the area for movement, then stop and observe for a few minutes, and then move on a little further doing the same thing. The terrain where you hunt may be too dry or treacherous for you to still hunt at certain times. If the hunting pressure is too great, then you should hunt from a stand and let the other hunters drive the deer to you. This is also the safest way to hunt when there are several hunters in the woods. Under the proper conditions, still-hunting can be one of the best and most productive ways to see deer. To take a nice buck by the still-hunting method is very gratifying and seems to be more of a challenge than sitting on a stand. It does, however, take a great deal of skill to pick the right spot to place your stand to maximize your chances of a successful kill.

If you enjoy still-hunting like I do, scout for still-hunting routes. You should do this in order to find directions of travel for you to hunt that will offer you the best possible concealment. You want to find routes that will allow you to be as quiet as possible. Look for areas such as a flat rock creek beds that have a lot of exposed flat rock, heavily worn paths on logging roads, or anywhere that is free of dry leaves, loose rock, brush, or anything else that would give your presence away to a deer. You want to find areas that you can traverse as quietly as possible in the hopes of sneaking up on an unsuspecting deer. Look for fresh-cut fields or sandy areas that allow you to step quietly. Take a little extra time during your scouting process to discover and map out these still-hunting routes. The extra time spent here might pay big dividends later, when still-hunting is the best method to hunt during a certain period because of bad or very windy weather.

This old logging road has been an excellent still-hunting route over the years after a rain.

When you are still-hunting, the distance you travel is not as important as the time it takes you to get there. You must walk as slowly as you possibly can, making no noise and no exaggerated or quick movements. The terrain and weather conditions will dictate just how slow or fast you may walk and still be quiet enough to go undetected. Concentrate on short distances at a time. Take no more than a few

I've been able to use this flat rock creekbed for still hunting on many occasions.

steps at a time, and do so very, very slowly. Practice this slow walking to determine just how slow you need to walk in order to keep any exaggerated movements or noise to a minimum.

Each time you stop to examine the area around you, before you begin to move again, pick out the next object you plan to stop at to examine the area again. You may select a tree, bush, rock, stump, log, or whatever, but it should preferably be something to offer both some cover for you, as well as an arm rest for your weapon should you get to take a shot, if you aren't carrying a shooting stick or tripod.

Every time you stop, look the area over thoroughly before you move again. Use a good pair of field glasses, and search the forest floor for any sign or part of a deer. Look for parts of a deer, because most of the time if you see the deer before the deer sees you, he will be feeding or bedded down and will probably be partially concealed. You may be able to see only a flash of the rack, the tail or ear twitching, the head bob, or an ever-so-slight movement. Look for legs moving or straight, horizontal lines that may be a deer's back. Look for any flash of white, which almost definitely will be a part of a deer if in motion. Occasionally, get down on your knees or stoop down and try to observe the area from the deer's point of view. Things look totally different from this perspective, and in many cases, this perspective is why a deer sees you before you see it.

When still-hunting, you must look for parts of a deer's body.

One of the best times for a hunter to still-hunt his way up on a browsing or unsuspecting deer is during a light rain or just after, when the leaves are wet and quiet. The deer are naturally more active when the weather is like this.

When still-hunting, you must always do so into the wind or with the wind in your face. If you prescouted and found some still-hunting routes, you should only use them if and when the wind is right for them. You don't have to hunt directly into the wind, but you should hunt either

During or just after a light rain is one of the best times to still-hunt your way up on a browsing deer.

directly into it or at a slight angle to the upwind direction. Keep in mind that you want the wind blowing your scent away from the direction where you are trying to spot deer.

If the wind is blowing quite hard, still-hunting is your best method of hunting, because the wind alone will help camouflage the sounds you make as you walk through the woods. Quite often the wind will blow hard, be still for a few moments, and then blow hard again. Use this to your advantage by moving only when the wind is blowing hard and stopping to observe the area when it dies down.

When you are still-hunting, you must constantly watch each step you take to avoid stepping on limbs, twigs, rocks, or anything that could snap or make a foreign sound and send any nearby deer fleeing the area.

If you are still-hunting through the woods and you jump a deer out of a bedding area, watch which direction he runs to exit the area. The chances are that if you walk this direction again and he is there, as he may very well be, he will probably exit in the same direction. You might want to take advantage of using the buddy system here, in which one of you sets up down the trail in the direction the deer exited. The other should approach just as you originally did, trying to jump the deer in the same direction, giving the partner the shot. This ploy could be productive.

When you jump a deer out of a bed, watch which direction the deer runs. It will probably run this same direction the next time.

When you come across a bedding area, if you feel the beds, one or more of them may still be warm from the deer that just left because they were frightened at the sound of your approach. It's difficult to spot a bedded deer most of the time, so you have to constantly be searching the area around you for the slightest movement or sign of a bedded deer before he sees you. If you get in the habit of searching the area

Try to spot bedded deer before they spot you.

as thoroughly as is necessary to see the bedded deer before he sees you, I guarantee you'll see more deer as a result.

Photo © by Mary Morris.

STALKING A DEER

There are times when you are walking to or from your stand or still-hunting and you spot a deer browsing off in the distance. This is when good stalking capabilities come into play, when the contest is truly one-on-one, with you on his battlefield and in his backyard. You must put everything you know about the whitetail into use here. Keep in mind that you are lucky to see a whitetail browsing before he sees you first and runs away. The trick is to keep him in the dark or unaware of your presence until you can get close enough for a shot.

When stalking up to a browsing deer that you have spotted, pay close attention to his body language. Knowing all you can about a deer's body language can make or break this effort. (For more on this, refer to the chapter on whitetail body language.)

This browsing doe is unaware of the hunter nearby.

If the deer has his tail down and twitching, this is usually a sign that the deer is fairly calm and unaware of any possible danger. If the head and tail is up and the ears are outspread, the deer is on the alert, somewhat uneasy, and probably suspects danger.

These does are relaxed and likely to hang around for awhile.

If a deer begins to bob its head up and down and stomp his foot, it is definitely on the alert and will probably vacate the scene shortly.

If you are walking or stalking along and you hear a sudden snort or blowing sound, your presence has been discovered, and the deer making the sound will soon be out of there. (This sound will also alarm other deer in the area.)

If deer are performing certain body functions such as scratching or licking themselves or defecating or urinating, then you can assume that they are unaware of any potential danger. These are all signs that the deer are probably unaware of your presence.

These deer are highly on the alert and suspect danger. They are likely to bolt at any second.

This doe is relaxed and content for the moment.

Move toward the deer in as straight a line as possible. Deer can spot sideways movement much more quickly than they can spot movement headed straight toward them, depending on how quick the movement is. Move toward the deer only when the deer is looking away from you or has its head down.

Stalk toward your deer only when its head is down or it is looking away from you. Photo © by Peter Eades.

If you are stalking a deer and it senses danger, sometimes it will pop its head up looking in your direction, put it down, and quickly pop it back up again in an effort to catch a would-be predator off guard. You must be able to quickly read this situation and know how to proceed. Do not move again until the deer resumes its original position of browsing and becomes relaxed again—and constantly be ready for that head to pop up.

When moving toward the deer, also try to stay as low to the ground as possible. This way, you are that much less obvious to him and stand out

If a deer senses danger, a common behavioral tactic is to pop its head up looking in your direction, put it back down, and quickly pop back up to catch its predator off guard.

that much less if he looks straight at you.

Look ahead of you at where you plan to step each time prior to actually moving so you don't step on anything that will sound an alarm to the deer. It is critical that you avoid any dry twigs, leaves, or rocks, and anything else that will make noise.

It is very important to move from one point of concealment to another as you stalk toward the deer. Make it your goal to get from where you are to that next bush or tree that will offer you conceal-ment and a chance to collect yourself for your next move.

Sometimes you can use your call to entice the deer to move in your direction, and in other situations, with no effort on your part at all, the deer will begin to browse in your direction and thereby close the gap somewhat. Take advantage of this situation and let the deer do as much of the work as possible. The closer the deer moves to you, the less you have to move in its direction.

This doe is browsing in my direction and by doing so is making the stalk easier.

Don't move any closer to the deer than you absolutely have to in order to make the shot, and try to do so from some sort of arm rest, such as a tree or log, to steady your shot.

Stalk into the wind toward the deer, or the deer will get your scent and be gone. If the wind changes as you are stalking toward the deer, you may be forced to change your stalking strategy and stalk toward it in a different direction.

One of the best times to stalk your way up on a browsing deer is during a light rain. The rain dampens the deer's senses somewhat and also deadens the sounds that you make in the stalking process. Deer love

If the deer gets your scent he will take flight. Photo by Scott Bauer, U.S.D.A.

this type of weather and are often quite active during and after a light rain.

Just after a light rain is an excellent time to stalk your way up on a casual deer. Photo courtesy of Beth Andrus, www.nenature.com

Deer are used to hearing the sounds that a wild turkey makes as it walks through the woods. A lone hunter walking up on a browsing deer can sound very much like this wild turkey, just as you would when still-hunting. A turkey call may or may not save the stalk, but it's worth a try. Just remember that you can never have too many tricks in your bag. Always have a variety of calls in your bag to be used in situations like this.

A hunter walking in leaves sounds just like a wild turkey.

Try to choose quiet stalking routes if at all possible. If you need to stalk your way to another point from which to begin closing the gap between you and the deer, do so.

A flatrock creekbed such as this can offer a reasonably quiet stalk on a deer.

In the process of attempting to stalk up on your deer, try not to jump or stir up any of the local critters. It might only take a jumped rabbit tearing off through the weeds or a covey of quail suddenly flying off in all directions to scare off your deer. Even a possum waddling his way across the leaves could be just enough to stir the curiosity in an otherwise calm deer.

Try not to disturb any of the local critters in your attempt to stalk up to your deer.

Photo © by Mary Morris.

DRIVING DEER

There are many different ways to set up to approach a deer drive. Several factors will play a role in how to set up for the drive. You must determine how many drivers there will be and from what direction the drive will commence. Consider such things as the terrain, the number of hunters participating in the drive, the time of day, and so on to achieve the best results based on other hunting pressure. The weather conditions are very important and may or may not be conducive to a drive. Will the drivers be approaching the deer from the proper wind direction to accomplish what needs to be accomplished? Is there a clear understanding of where everyone will be?

On deer drives, it is extremely important that everyone wear blaze orange clothing and caps and know exactly how the drive is supposed to take place. Everyone should know from where the drivers will approach and where the shooters will be. Depending on circumstances, you will probably want the drivers to drive downwind so that the deer approaches the shooters from the upwind direction, or at least the crosswind direction. The drivers will be giving their presence away to the deer anyway as they walk through the area, but the shooters are the ones who need to go undetected.

Keep in mind that the natural tendency of the whitetail deer is to try to circle around behind the danger and slip away or to slip away by way of a heavily thickened corridor somewhere along the way. Try to place your shooters at certain key spots that slightly overlap the next shooter position. This is the preferred method provided there are enough hunters.

If the number of hunters is too few (for example, only one or two) then the driver's work is more difficult, and the shooter must be even more alert. The drivers may have to do some still-hunting–type driving in order to give the deer a decent opportunity to move past the shooter. In the situations where there are only two or three of you setting up a drive, you must take advantage of natural escape routes and funnels. This eliminates the need for flankers, in many cases, or hunters to force the deer to go in a certain direction. The deer will have a natural tendency to take these escape routes, so a lone shooter strategically located at the end of a route should do well.

In most cases, you should have at least three to five hunters for a good drive. This would be a minimum of one driving and two shooters or vice versa, depending on the terrain. It is a tremendous advantage to have a couple of flankers between the driver and the shooters, one on each side of the drive. There are many other wind direction considerations, but the bottom line is to not drive the deer into a prevailing scent that would push it in an undesirable direction. For example, if you drive the deer into the scent of the first shooter, be sure that the only other direction for the deer to go is in the direction of another shooter.

On any deer drive, safety is the foremost consideration, and only with this in mind should any hunter be strategically positioned to outsmart a deer on a deer drive. The following are a few hunting scenarios for you to analyze to get the idea. Keep in mind that there are many different scenarios, and each one is based on individual existing circumstances.

Notice in this illustration that there are two drivers walking downwind, approximately fifty yards apart. They are staggered, one in front of the other, by approximately thirty yards. They are driving toward one lone hunter.

The illustration above takes advantage of the terrain, deer habits, and having only two hunters. One driver walks down the side of a bluff, very steep hill, or any area that is not likely to be considered an escape route. He walks into the wind and either hopes to get a shot at a deer himself or force a deer to circle around behind him in an attempt to get downwind of him, as they quite often do. As the deer moves in this direction, hopefully he will move into the shooting path of the other hunter strategically set up waiting for him. The wind will be in both hunters' faces in this scenario.

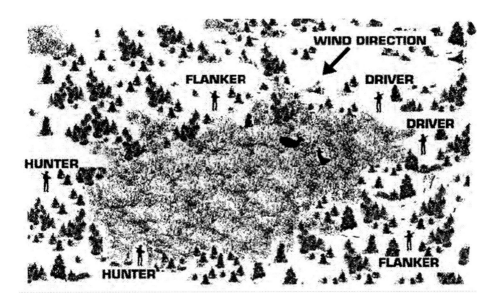

We have two drivers walking through a field with the wind blowing their scent toward two hunters strategically located at the opposite side of the field. There are two flankers, one on each side of the field to help funnel any deer toward the hunters.

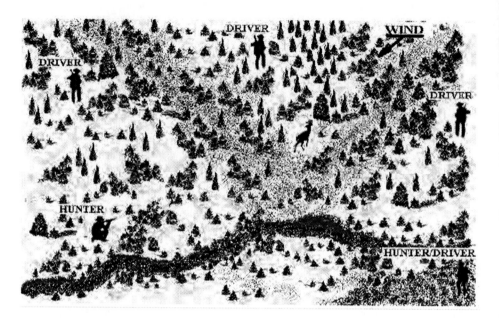

The illustration above shows three drivers, each driving down one of three points that converge at the bottom of the hill near a stream. Two hunters are strategically located, one on each side of the stream as well as each side of the conversion point of the three points. The drivers drive downwind, so if the wind is wrong, you can possibly reverse the driver and hunter roles.

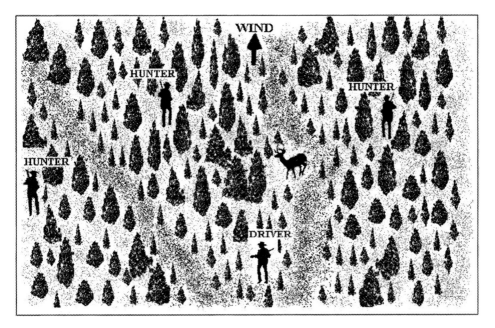

In this illustration, there is one driver slowly walking up a ravine or hollow down-wind. This ravine forks into two hollows that rise uphill, creating three points. Each of the three hunters positions himself on these points, anxiously awaiting an unsuspecting buck being driven by the one driver.

This illustration shows one single driver walking down a draw with the wind in order to disrupt any potential deer in the draw and force them back toward the two hunters. Each of these two hunters is strategically located on each side of the draw in concealment and with the wind in his face.

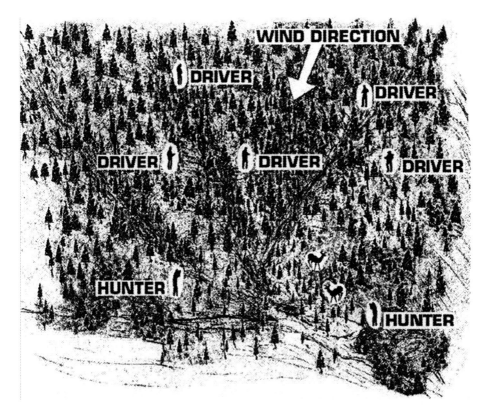

The above illustration reveals five drivers slowly and carefully walking down three draws or hollows and the points of these draws. They are walking downwind toward two hunters strategically located in good ambush positions. These drivers are revealing their scent to any potential deer ahead of them in the hopes of causing them to move toward the hunters. The two hunters are concentrating upwind, toward the direction of the drivers, for unsuspecting deer escaping the driver's pursuit. With this many people, it is much easier to cover more territory for a successful drive.

Photo © by Mary Morris

RATTLING FOR BUCKS

Rattling can be another very productive way to attract bucks if done properly and at appropriate times. The time of the season will determine what type of rattling you do. No matter how good you are or how hard you work at it, you won't always rattle up bucks when you try, because the whitetail doesn't always do what you expect him to. The few days just prior to the rut, during the rut, and just after the rut are the very best times to rattle. These are the times when the bucks are doing most of the clashing of horns themselves. Don't rattle too aggressively during the period prior to the rut. The more aggressive sounds come during the two to three weeks of the peak rut period. This is also when the bucks are most preoccupied, and most likely to make mistakes.

During the early season hunting period (or primarily bow season) prior to the rut, bucks are normally hanging out in bachelor groups. It is very common to see several bucks together feeding, sparring, and sharpening their skills for the rut, when the really serious fights will begin. During this early part of the season, a light tickling action with your rattle bag or rattling horns might stimulate a buck's curiosity and bring him in for a closer look. You want to simulate the sparring sound made by these young bucks and offer them an invitation to come join the fun.

Bachelor group at a feeding site.

As the rut begins to unfold and the bucks begin to aggressively fight over the right to service the does, the sounds you make when rattling must be much more aggressive and threatening. Clash the horns together and rattle them as you pull them apart. Thrash them against the ground, bushes, or trees. You want to challenge a buck to a contest for the rights to his territory. He will not freely volunteer these rights to you, but hopefully he will come in to "discuss" the issue.

Yours truly attempting to rattle in a good buck.

There are many devices on the market for rattling, and many of them have distinct advantages over others. You can use actual buck horns, synthetic horns, or a rattling bag, but whatever you use, it must be done properly at the proper time and must sound like the real thing. One advantage of the rattling bag over the horns is the reduced movement required to make the sound. This means a lesser chance of being detected, but if you use caution, a more realistic sound can be produced with a good set of rattling horns. One of the newest additions to my bag of tricks is a set of Big Buck 4n2 Rattling Antlers. They were developed by my friend Tom Tann. The unique aspect of Tom's antlers is the fact that there are two sets of antlers on each half. Consider that in an actual buck fight, there are almost always two complete sets of antlers (four half sets) creating the sound you hear. This is a more realistic sound than when you simply clack two half sets together like we have been doing for years. In an effort to put his theory to the test, Tom and his associate spent six weeks in the field and woods rattling for bucks with his Big Buck 4n2 Antlers. During this six week period, Tom rattled in over one hundred bucks, and this didn't even include the two weeks of peak rut. He videoed all of these events and will have many of them on his website, www.bigbuckrattlingantlers.com.

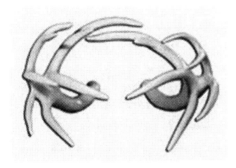

The Big Buck 4n2 Rattling Antlers

Tom has just rattled in a pretty nice buck with his 4n2 Rattling Antlers. Photo courtesy of Tom Tann.

The rut progresses to a peak period that normally last for two to three weeks depending on the geographical location, and during this time is when the bucks are most vulnerable to all of our tricks. This is the time when aggressive calling and rattling is most productive.

During the rut, bucks are most vulnerable to our tricks. Photo © Kevin Lammi, Northland Images.

It is extremely important to be as concealed as possible, especially if you have to do much moving at all when you are rattling. You must be very alert and anticipate a buck to come running in from any direction—not just from the downwind direction—during the peak rut period. Once you spot an approaching buck, stop rattling to prevent being detected until you can determine what his intentions are. If you are well concealed and can continue rattling as needed to bring him in closer, do so. Whether you rattle any more at this point must be determined by how well you read the deer and his body language.

Concealment goes hand in hand with rattling for bucks.

The buddy system can be very productive when rattling, too. Have a friend conceal himself and do the rattling for you while you strategically locate yourself for the actual shot. This way, the buck's attention will be focused on the sound and away from you, so you can concentrate on good shot placement and not as much on what you have to do to be able to take the shot. You should use field glasses when using this method in order to get on the buck as quickly as possible as he approaches. By having someone else do the rattling, you are more flexible in what you can do to be ready when a buck comes in.

Have a buddy conceal himself and rattle for you while you prepare for the actual shot. Photo courtesy of Tom Tann.

There are various books and tapes available to help you learn the proper way to rattle in different situations. The tapes acquaint you with the sounds to strive for in each scenario. You want one sound to come across when you are trying to emulate bucks sparring, another when two aggressive bucks are fighting, and still others when a buck is rubbing his rack on trees or limbs.

Photo © by Mary Morris

DEER CALLS ARE VERY VALUABLE TOOLS

Deer calls are extremely valuable to a deer hunter if they are used properly. Young hunters should try to acquire and become proficient at a few calls early in their hunting careers. When, where, and how the calls are used are extremely important. There are several different types of calls made by different manufacturers. Some of these calls do a better job than others, and this is where your own experimentation comes in. What works best for some might not work best for others, so you should find out which ones work best for you. Much as a good fisherman always has a variety of lures in his tackle box to be able to find the one lure that the fish are hitting at a given time and under certain circumstances, you should have the deer calls you find you need. Some people have the ability to use certain calls better than others. Always have a variety of call capabilities in your bag to be able to find the one that will attract the deer to you. Sometimes you may get no response at all, and on other days you may get a great deal of response. It is important to use the proper call for the proper situation. For example, you would not want to use an aggressive buck grunt if you know you are hunting a subdominant buck; the subdominant buck may feel threatened and not approach. You would do better to use a doe grunt or subdominant buck grunt. On the other hand, if you are hunting a dominant buck, you could use a variety of calls such as an aggressive buck, subdominant buck, doe grunt, tending grunt, or breeding bellow.

If you are hunting during the rut and are trying to attract does, you could use a variety of calls, such as those above as well as the doe bleat, yearling or fawn bleat, or fawn-in-distress call. If nothing else has worked for you, use the fawn-in-distress call as a last resort since this call tends to disrupt an otherwise calm atmosphere. This sound appeals to a doe's maternal instincts and in many cases will bring in does to try to assist a fawn in trouble.

Much like a fisherman uses several different lures, a deer hunter should use a variety of calls.

Take advantage of certain books and tapes available to learn as much as you can about deer body language and communication. There are a large number of resources available, and many of them are very helpful.

Talk to other deer hunters to find out what works best for them, and try to get them to show you how they use their call. What sounds do they make when using their call?

Sometimes deer just don't do what you think they should in a given situation, but don't get discouraged; this is a big part of deer hunting and what makes hunting deer such a challenge. No deer call will work all of the time—there are too many variables involved.

Many times you can see deer off in the distance that are not approaching your position. In many of these cases you can watch them through field glasses while trying a series of calls. Determine with your field glasses if you are getting their attention and arousing their curiosity. Calling deer in this manner will often reward you with an opportunity at a deer that you would not otherwise have gotten.

Watch the deer's body language as you call.

When a deer is running through the woods and you want to momentarily stop him for a quick shot, try a whistle or a verbal "Naaa!" or even just a yell. In many cases, this will do the trick. They normally will stop just long enough to try to determine where the sound is coming from, offering you a shot at a standing deer. Be ready to take a quick shot when the deer stops.

A call with a removable mouthpiece or one that allows your hands to be free has the distinct advantage for bow hunters of allowing you to be at full draw when you try to stop a deer in his tracks with your call for a split-second shot opportunity.

A lone turkey walking sounds much like a lone hunter walking.

When a lone hunter is walking through the woods, he or she may sound much the same as a turkey walking through the woods. Keep a turkey call with you—nothing aggressive, but merely some simple clucks to fool a listening whitetail into thinking that you are just another natural resident of his domain.

Don't overcall, or you will give yourself away. Depending on the type of call you are making, hit your call once or twice, wait a moment or so, then hit it again and put it aside for a while and see what happens. After thirty minutes or so, if you get no results, repeat the same procedure and wait again. Deer hunting is a lot of waiting to see what will happen. If you have waited for another thirty minutes or so and still have seen nothing, you might want to try a different call, using the same procedure or perhaps getting a little more aggressive with the first call. You will only learn what works best for you by trial and error.

Take care not to overcall; this could give you away.

Photo © by Robert Kraft

Photo © by Mary Morris

BOWHUNTING FOR WHITETAILS

While I love deer hunting no matter what type of weapon I use, I never feel quite the same exhilarating feeling as I do when I take a nice buck with a bow. It's much more challenging, and it helps me to relate back to our forefathers and the primitive skills they were forced to master just to survive. Our fine, high-tech compound bows of today are no comparison to the weapons they were forced to use back in those days. They had to become true hunters in every sense of the word in order to survive. I think it's very important that our young hunters following in our footsteps realize this and develop an appreciation for their ancestors and what they had to accomplish. Bowhunting also offers me the opportunity to get out into the woods with the deer before they have become skittish due to all of the surrounding gunfire. They are still calm and going about their normal activities. You can learn a great deal about the deer during this time of year.

If you choose to take up bowhunting, you must make a commitment to develop your skill and knowledge of the bow to the absolute best of your ability. You should strive to do this in anything you undertake, but especially in bowhunting, because the quarry you seek deserves the most humane and accurate kill shot you can provide him. Since practice makes perfect, be sure to practice a great deal.

Practice as much as possible to achieve good
shot placement on a deer.

Do some research into the various bows and equipment available
in order to make the best-educated decision on which one is right
for you. Visit your local archery shop to speak with someone who is
very knowledgeable on the subject. Most archery shops of respectable size have a technician on staff who can advise you about what
will suit your needs. The larger shops also have an indoor range to
allow you an opportunity to try out your selection and can help you
set it up to your specific draw length and weight. They can help you
decide what type of release to use, whether or not to use an overdraw, what type of shafts, broadheads, arrow rests, and fletching to
use, and so on.

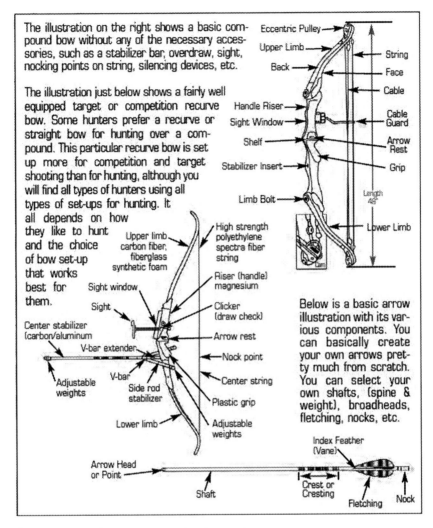

The illustration on the right shows a basic compound bow without any of the necessary accessories, such as a stabilizer bar, overdraw, sight, nocking points on string, silencing devices, etc.

The illustration just below shows a fairly well equipped target or competition recurve bow. Some hunters prefer a recurve or straight bow for hunting over a compound. This particular recurve bow is set up more for competition and target shooting than for hunting, although you will find all types of hunters using all types of set-ups for hunting. It all depends on how they like to hunt and the choice of bow set-up that works best for them.

Eccentric Pulley
Upper Limb
Back
String
Face
Cable
Handle Riser
Sight Window
Shelf
Stabilizer Insert
Limb Bolt
Cable Guard
Arrow Rest
Grip
Length
Lower Limb

Upper limb carbon fiber, fiberglass synthetic foam
Sight window
Sight
Center stabilizer (carbon/aluminum
V-bar extender
V-bar
Adjustable weights
Side rod stabilizer
Lower limb

High strength polyethylene spectra fiber string
Riser (handle) magnesium
Clicker (draw check)
Arrow rest
Nock point
Center string
Plastic grip
Adjustable weights

Below is a basic arrow illustration with its various components. You can basically create your own arrows pretty much from scratch. You can select your own shafts, (spine & weight), broadheads, fletching, nocks, etc.

Index Feather (Vane)
Arrow Head or Point
Shaft
Crest or Cresting
Fletching
Nock

Learn as much as you can about your bow.

Do not choose a bow of too great a draw weight. If your bow requires too much strength to draw, you will become fatigued too quickly during those times when you need to hold your draw while you wait for the buck to get in a good shot position. This is a common mistake that a lot of hunters make. You want to be able to make a smooth draw. For whitetail deer, you should choose a draw weight of at least forty-five to fifty-five pounds.

If you plan to shoot longer distances, you will want a flatter trajectory shooting bow—in other words, a faster bow. You should be aware that a faster bow is less forgiving than one that is slower, though both bows require the development of a certain amount of skill. The faster bow requires a little more skill than the slower one, however.

Your draw length is another area that deserves serious consideration. The bow design itself and your physical anatomy will determine the draw length. The design of some bows has the string closer to the riser or handle of the bow than others, and some limbs are longer than others. The further you have to draw your bow to achieve full draw, the longer your draw length. You want this draw length to fall into a comfort zone for you; the archery representative should be able to advise you in this area.

You should always shoot the bow you intend to purchase to determine just how much noise it makes and how much vibration you get with each shot. This noise and vibration represents dispersed energy that is not going into your actual shot. In other words, the energy you put into your draw that you expect to get out of the shot is reduced by the amount of noise and vibration because this is useless, wasted energy. Do some checking in this area and rule out those that are fairly noisy and vibrate a great deal. Talk to other hunters and archery enthusiasts to get their input, too.

There are many choices to make regarding your bow and its various accessories. You must whether to get a compound, recurve, or straight bow. In years past, you had to be handicapped in order to use a crossbow for deer hunting purposes, but now it is legal for anyone to use a crossbow in most states. If you get a compound, for example, what brand and style do you get? Do you want a bow with solid limbs or split limbs, single- or double-cam? You must consider the weight of the bow, since you will be carrying it in the field. Will you choose to use a bow sling, and if so, what type? What type of silencing measurers, what type of release, overdraw or not, appropriate stabilizer bar: are all important considerations. You will also need to decide what type of arrows or bolts to use and what type of arrow rest, broadheads, camouflage pattern, fletchings, quiver, and sight to use (unless you plan to learn to instinctively shoot, in which case you would prefer no sight).

Learn the proper care of your bow and how to perform some basic adjustments and repairs in the field. Be sure to keep the axles and bushings of your bow well lubricated to prevent unnecessary wear on these parts due to friction, which causes damage to your bow. To reduce any unnecessary noise, these parts should be lubricated with bow oil every other time that you use your bow. Keeping your bow-string waxed will greatly prolong its lifespan if done correctly. Be sure to rub the wax into the strings—don't just coat the outside of it. As you are waxing the string, look closely for any worn or frayed portion that may require the replacement of the string. Waxing your arrow shafts will make them slide across the rest more freely and offer less resistance for smoother, quieter shots. Regularly inspect the bow limbs and all other parts of your bow for cracks or wear, and either repair them yourself or have them repaired at a bow shop. Be sure that your limb bolts have not backed off, changing your draw weight. A good way to manage this is to scribe a mark across the bolt head onto the limb so you can see at a glance if the two ends of the line are mismatched.

There are many different styles of broadheads available on the market. Do some research to determine which broadheads you prefer to use. Your arrow shafts or bolts must be compatible with your bow as well as your broadheads. The length, weight, and wall thickness of the shafts must match your specific bow and cannot be too light or too heavy. The grain weight of the shafts and broadheads must complement each other. You should consider certain factors in choosing your broadheads, such as how well they will retain their edge and how sturdy they are when sustaining impact. Will they power through that deer and offer a clean kill by slicing through veins and arteries in the process?

You must make decisions regarding your fletchings, too. For one thing, you must decide whether to use three or four vanes based on what type of rest you have chosen. You don't want the vanes to hit your bow or rest improperly and affect your arrow flight. If you are shooting broadheads, depending on the style, you may want your fletchings installed on your arrow shafts at a slight angle. This will cause your arrows to rotate in flight and help stabilize the effects of your broadheads on them. The color of the vanes also should be considered. The lighter, brighter colors would be easier for you to see or spot, but they also make them easier to spot by a deer.

It is important to establish your anchor points when you first begin shooting your bow. These are specific points that you or your bow-string, kisser button, or other devices you may have on your bow touch each time you come to full draw.

I prefer a three-point anchor method. Using a mechanical release, when I am at full draw, my thumbnail hits the corner of my mouth as my forefinger's second knuckle hits the center of my cheek bone and the string hits the center of my nose. Everyone's anchor points will be a little different, but the more points like this you can establish, the more likely you will be to be able to anchor and release the

Establish your anchor points early on, and learn to depend on them to make the shot.

exact same way each time you shoot. These anchor points will vary depending on whether you are using a mechanical release, tab, or fingers.

Learn to shoot from a sitting or standing position. You never know what position you may be in when you get a shot at a buck. Your anchor points should be the same even though you may have to change the posture of your body to shoot under low-lying limbs or around a tree.

Be very careful not to make your draw too soon when you see a deer, because the deer may

Learn to shoot from the sitting and standing positions when you are bowhunting.

hesitate and stand still for several minutes, deciding whether or not to continue on into your shooting lane. You don't want to have a deer close by, just out of a shooting lane when you are standing there at full draw, waiting on him. If the deer takes very long to make up his mind as to what to do, you will begin to fatigue and shake. The end result will probably be that you will make enough noise to frighten off the deer without ever getting a shot at him. Sometimes it's hard to determine exactly when to come to full draw without doing so too early or

Don't make your draw too soon, in case the deer hesitates behind a tree.

waiting too long. We all hate to run the risk of drawing when a deer can see or hear our movements. This is simply a call you must make each time the situation presents itself.

When you practice shooting your bow (and be sure to do this a lot), practice from an elevated position; the arrow will travel a little differently when shooting down than when you are shooting on the level—it will actually rise slightly when shooting downward. Try to simulate actual hunting scenarios. Have an elevated platform at home set up to practice on. Set up milk jugs or any such objects around you so that you can shoot in all directions. Take shots from different positions: standing, sitting, kneeling, and so on. Wear the same type and amount of clothes that you will have on when you are hunting. Take

Practice, practice, practice.

shots from different distances and concentrate on judging distances. Step off certain distances you feel comfortable shooting from, and mark them by tying a ribbon around a tree or placing an object at this point to become accustomed to the distance. One of the best objects to practice with at these distances is an actual 3D deer target, a life-size target of a deer that will help you even more to judge the distance as if it were a real deer standing in the same spot. If you practice enough— and I'm talking about a serious practice strategy—you will become a proficient archer.

Practice from different eleva- tions, including from your tree stand.

Competition shooting is a very good way to keep you sharp, and this doesn't necessarily have to be at a real club or sanctioned compe- tition. You and some of your hunt- ing buddies can get together in your backyard, set up targets, and try to outshoot each other. Try to have these types of get-togethers fairly often.

Never climb into your stand with your bow, but instead use a pull rope to pull your bow up after you are settled on your stand.

When I get settled in my stand, I take my quiver off and hang it on a limb or on my stand. I figure I reduce the potential noise prob- lem and the additional chance of being spotted because of the bright-

Always pull your bow up to your stand with a pull rope.

colored fletchings by doing this. This way, the only arrow that gets moved around is the one I have nocked. One of the arrows could work loose in the quiver, or the bolt that holds the quiver to the bow could loosen up a little. All of these things could cause you problems.

Never leave your bow in a hot vehicle, since the heat can do serious damage, making the bow unusable or inaccurate.

Transport your bow in some sort of case to prevent any accidental damage in transit. You don't want to go to all the trouble of getting your bow all tuned up and sighted in just perfectly only to accidentally knock the sight off in the back of your vehicle on your way to the hunting site. I highly recommend a hard-shell case for your bow.

Because you must be much closer to your quarry with a bow than with a rifle or muzzleloader, your scent, your camouflage, the noise factor, and everything else becomes much more critical. You must overcome all of these obstacles in order to be successful. You must be familiar with deer body language and all of their keen senses, as well as wind directions, up- and downdrafts, and the effects weather changes have on the movements of deer.

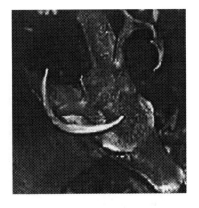

Be prepared for what to do if a buck shows up somewhere unexpected—perhaps just beneath your stand.

When you make your release on a deer, in most cases the deer will hear the release and instinctively drop its body several inches in and effort to bolt away. With this in mind, you may need to make some allowance for this movement when you take your shot. If its head is down feeding, or if it is preoccupied in some other way, the deer might not react to your release, so try to pick the best possible time to make your release.

Sights vary a great deal, so spend a lot of time deciding which one will suit your needs best. There are many styles to choose from. For example there are pin sights, crosshair sights, fiber optic sights, pendulum sights, lighted sights, peep sights, and other sights that are mostly variations of these. Discuss the advantages of each with a specialist at your favorite bow shop. Remember: just because one person prefers a particular style does not mean that it is the right style for you.

Be sure to learn the proper way to tune your bow. Just because you can shoot a tight group with field points does not mean that your bow is perfectly tuned for hunting. Broadheads will almost certainly make your shafts fly differently than with field points, even though they may be the same grain weight. There are a few different methods for tuning your bow, and they all are based on using shafts of a proper spine for the bow and cam you are using. If you have a consistently smooth release, then paper-tuning your bow will probably be the most accurate method to use. Build a wooden frame about two or three feet wide and about five or six feet high, and cover it with paper stretched as tightly as you can stretch it. Stand about six feet away, and shoot an arrow in a straight, horizontal direction through the paper to a target. Note the configuration of the paper cut after the shot. If the tail of the nock is high, this indicates that the nocking point is too high. Either lower the nocking point or raise the rest slightly. If the tail of the nock is low, then do the opposite. If the tail of the nock is off to the left or right, move the rest to the left or right in the direction that it is off. This is for those shooters that shoot a release; finger shooters would do just the opposite. Once you get your bow tuned to where you are shooting a consistently symmetrical hole, then move back a few feet and check it at different distances. Another method of tuning your bow is by using a bow square. Affix a bow square to the string and lay the arm on the rest. Position the nocking point on the string the shaft diameter distance above the plane of the rest or lower side of the shaft. This should take care of your elevation or vertical aspect of your arrow flight, and for the windage or horizontal flight, adjust your rest as necessary as in the paper method above. You must realize that bows do vary somewhat in the exact placement of the nocking point on the string. Some single-cam bows may require the nocking point to be slightly higher than normal in order to get good performance. Discuss these various options with a bow technician where you purchase your bow, and get him or her to help you tune your bow the first time. For clarity purposes, think of these adjustments in a different way. If your arrow in flight porpoises or the tail of the arrow flops up and down, the nocking point on your string needs to be adjusted up or down, but if it fishtails or flops side to side, adjust your rest to one side or the other.

One very important safety tip—not only for you personally, but also for the safety of your bow—is to never dry-fire your bow. This means that you should never draw your bow to full draw and release the string without an arrow knocked. This action could seriously damage your limbs, and maybe you in the process.

Photo © by Mary Morris.

MUZZLELOAD HUNTING FOR WHITETAILS

Here in Tennessee, my favorite time of the year to be in the woods hunting for the whitetail is the opening week of muzzleloader season. This is the first time that we can be in the woods with a long-range weapon, when the deer are still calm and going about their regular routine. The bucks are becoming more active and starting to rut. They have begun to chase the does and create scrape lines. There is much more rub and scrape activity going on at this time of year. Naturally, muzzleloader hunting presents a little more of a challenge than rifle hunting, but it also has many of the same advantages as rifle hunting. This is deer hunting more like our forefathers did, and a perfect opportunity for certain family members to be together and relate back to these early days. Our youths of today in most cases have no idea of what it was like for the early pioneers to just survive. I always plan some vacation time around this time of year, and I recommend that you do the same.

Choosing a good muzzleloader rifle that pleases you is very important. I highly recommend a .50 caliber with a composite stock for durability and lightweight. You do not want a shiny finish that could reflect the sunlight and betray your presence to the deer. Your weapon should be able to be loaded quickly and cleaned easily in the field. I personally use a .50 caliber Black Knight and have been very pleased with it, but there are several very fine makes available. Check them out, and choose one that suits you.

I recommend a good scope for your muzzleloader rifle. A scope will greatly improve your odds of being successful and getting a clean kill. Be sure and choose a scope that is good in low-light conditions since there will be many situations when you will be scoping a buck either very early or very late in low-light conditions. Be sure to put scope covers on your scope to protect the scope lens from getting scratched and to keep rain and moisture off the lens. I prefer the flip-up type so you don't have to pull them completely off of the gun when you get ready to shoot.

Be sure to use a sling of some type so that you can shoulder your weapon when you are not hunting. Remember that you may be in the field all day—after a few hours, the gun is going to get heavy. If you are successful and bag a deer, then you will need to be able to sling your gun over your shoulder in order to drag your deer out. Wrapping the sling around your forearm can also steady your shot in certain scenarios.

If you don't have a camouflage finish on your gun, regardless of what type it is, you should get a camouflage gun sock to pull over it to help conceal it while you are in the field hunting. These also soften the noise your gun makes against limbs and protect your gun as you hunt with it.

You will need an accessories bag of some type or a butt-pack to put your various necessary items in. You will need extra powder or pyrodex, extra projectiles (balls, sabots, bullets, etc.), primer caps, dry-clean patches to run down the bore, bore cleaner, and a ball starter and ball puller if you cannot access the bore from the breech end. I like to use quick loads because they are much faster for getting off a second shot if necessary. You can premeasure your powder and place it in a quick load with a projectile and a primer cap on the side, ready to apply.

You must always remember to pop two or three primer caps before loading your weapon. This ensures that your nipple is clear and that you have a clear path from the primer cap to the powder to the projectile to the end of the bore, and hopefully to your deer. With your gun empty (unloaded), place the primer cap on your nipple and pull the trigger while holding the end of the bore down to a leaf or piece of paper. If the path is clear, the sound will be loud and hollow and will move the leaf or paper somewhat. You should do this two or three times, or until you are satisfied that there are no obstructions. If you still don't feel comfortable that your gun is clear, then you should clean it. It's better to take the time now than to attempt a shot at a big buck and misfire.

Always check how your gun is firing before the season opens. Be sure to use the exact grain projectile and the exact number of grains of powder that you will be hunting with to site your weapon in. Each time you fire the weapon, the grains of powder must be the same, or the shots will not group for you. I always site my Knight rifle in at 100 yards and then check how it shoots at 150 yards. Shoot the weapon enough that you are confident that you know how it will shoot in the field at a deer.

Carry your powder, primer caps, and projectiles in some sort of waterproof container or bag in case it rains. Above all else, you must keep your powder dry.

It is imperative that you clean your weapon thoroughly when you get back to camp after having fired it. Once you fire the weapon, rust will begin to form very quickly. Thoroughly clean everything but the trigger housing with gun cleaner or soap and water, and then give every part a light coat of oil. Be sure to oil the trigger assembly to displace any moisture that may have gotten into it. Always thoroughly read the owner's manual that comes with your weapon, especially the cleaning portion of your owner's manual.

Use a great deal of care to protect your scope and its relationship to your weapon. In other words, be careful that you don't accidentally bump or hit your scope against something and knock it off line to where it is no longer zeroed in. This could ruin your hunt, especially if you get a shot at a good buck.

There are a few things to pay close attention to after shooting your weapon. Be sure to get rid of the spent primer cap that sometimes may fall into the action chamber and need to be dumped out. When ramming a bullet or sabot down the barrel, force it with steady pressure tightly against the powder. Don't tap it several times once you have it firmly in place or you will deform the projectile and impair its flight capability. Don't forget to put powder in before you ram the projectile. Be sure your ramrod is seated properly back in your weapon so that it doesn't slip out and fall to the ground. Don't forget to place a new primer cap on the nipple when you are ready to hunt. Be sure to flip your safety back on until you are ready to shoot.

Photo © by Mary Morris

WHITETAILS WITH A RIFLE

One of the most wonderful feelings in the world for a deer hunter is to be sitting on a deer stand on opening morning of rifle season knowing that he or she has done good preseason scouting and found a good spot. The fact that the hunter has a high-powered rifle that he or she has patiently sited in, capable of reaching out two or three hundred yards if necessary to take a nice buck, is the cherry on top. I personally don't like to take extremely long shots, such as three hundred to four hundred yards, but it's nice to know that I can if the circumstances are right. Hunting the whitetail with a rifle is as natural to many of us as skipping a rock across a pond. It always takes me back to my boyhood, hunting squirrels on my grandfather's farm with a .22 rifle. There's a certain amount of relaxation when you're hunting deer with a rifle that you do not have with a bow, because you have to be in such close proximity to the deer with a bow that you are on your toes at all times. I enjoy knowing that if a nice buck appears out of bow range, I don't have to worry about whether or not he responds favorably to my deer call. It's true that the challenge is not as great with a rifle as it is with a bow, but when you're trying to put venison on the table, that challenge is not all it's cracked up to be.

My personal preference for deer hunting in my particular area of Tennessee is a flat-trajectory type of weapon. My Remington .270 has served me well over the years. I don't hunt in consistent thick-cover areas. In fact, in most areas, I could take a 150- to 200-yard shot, and in many cases longer than that. I also prefer a wide-field, variable scope conducive to low-light situations, since many of my shots are under these conditions. A .243, .270, .308, .30-06, or 7mm magnum all would be good calibers for the area I choose to hunt. I prefer a flatter shooting rifle, because within the range that I feel comfortable shooting and using a 130-grain bullet, I don't have to make as much of an adjustment as I would if I were shooting a .30-06, for example, with a 180-grain bullet. The thicker, brushier areas would suggest a heavier caliber, such as a .30-30 or maybe a .35. You should use a heavier-caliber bullet that can resist the rugged cover areas more readily. I am not suggesting that you shoot through brush at your deer, but if your bullet accidentally hits a twig, you'll want it to resist veering off course.

The following rifles and their capabilities are more than adequate for whitetail deer hunting no matter where you hunt. This is valuable information that you need to know in order to make an educated decision on a rifle selection. This is also necessary information for long- or short-range shooting accuracy. You need to know what your rifle is capable of doing with whatever projectile you choose to use in it.

1. The .270 with its oversized case holds enough powder to push a 150-grain bullet in the 3,000 fps range; its retained energy at 400 yards is nearly 1,200 ft/lbs.

2. The .308 Winchester has the bullet speed and weight to closely match the .30–06 at shorter ranges. In the .308 Winchester, a 180-grain bullet will retain over 1,200 ft/lbs of energy at 400 yards but will have dropped some 52 inches.

3. The .30-06 Springfield has a long history is still among the favorite all-around big-game calibers. For the hunter who will hunt everything from deer to moose or even prairie dogs, the .30-06 is a great choice. You get a range of bullet weights from the 110-grain bullet to the 220-grain bullet. Loaded with the 180-grain bullet, the .30-06 will retain over 1,300 ft/lbs of energy at 400 yards. That is plenty to knock an elk off its feet, although the bullet drop at that range is nearly 50 inches. It is available in almost every action and almost every brand of firearm on the market. This is an advantage for the .30-06. Find-

ing a rifle action, model, and style that you want is easy with the .30-06. Because of its popularity, you will have no problem finding or borrowing ammunition for the .30-06 no matter where you are.

4. The 7mm magnum has a slightly larger case and holds enough powder to push a 175-grain bullet faster than the .270 could move its lighter bullet. That means that the 175-grain bullet from the 7mm Magnum retains nearly 2,000 ft/lbs of energy at 400 yards. Bullet drop is about 42 inches at 400 yards, better than the .270 and without much more recoil. Minimal bullet drop and its knockdown power at the extreme range are its credentials. The 7mm Remington Magnum is a very good elk gun.

You must take extremely good care of your weapons. Keep them well-lubricated, clean, and sighted in for whenever you may need an accurate shot.

If your gun gets wet, always clean it as soon as possible to prevent rust. A wooden stock should be waxed periodically to protect it from the elements.

Always transport your weapon in a gun case, preferably a hard-shell case of some type. There are several different kinds available, and some are very reasonably priced for the quality you get.

Log the serial numbers of your weapons and keep them in a safe place. If your weapons are ever lost or stolen, these may help in recovering them.

After you have successfully taken a buck and have to drag him out, be very careful how you treat your weapon in the process of dragging him out. I have seen people tie a rope around the animal and the other end around their rifle and physically use the rifle to drag the deer out. This can damage your rifle in several ways and should not be done under any circumstances. You can easily substitute a stout stick or tree limb that you have fashioned for this purpose. Using a sling on your rifle, you should drape the rifle across your back or chest to keep it safe from damage while dragging your deer out. Different hunters use different means for getting their deer out, such as ATVs or specially designed carts, or leave the deer and bringing the vehicle to the deer. It helps a great deal if you have a hunting buddy along to help you.

There are many advantages to deer hunting with a rifle. One big advantage, of course, is the increased range from which you can successfully take a deer. Because of this increased range, you are not as likely to be scented, seen, or heard if you use normal caution. You don't have to worry as much about bringing the deer to you with a call of some type. A well-placed shot in the kill zone is easier to make with a rifle for most hunters. If a second shot is necessary, it is a great deal faster to do it with a rifle than with a bow or muzzle-loader. You don't have to worry about keeping your powder dry or a deer jumping the string on you either. Please don't get me wrong here—I love archery and muzzleloader season, but I think that the older you get, the more advantages you appreciate, and I sure do enjoy rifle season.

There are a few disadvantages to hunting deer with a rifle also, such as the noise factor. Once rifle season opens and hunters begin firing rifles in the area, the deer become skittish and start changing their habits. You have to hunt harder and stay in the woods longer to be able to get a shot. Luckily, rifle season here in Tennessee is normally scheduled in close proximity to the rut, so you have the extra advantage of Mother Nature's assistance, to a degree. Always try to do your preseason scouting, and make the most of the first couple of weeks of the season; it will be a little more difficult after that. Many bucks become nocturnal as the season progresses. You don't have the noise factor causing such changes during bow season, and the deer remain fairly calm. Another big disadvantage to rifle hunting is the increased danger to you or someone else. There is always the possibility that your shot could travel beyond your target and hit someone or something without you knowing. This is why it is so important to abide by the law and wear the required amount of blaze orange. There are hunters or bystanders shot accidentally every year due to someone's negligence.

When hunting with a rifle, if you aren't careful, you may tend to get a little lax or tend to be a little off guard. The knowledge that you are carrying a high-powered rifle capable of reaching out a great distance to take your deer may make you a little overconfident and prevent you from being as alert as you should be. You must not forget the keen senses of the whitetail deer and what he is capable of. In many cases, under ideal conditions, the whitetail deer can see, hear, or smell you from as far away as you can shoot him with a rifle. I am merely saying that you must always be on guard regardless of what weapon you are carrying. Relax a little in the knowledge that you don't have to lure him in as close as you do with a bow, but always be alert to his possible presence when you least expect him.

Do a little manicuring to the area where you intend to hunt to give yourself the best possible visibility or shooting lanes without obviously changing the look of the area. You don't want to do anything to alert the deer to your presence. It will help you to feel out the range when a deer appears if you automatically know the exact range to certain specific points, such as a particular tree, creek bed, or boulder. This gives you a reference point to compare where the deer happens to be when you do see him. This tip is more helpful in bow hunting, but I find it helps me with all three weapons.

RECOVERING YOUR DEER

One very critical part of deer hunting is actually recovering your deer once you have gone through all of the time and effort to do everything else right and you actually get that shot at a nice deer. This is when the followthrough aspect of deer hunting comes into play. If you take a shot at a whitetail—or any other game for that matter—and hit the target, you must exhaust every effort and means possible to locate it. Once you have done everything you think you can to locate it, get help if you can, but try to never leave a wounded animal to suffer and die a slow, painful death. This is one of our most important rules in our hunting ethics code. The following suggestions will help you in this regard or at least point you in the right direction.

If you shoot a deer, wait at least thirty minutes before attempting to pursue it. If you achieved a good solid hit in a vitals area, it won't be far away. Also, if you did get a good hit in a vitals area, by staying in your stand for a good half-hour after shooting, it allows the animal time to go down and expire with less trauma than if you push him. By doing this, the animal will be much easier to find. If you jump down and immediately go after it, it may continue on much further just out of sheer adrenaline.

Wait thirty minutes after you shoot a deer in most cases before pursuing it.

There are times when you may not have gotten a good hit on the deer but one that would guarantee you the kill if the deer kept bleeding. Once shot, deer will eventually lie down and attempt to close up the wound with mud or other debris; this will either prolong its death or prevent it. If you can read this situation accurately enough, you may want to start pursuing your deer immediately in an effort to keep him moving and losing blood; however, this is a very questionable retrieval. If you fail to get a good shot placement on your deer, the odds go way down for a recovery.

Once you shoot a deer, be very cautious in your attempt to retrieve it.

Train yourself to automatically look for that vitals area as soon as you spot a legal deer. As soon as the deer is in shooting range, take note of exactly where the deer is standing in order to locate this exact spot later. Aim for the vital area and release or fire the weapon. If you are bowhunting, try to follow through with your shot by watching the arrow as far as you can to the target. If you concentrate hard enough, you can actually see the arrow penetrate the deer. Always do your best to hit the deer in a vitals area, and watch how the deer reacts to the hit, as well as which direction the deer runs.

I prefer to use a compass to check the direction that a deer went once it was hit. Check your compass heading to the last place you were able to actually see the deer so that when you climb down out of your stand, you will have two points and a line of travel to try to pick up the blood trail: you have the point of impact and the point at which you were last able to see the deer. The view from up in your stand looks entirely different from how it looks on the ground, and these points may be difficult to find without the use of a compass.

You should try to watch the deer as long as you can once it is hit, and when it disappears, listen for it as long as you can hear it. Try

to pick out some land-
mark—a tree, a stump,
a log, anything to help
you find the spot bet-
ter once you are on the
ground. When you climb
down out of the stand,
you should go to the
point of impact follow-
ing the same compass
heading you noted up
in the stand as being

Pay special attention to the last place you saw
your deer once it was shot.

where the deer was hit. Once you arrive at this spot, look for blood
and hair signs and your arrow if you were bowhunting. If you locate
the arrow, inspect it thoroughly to see what the blood looks like. The
blood on your arrow will tell you a lot about how badly the deer was
hit, and this information will help you recover your deer.

If you hit a deer in the lungs, there will be air bubbles or a frothy or
pinkish appearance on your shaft due to oxygen content in the blood.
Any hair sign would likely be long and brown or gray in color. The
deer may travel thirty-five or forty yards before going down. If you
hit it in the heart, the blood will be a dark red with similar hair as the
lungs. Normally you will find a blood trail within ten or fifteen yards.
A friend of mine once shot the heart out of a deer, and we found the
deer over sixty yards from the heart. Either of these shots would be
a clean kill. If you hit the deer in the liver, however, the blood will be
very bright red. The deer may run one hundred yards or more before
going down or slowing to a walk. This could simultaneously be a
lung shot as well, so you might also see tiny air bubbles in the blood.
You might penetrate the lungs and the liver at the same time because
of the proximity of each location to the other. There will be a stench
and stomach or intestinal matter on the shaft if you penetrated the
stomach or intestines, and the blood will be blackish in color. The
hair will normally be white and coarse. This will be a slower kill and
harder to recover. One of the easiest blood trails to follow is a kidney
hit, because of the extensive bleeding. If the deer is hit in this area,
it will normally walk or slowly run for seventy-five yards or so, and

then bed down. Should you hit the deer in the neck, hindquarter, or hind legs, you might get lucky and penetrate a main artery such as the femoral or carotid artery, which will be a clean kill. If you can determine that you hit the deer in one of these areas and fail to penetrate one of these arteries, you should begin tracking it immediately to force it to continue bleeding. Once it loses enough blood, it will expire. If it is allowed to lie down and rest, it may be able to stop its bleeding and survive.

If the blood trail stops, try to establish a definite direction of travel by lining up the last few blood spots. Place markers of some type at the last few, and then follow that line of travel beyond the last blood spot and check right and left of this line, a few steps each way, to attempt to pick up some sign of the deer's passing or more blood spots. Try this for twenty-five or thirty yards, and

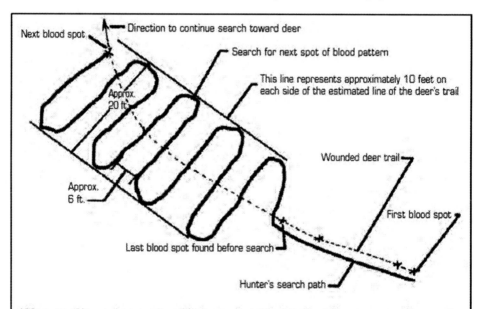

When tracking a deer, and suddenly you lose the blood trail, attempt to line up the last few spots to determine a line of travel. Follow this line of travel, zigzagging back and forth approximately ten feet on either side of the suspected line of travel. Do this for approximately thirty or forty yards, and if you fail to find any new blood spots, then revert to the semi-circular pattern in an attempt to find new blood spots.

When tracking a deer, you may suddenly lose the blood trail, requiring you to track the deer using other methods.

if you don't find any new blood, resort to the semicircular method mentioned next.

When you are following a blood trail and the trail stops, tag the last spot of blood in some way. Tie a ribbon on a tree or use a reflective marker of some type if it is getting late. Now start semicircling the last spot of blood, gradually moving forward as you look for new blood or other signs of the deer's passing. Start looking for the

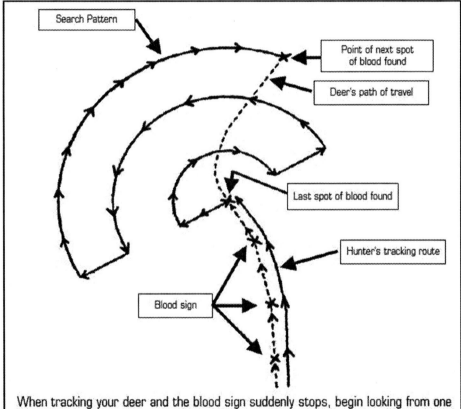

When tracking your deer and the blood sign suddenly stops, begin looking from one side to the other in a 180° semi-circular pattern in the direction the deer was traveling, based on the blood sign previously found. Do this until you find some sign, such as blood, turned up leaves, or some other sign where the deer went. If this fails to reveal any new sign, you should try complete circular patterns around the last visible sign found, increasing the circle gradually.

When you are trailing your deer and the blood trail stops, look for other signs of the deer's passing.

not-so-obvious signs, such as blood that failed to hit the ground. Sometimes blood will spurt out to the side of a deer as it is traveling or running and may land on the side of tree trunks, tree limbs, or bushes. Look for turned-up leaves and rocks, or a place where the deer may have stumbled or fallen.

A badly wounded deer will try to exit by the easiest possible route when it can. It will tend to run down the hill rather than up it or across it, or around the bottom of a point as opposed to straight up it. There are exceptions, though, and it depends on how badly the deer is hit, and how alert it still is after being shot. Remember that the deer knows the area well, and will run for safety regardless of what it has to overcome, depending on how critical its wound is. If the wound is a fatal one, the deer will in most cases just drop or run a few feet out of shock until it drops, with no conscious direction in mind. Depending on how badly a deer is hit, a deer tends to head for water if it is hit in the gut or kidney.

If you are tracking a deer and you come across a large area of blood but no deer, temporarily stop your search. You are probably pushing the deer, and it may keep this up for a long time. Wait a while and let the deer bed down again and expire before taking up the search again. Potential bad weather would be the only reason to push the deer any further at that time.

Never let a blood trail wait until the next day if you can find your deer today. If you don't have sufficient light, go get a flashlight or lantern and return to search again. Lanterns are good light sources for tracking at night. You never know for sure what the weather is going to dish out. A rain shower could come up when you least expect it, depending on where you hunt. If it rains, the

Once you shoot your deer, find it.

blood trail will wash away and make it almost impossible for you to find your deer. A hungry pack of coyotes could sniff the deer out and have their way with it during the night, or if the weather is too warm (above 42 degrees), the deer could spoil during this period.

If you are tracking a wounded deer, it may lie down, settle in, and more or less freeze in place in an attempt to evade you as you pass by. You would almost have to walk over it in order to stir it from its seclusion. Once you pass by the deer and fail to detect it, it may slip away quietly. Don't get so caught up in the search for blood or other sign that you fail to look for the deer itself.

A wounded deer may lie down and freeze in position in an attempt to elude its hunter.

Don't underestimate a whitetail deer's stamina once it is hit. If you fail to get a good solid hit on your deer by penetrating the vitals area, you could lose it altogether if you aren't extremely careful. I'll mention again the deer that ran over sixty yards without a heart. The heart was lying on the ground where the deer was hit—and the carcass was sixty yards away. A badly wounded deer can travel great distances, so it is extremely important to concentrate heavily on first-shot placement so that you can bring the deer down with the first shot.

Always approach a downed deer cautiously and safely, since the deer may not have expired yet. Try to approach in such a manner as to be able to get off another shot if necessary to finish it off. If you approach too suddenly and the deer is still alive, it may have enough life left in it to thrash out toward you, causing you bodily harm. Deer have been known to cause harm to hunters before under such circumstances.

If you approach your deer and it is still alive, try to finish it off as humanely as possible. If there is no danger in getting close enough, place another shot behind its ear into the head. This should be a quick and clean kill. Do not slit the deer's throat; this is not a very humane method of killing.

Some hunters use a string tracker device when bowhunting, but this device usually works best when you expect to get close shots. Others prefer to use lighted nocks that help determine exactly where in the body you hit the deer and that can help you find the deer in low-light situations. In this high-tech world we live in today, some choose to use a game finder of some sort that picks up body heat and can locate a down deer for several hundred yards in the woods, and even further in the open field, though these are usually somewhat pricey. And

Always treat your quarry as humanely as possible.

then again, you just might prefer the old-fashioned way of using your head as best you can.

Be sure to use your field glasses to search the area ahead for your deer if you have lost the blood trail.

After an extensive search of your own fails to produce your deer, but you know you hit the deer, recruit the assistance of a friend or hunting buddy to help you before you give up the effort. Always exhaust every effort to retrieve a wounded deer. If you don't find it during the night, go back the next day and try again.

Always try to take your deer with you when you leave.

Photo © by Mary Morris

Photo © by Mary Morris

FIELD DRESSING YOUR DEER

When you locate your deer, there are certain things you should and should not do. This is a very important part of deer hunting, yet it is surprising how many hunters don't know the proper way to field dress a deer. A few precautionary measures here can save you many problems later. There are different methods—or, I should say, sequences of order—to arrive at the same end result. Different hunters may approach this process differently but follow the same basic guidelines. Over the years, I have learned that regardless of how you go about it, the goal is the same: to get the meat to the cooler in the cleanest, safest, and quickest way possible. If you have taken a nice trophy buck, the field dressing process must conform to the preservation of that portion of the cape necessary to mount your buck.

Once you have located your deer and begin to approach it, do so very cautiously just in case it is still alive. If you suspect the deer is still alive, try to work yourself into a position to place another projectile into a vital area. As you approach the carcass, be prepared to shoot again if necessary. You do not want to leave a wounded animal in the woods. One last safety precaution when you arrive at the carcass: if possible, stay on the side away from the hooves, and poke the deer with a stick or kick it to verify that it has indeed expired. You don't want to go on a wild ride through the woods on a bucking buck.

Now that you have verified the deer is definitely expired, try to position it in the best and most comfortable position for you to field dress it. I prefer to position the deer lying on its back on as level ground as possible side to side with its upper body slightly uphill.

This keeps the innards fairly evenly distributed throughout the cavity but still allows the blood to flow toward the rear of the carcass. Sometimes, depending on where the deer falls, you may need to try to find a small log or two to help you keep the carcass positioned. There are different approaches to field dressing deer, and the more you do it, the sooner you will develop your own technique. The following is simply what seems to work best for me.

If you feel comfortable removing the tarsal glands from the inside of the hind legs, by all means do so, but only if you can do so without penetrating the glands themselves. You will probably end up contaminating the meat if you accidentally puncture a gland and get the contents on your knife. If this happens and there is no water available, use a separate knife and a pair of rubber gloves so you don't get any of the musk oil on the meat. These tarsal glands are quite obvious by the darker-haired, puffy areas on the inside of the hind legs and are really very easy to remove once you have learned the proper way to go about it. Many hunters don't remove them at all and leave them alone because they simply drop their deer off at a packing house to be processed anyway. If you process your own deer like I do, then when you hang your deer by the hind legs to skin it out, the gambrel hooks go through the hind legs where the tarsal glands are located, so they would need to be removed at this point anyway. To

Removing the tarsal glands should be done with great care.

remove them, cut at least a couple of inches out away from the dark puffy area, in a circle all the way around this area. Once you have cut the hide all the way around, peel this portion of the hide away. The tarsal gland will peal off with the hide on each hind leg. If these tarsal glands get punctured, the meat could get contaminated, so be very careful doing this. Remember: cut as far away from the dark puffy area as you feel comfortable doing so you don't puncture the gland.

With a clean knife and a pair of rubber gloves and with your deer lying on its back, straddle the carcass. Push down at the base of the rib cage, and, using a sharp knife with the blade turned up and away from you, puncture the carcass. With a sharp jerking motion, rip through the first few ribs, or until you can reach up into the neck cavity far enough to sever the jugular and windpipe. If the deer is to be mounted, don't cut too far up through the rib cage; leave plenty of hide for a nice shoulder mount. Do not go ahead and sever the windpipe just yet, as you do not yet have good accessibility to this area.

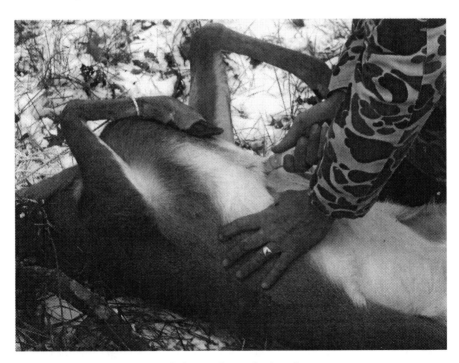

Penetrate the carcass and rip up through the rib cage.

Reposition yourself straddling your deer, facing the rear of the carcass. Insert your index and forefinger into the opening, and pull up and spread the opening slightly with your fingers. With the knife blade turned in the same direction, with the blade up, and cutting away from yourself at a shallow angle, insert the knife between your fingers, and go ahead and complete the cut from the sternum to just in front of the penis (or milk sack, for a doe). As you are making this cut, pull up on the carcass wall at the same time you are cutting so that you don't puncture any of the innards. While holding the penis and testicles or milk sack in one hand, cut around each side of them and down between the hams to the anus and pelvic bone, severing these organs from the carcass.

Straddle the carcass, facing the rear of the animal, and insert your index and middle fingers into the carcass. With your knife between those two fingers, blade edge up, cut back toward the rear.

If your deer is a young deer, after removing the genitals, you can take a sturdy knife blade and with a rocking motion carefully cut through the pelvic bone, exposing the bladder. You can now apply pressure to the inside of both hind legs and push them down toward the ground and spread this cut apart. This is easier to do if it is a young deer. With this cut spread apart, carefully sever the attachment to the rectal area and remove the bladder.

Cutting through the pelvic bone with a good sturdy knife or small saw.

If the deer is an older, tougher deer, you can use a small bone saw or a hacksaw blade and cut through the pelvic bone, or you can carefully cut around the rectum following the bone in a circular motion from the outside of the carcass. After making this cut, you should be able to pull the rectum and the bladder to the inside of the cavity with the other innards to remove them.

Cutting around the rectum to remove along with the bladder.

Remove the heart and the liver from the innards, and place each in a plastic bag for later cleaning if cleaning is not possible at this time. To remove the heart and lungs, you will need to cut around the inside of the diaphragm to sever the membrane that contains these organs. Prior to bagging the heart, make a slit in it to bleed it out. The liver may be removed by severing a blood vessel that is attached to it. Inspect the liver for any obvious defects or diseases. If the liver is a healthy one, it will present a consistent color throughout and have no obvious deficiencies. The condition of the liver will give you an idea about the condition of the deer itself.

Remove and inspect the liver.

Now is the time to spread the rib cage apart enough to reach up into the neck cavity to sever the jugular vein and windpipe. Gently pull the jugular and windpipe from the neck through the sternum or rib cage area to remove them with the remaining innards.

Reach into the rib cavity as far as you can to sever the jugular and wind pipe, and pull back on it.

It is now time to clean the innards out of the carcass. Try to do so as neatly as possible so that you don't contaminate the meat in any way. There is an internal sack or connective tissue around a portion of the innards that will need to be cut to release these innards from the carcass. Take a hold of the jugular and windpipe and begin to drag them out. With both hands, rake the innards out of the body cavity.

Remove the innards from the carcass.

If you are near water, try to wash out the carcass as soon as possible and as thoroughly as you can. If the weather is warm, be sure to cover the carcass with a fly net as soon as you can, and get to a cooler, preferably set at 32 °F, or iced down, as soon as you can.

In most states, including Tennessee, we are required to tie the kill tag on the deer as soon as we arrive at the carcass. Be sure you are aware of your state regulations, and follow them precisely.

Once you have field dressed your deer, before leaving the area, open the stomach and try to determine what food sources the deer was currently feeding on. As the year progresses, the food sources change somewhat. This effort may just clue you into a food source that you didn't even know was present where you are hunting, or it might let you know where the deer have been hanging out for future hunting trips.

If you would like to use the tarsal glands for future scent purposes, these should be placed in sealed plastic bags and frozen until you plan to use them. Some hunters like to use these in the creation of mock scrapes.

If you don't plan to mount your deer and have to drag the deer out, tie the two front legs to the head to reduce the amount of drag resistance. Two less legs hanging on rocks, limbs, and anything else that will tend to catch them will help save your energy.

Tie the two front legs to the head to make the dragging process easier.

You are now ready to transport your deer back to camp. Use care when transporting it back to camp. Be careful not to tie a rope around the neck or drag it on the portion of the hide that would be used for your mount.

If you plan to mount your buck, use care transporting him out.

Photo © by Mary Morris.

Photo © by Mary Morris.

HUNTING ETHICS

Most of us strive to be good, respectable, honorable people in everything we do. We want to follow the golden rule and do unto others as we would have them do unto us. We all make mistakes along the way, because we are only human, and as a result, many of us will tend to question our ethics. What do we believe in as human beings, and how do we choose to carry these beliefs over into our lives as deer hunters? Our basic ethical beliefs are formed in us over years of exposure to our environmental situations. These beliefs vary in all of us, and this is why we need to set an example for all of those we come in contact with. Good hunting ethics will carry you a long way in your hunting future and will also show a positive side of all us hunters who are criticized and put down by special organizations or others who tend to criticize without knowing all the facts. On the other hand, one unethical hunter can do a tremendous amount of damage to us all in the eyes of nonhunters and others. If we do something positive as a hunter, it reflects on us all in the eyes of the public—just as it does if we do something negative. Good hunting ethics are one of the most important aspects of deer hunting—second only to safety—in becoming a totally responsible hunter.

Our hunting rights are under attack unlike ever before in our history. The primary target is the image of an unethical hunter who has no respect for wildlife, private property, landowner rights, or other nature users. We have to do everything in our power to help educate the public about our deep respect for our sport and show them our positive efforts to pursue our forefather's intentions and belief in our Second Amendment rights.

We must respect the rights of all wildlife users and their ways of enjoying the outdoors. There are many ways to enjoy nature, and we all must coexist and cooperate with each other for the enjoyment and pleasure of us all.

We deer hunters, for the benefit of all, must hunt ethically, respecting our quarry and the rights of the landowners, other hunters, and all those we encounter in our love of deer hunting. It only takes one of us to jeopardize the privileges we have all come to share and enjoy. Don't destroy property, litter, be careless, trespass, take chances with fires, leave gates open, hunt without proper permission, or be rude to others. Always offer help or assistance to those in need of our help. Never do anything that would harm the environment or natural resources or our rights as hunters.

Respect your quarry, and don't take cheap shots at him. We owe him the right to as clean and humane a kill as possible. We must strive for good shot placement to accomplish this type of kill. Too many times shots are made too quickly, with too little focus on or regard for good shot placement; as a result, the deer is left, wounded, to go off and die a slow, painful death, never to be recovered. A conscientious effort and awareness of good shot placement can improve these statistics tremendously.

Focus on good shot placement to avoid losing your deer. Photo © by Peter Eades.

Respect other hunters' rights just as you would expect them to respect yours. If other hunters get to an area on public hunting land ahead of you, move on and don't disturb their hunt any more than you have to. They probably went to a great deal of effort to locate that spot, just as you did, but they went one step further than you did and got there first. If it's public hunting land, the spot is theirs for this hunt, so do the honorable thing and quietly move along to another area.

Throughout your life as a deer hunter, you will have many encounters with farmers, landowners, forest rangers, game wardens, and other hunters. Always be as sincere and respectful to all of these people as possible, and make as many of them your friends as possible. This could open up many future opportunities to hunt that you would not otherwise have had. If you run across another hunter who needs help dragging a deer out to his vehicle, help him; next time, the table could be turned, and it could be you who needs help. Remember: what goes around comes around.

If a farmer offers to let you hunt deer on his property, offer to help him with some task around the farm, bring him some venison, or do something to show your gratitude. This is a perfect opportunity to cement a good, permanent relationship for regular hunting rights on his property.

Always transport your deer as inconspicuously as possible. If you drive a truck, four-runner, or station wagon, place the carcass inside, and close the tailgate to conceal it. Depending on the condition or

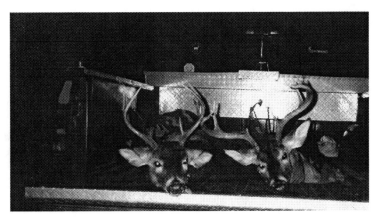

Try to conceal your carcass when transporting it.

type of vehicle, you could wrap the carcass in a tarp or other cover in some way to conceal it for transporting purposes. Never display the deceased animal over the hood or bumper. This type of action will draw animal rights activists and antihunting enthusiasts out of the woodwork if they see you. Let's face it: we have got to overcome the old stigma of being Bambi-killers.

It is our responsibility to try to prevent an unsafe act by another hunter if we notice it in progress. Try to be as discrete as possible. While you don't want to offend anyone, you don't want to let it go unnoticed, either, because it could cause problems for someone in the future. Many of us do unsafe things at times without even noticing and would appreciate someone pointing it out to us.

If another hunter seems to be seeking advice or suggestions from you on deer hunting, freely provide it if you are qualified to do so. Always try to offer your knowledge based on your own experience as a deer hunter to anyone who wants it. Hunters normally love to talk to other deer hunters and share their knowledge and experiences. We can all learn from each other, and we can never learn everything about the whitetail deer. It will eventually amaze us in some way. After forty years of deer hunting, I am still learning about the animal, and will until my last hunt.

We can all learn a great deal from each other about whitetail deer hunting.

If you take a shot at a deer or any other quarry, be sure to exhaust every effort to find the animal. It may not be easy and may take a great deal of time, but try to spend whatever time necessary to determine if the animal is fatally wounded. If you can determine this, then try everything you can think of to find it in order to do the humane thing and put it down as quickly as possible.

Always leave any wild area you visit just the way you found it. Don't litter or leave behind anything that does not belong there or leave anything to indicate you were there in the first place.

The successful end to a long search for your deer.

The next person should feel that he or she is the first person to enter the area. While this may sound a little farfetched, the next person should at least be able to get the same degree of pleasure out of the area that you did, so leave it as natural as possible.

Don't be outwardly critical of another hunter who doesn't know as much about deer hunting as you do. Instead, offer to help him or her. That hunter's lack of knowledge may be strictly due to a lack of experience—we were all there at one time or another.

Don't lie or overly exaggerate a hunting experience just to make it sound better. We need to be able to rely on the advice and reports of each other about certain hunting possibilities. We are all going to keep a few signs we find under our hat, so to speak, but if we can put an unlucky hunter on to a potentially good spot for a buck, we should do so if we have already scored. We need to try to help each other out every chance we get because of the common bond of deer hunting that we all share.

Don't use No Hunting signs, management area signs, or other signs for target practice and jeopardize your relationship with the people that put them up or negatively influence anyone with you at the time.

Always obey the laws of the land. Follow the hunting regulations and guidelines to the letter. Be an example to others in this regard so that they may be influenced by you and become ethical hunters themselves.

Respect these signs wherever you find them, just as you would want your signs respected.

SECTION IV

◆

NOW THAT YOU HAVE YOUR DEER IN CAMP

Photo © by Mary Morris.

NOW THAT YOU HAVE YOUR DEER IN CAMP

Almost simultaneously with selecting the title for this section, I was reminded of a hunt several years ago where I invited a work associate, Jim, and his son, Tim, to go deer hunting with me. Neither of them had ever been deer hunting before, and Jim wanted to introduce his son to nature. I felt this would be a good opportunity for the two of them to enjoy a good bonding experience, much as my son and I had done many times before. I explained that they were welcome to stay in my old, beat-up over-the-cab camper with me, but Jim declined, stating that he had a mobile home that he would like to bring. I had to tell him that he would have to park it out on the road because he would be unable to negotiate the old half logging road, half dry creekbed to our camp site. He indicated that this would be fine, but he definitely wanted some of the modern conveniences of home, and he would tow his International Scout behind to drive to the campsite. We made plans for them to meet me at my camper at three o'clock the next morning, and from there, we would take his Scout part of the way to where I would place them for the actual hunt. We would walk to our actual hunting stands from there.

The location where I placed them was a high-traffic bottleneck-type area leading to a good stand of clover with a great deal of doe activity. I was sure they would see deer if they took the necessary precautions, all of which I tried to explain to them. I was about to leave them when I asked if they knew how to field dress a deer. The look on their faces told me no, so I proceeded to give them a crash course and also drew them a little sketch to keep with them. We said our good lucks and split up.

Throughout the morning, I wondered how they were making out, because I hadn't heard a shot and felt they should have seen plenty of deer. It was a very cold morning, and I wondered if they had dressed warmly enough since they weren't used to sitting out in the cold waiting for deer.

Just about mid-morning I heard a shot, and a few moments later, another shot rang out, and then a final third shot. I figured that with that many shots and the way they were spaced out, they must have at least hit the deer. I sat there for about another hour-and-a-half and decided that since my particular hunt had not fared very well from the standpoint of producing a buck, I would go see if they needed any assistance. I figured they might have trouble tracking a deer.

As I arrived back at the Scout, I heard Jim call out to me. I went over to the base of a hill where they were in the process of field dressing a six-point buck. They had my sketch, smeared with blood, lying out on the ground, and were doing a pretty fair job. Jim proceeded to tell me the story of how the morning had unfolded. He said they sat on their stands for about an hour and got so cold that they kept thinking of their hot coffee they had in their Scout, and the thought was too much for them. They walked back to the Scout and started the engine, fired up the heater, and enjoyed the hot coffee.

About 8:30 or 9:00, they had warmed up to the point of hunting again. They got out, walked up and down two ridges and up to the top of the third one, and sat down on a stump. After about five or ten minutes, they saw this six-point buck walking through the woods. Jim threw up his rifle and shot, after which the deer ran a few yards and stopped partially hidden behind some brush. As he watched the buck, he saw it lie down, so he figured it had expired. He and his son proceeded to walk toward the buck, and it jumped up and ran again, at which time Jim shot again. This time the buck went down but was still kicking, so he walked closer and finished him off with the third shot.

Once they got to the buck, they realized they had left the drawing I had given them in the Scout. Since they were unable to remember the proper procedure to follow, they decided to drag the buck back to the Scout and get the drawing before proceeding to field-dress it.

If you have ever experienced dragging a buck on flat ground that has been field dressed, you can appreciate what they went through by having to drag that non–field dressed buck up two long, steep hills and down three. They were probably dragging about thirty-five pounds of unnecessary dead weight. I think every stitch of clothing they had on was wet from sweat. This would be considered the extreme high-end of the saying that once you get your deer, that's when the work begins.

A great deal of deer hunting is work, but it's the type of work you can enjoy if you learn to do things properly. If Jim had spent a little time asking questions and checking out what all was involved in deer hunting beforehand, his hunting experience with his son would have been much more enjoyable for both of them.

These remaining few chapters deal with what comes after the field dressing process.

Photo © by Mary Morris.

SKINNING YOUR DEER

Keep in mind that there are different approaches to skinning a deer just as there are to field dressing one. You should be aware of the different methods and settle on the one that works best for you. Skinning your deer is a fairly simple process, the more so if your deer is still warm—it's a little tougher to peel the hide off of a stiff, frozen deer. The following is the method that seems to work best for me, and hopefully it will help you. After you have skinned out your first two or three deer, it will seem quite simple.

If you have not yet removed the tarsal glands, you must do so in order to hang your deer from the hind legs for skinning purposes. You do not want the tarsal glands in any close proximity to the exposed carcass, and you do not want to handle the meat with your hands or the knife used to remove the tarsal glands unless you have thoroughly washed them. As I explained in the chapter on field dressing your deer, using a sharp knife, preferably while wearing rubber gloves, cut the hide around the tarsal glands, located on the inside of the hind legs, staying at least an inch or two away from the dark-haired puffy area. This is the area to be sure not to puncture since it would contaminate the meat. Once you have cut the hide all the way around this area, the tarsal gland will simply peel off the leg. You must do this on both hind legs.

With the tarsal glands removed, take your knife and cut a slit in the outer hide in this area. The objective is to open this area and place a gambrel stick between the two knees, hanging the deer upside down from a tree limb or skinning pole. Once you have made a slit in the hide where the tarsal glands were located on each leg, you may now insert a gambrel stick or anything you desire through these openings to keep the hind legs apart. This will also provide something to attach a rope to in order to hoist the deer up into a tree far enough to clear the ground.

If you are hanging the deer by yourself, you may need to use a pulley system, block and tackle, chain hoist, or rope fall. You could also throw a rope over a limb and tie it to the bumper of your truck and pull the deer up in this manner. You may simply be able to throw a rope over a tree limb with the other end tied to your gambrel stick and manually pull your deer up to the desired height, depending on the weight of the deer and just how strong you happen to be.

Take a drinking-safe water hose and wash the entire carcass thoroughly on the inside and out. Have a pan of water handy for occasionally rinsing your hands and your knife, saw, and other tools.

With your deer now hanging upside down, cut the hide on the inside of the hind legs from the cut made during the field dressing process, up the inside of the legs, to a point just above the knee

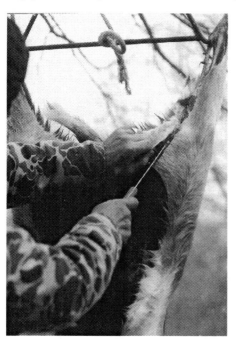

Initial cuts to make it possible to peel the hide down off the hindquarters.

joint. With the deer in this position, it would be on the side of the knee closest to the deer's body and not the foot side of the knee. Now cut from where you stopped your cut, all the way around the leg. You want to cut the hide in such a way to make it possible to peel the hide off each hind leg and down off the rump.

Now peel the hide off both hindquarters.

Peel the hide on both inner thighs up over the top of the hindquarters, and peel the hide down off the inner thighs, around the back side of the hind legs.

Take the tail, and as you pull down, cut the tailbone with your knife, using short chopping motions. As you pull the hide away from the carcass, begin peeling the hide down and away from the rump, all the while making short slicing motions as necessary with your knife to continually separate the hide from the carcass. The hide will peel down with very little work until you get down to the front shoulders.

After severing the tailbone, peel the hide down the backside.

After cutting the tail and peeling the hide down the carcass to the shoulders, you are now ready to make the cuts to pull the hide off the shoulders.

After you peel the hide all the way down to the shoulders, you must cut the hide again in such a way as to be able to peel it off the front legs. You will need to cut the hide that you have accumulated down in front of the front legs, back to each of the front legs. This is necessary in order to get this hide out of your way and to be able to cut down the inside of each front leg to a point just above the front knees as you did on the hind legs. Once you cut the hide back to each of the front legs, you will

Making the necessary cuts to peel hide off the front shoulders.

have part of the hide hanging down from the underside of the neck and a part of the hide draped over the outside of each front leg, exposing the hide covering the front legs. This makes it possible to now make the cut I mentioned above, down the inside of each front leg to the knee and then around the entire knee so that

it will now peel off and down over the neck.

At this point, you will want to peel the hide as far down the neck as possible in order to both conserve as much of the neck meat as you can and also be able to sever the head and hide from the remaining carcass. You will find it necessary to use short slicing motions with your knife here in order to peel the hide back far enough to conserve as much meat as possible.

Once you have peeled the hide back as far as you feel neces-

Peeling the hide down the neck to sever the head and hide.

sary, take your knife and cut all the way around the neck to the bone, then use a bone saw or some other type of saw to cut the bone, finally severing the head and hide.

Look over the carcass thoroughly for any hair that was accidentally left on the meat. You can use a propane torch to quickly run over any part of the carcass that has hair; since these hairs are hollow, they will pop right off with very little heat.

With your bone saw, go ahead and cut off each of the lower por-

Sever the head and hide from the carcass.

tions of each front leg at the point where you skinned the legs. You are now left with only the part of the carcass that you will need for butchering purposes, except for the two hind legs, which will be cut off when you are finished hanging your deer.

Some people go ahead and make all the same cuts to the hide that were made above at one time. Instead of cutting the head off, however, for the purpose of this technique, it is left intact. The deer is hung right-side up instead of upside down, and the hide is cut all the way around the neck. Peel back a small area of the hide at the base of the neck on the top of the shoulder. Place a small rock, golf ball, or other item inside the hide at this point, and fold the hide over it enough to allow a strong nylon rope to be tied around the hide and around the item inside the hide. You can now tie the rope to the bumper of a vehicle and literally strip the hide right off the carcass in one brief pull.

This completes the actual skinning process and only leaves a couple of tidying-up steps.

Be sure to use a drinking-safe water hose and thoroughly hose off the carcass to remove any excess blood or other foreign matter remaining on the carcass after the skinning process.

If you do not plan to go ahead and quarter your deer or butcher it at this time, it should be placed in a cooler or covered, depending on the outdoor temperature, to prevent any flies from getting to the meat. I prefer to butcher it immediately after the skinning process to keep the meat safe from any potential problems. The meat can still be aged in a refrigerator after it has been quartered or cut up.

Photo © by Mary Morris

Photo © by Mary Morris

BUTCHERING YOUR OWN DEER

I get a great deal of satisfaction out of my own personal, exclusive involvement in my deer hunting from preseason scouting to the table. I also feel like I do a much better job of processing my deer myself—because my family and I are the ones who will be enjoying the harvest, I want the meat to be properly cared for. Some butcher shops are so busy during the winter months that they may not care quite as much about how clean the meat is, what cuts we prefer, or how many bone fragments and hairs are scattered throughout the meat. This is the exception rather than the rule, but it has happened to me more than once. All of this is very important to me, and there's also the fact that you save a little money by processing your own deer. As expensive as deer hunting has become over the past few years, it's nice to be able to save in a few areas.

You should be very cautious when skinning your deer not to get a lot of hair on the carcass. You may want to refer to chapter 32, on skinning your deer, to learn how to avoid this, and to read about what to do if you do get hair on your deer.

It is very important to wash the carcass very thoroughly inside and out before cutting the meat off of the bone. You must be sure there are no feces or urine on the meat as a result of the field dressing process. If there are, the carcass must be completely cleaned as soon as possible prior to freezing. It is best not to get water into the grain of the meat prior to freezing, which is why it is so important to clean the meat prior to cutting it off the bone and exposing the open grain of the meat.

If you can age your deer or let it hang for at least two or three days in a safe, controlled environment such as a commercial cooler of some type, where the temperature is a constant 35–38 °F, the meat will be more tender and have a better flavor. In some cases, it may not be practical if you don't have access to a cooler, and you may not live in an area with consistently cold temperatures to chance leaving the carcass hanging unattended. You can, however, age each package at a time somewhat prior to cooking it. Place the meat on a bed of two or three paper towels in a pan in the refrigerator, and let it thaw out and drain for two or three days.

I prefer to debone the meat from the carcass while the deer is still hanging and then determine how I want to process the meat. Some years we want to make more jerky, and in others we may want to grind up a substantial amount into ground meat, while in other situations we may want more steaks or chunks for stews. I always use the same basic technique even though the cuts vary from time to time depending on our preference.

From the following photos under "Separating the Meat from the Bone" and the drawing "How to Cut up the Sections for Packaging," you will notice the sections of the carcass that are best used for certain types of cuts. I would debone the meat first, then refer to the drawing for the actual cuts to make. You may also vary these cuts as you prefer. You may wish to use some of the choice backstrap meat for grinding, or you might want to use this section for chunks for stew or to dice up into small pieces for venison tips and rice or noodles.

It is best not to wash the individual pieces of meat that you are packaging prior to freezing. If you have already thoroughly cleaned the carcass prior to cutting up the meat, it is unnecessary to wash the meat at this point. You will always wash the individual pieces prior to cooking, but you don't want water freezing inside the grain of the meat.

When I make the individual cuts in preparation for packaging, I trim off the excess fat. Venison does not have a great deal of fat, but how you go about processing the meat will determine how much fat you have to deal with when packaging. You should try to get rid of as much of it as you can while the deer is still hanging with the meat still on the bones.

There is a great deal of meat in the neck of a deer that is often cut away with the hide and left to ruin or thrown away. You should remove this meat after peeling the hide back to expose it. I normally use this section for roast or stew meat.

You may prefer, as some people do, to quarter or section up the carcass while the meat is still on the bone. I personally feel that it is much simpler to debone the meat and discard the bones as soon as possible, but if you choose to section him up without first deboning for later butchering, this will be fine. With the deer hanging from the skinning process, use a sharp knife to remove the front shoulders. As you pull the front shoulders away from the carcass, cut all the way around the backside of the shoulder blade, and as you do, the shoulder will separate from the carcass. The hindquarters are a little more difficult, but if you apply basically the same procedure, they should pop right off with a little effort. Once you have cut all the way around the outside of the rump, letting the bone guide you, cut down to the rear ball joint. You should be able to pop the ball joint apart by twisting the hind leg. If this is a little difficult, simply take a heavy knife and apply a slight pressure to pop it apart. You now have the neck connected to the backbone, which still has the two ribcages attached to it. The backstraps are still intact, as well as the inside tenderloins. Go ahead and fillet these backstraps away from each side of the backbone, and don't forget the tenderloins on the underside of the backbone. With the backstraps removed, cut the ribcages off the backbone and then remove the neck from the torso. Both of these two procedures will need to be done using a saw.

I prefer to wrap the meat in plastic wrap first to squeeze out as much air as possible to prevent freezer burn, and then in freezer paper, with the glossy side toward the meat. Wrap the meat nice and tight by making folds as if you were wrapping a present. Label these packages as you see fit. With the meat tightly wrapped in freezer paper, place it inside resealable freezer bag. Force any excess air out of the bag before sealing it. These bags also serve as freezer organizers. I will place two or three packages of the same cuts of meat in one freezer bag together.

Be sure to package the meat in packages of adequate size suitable for your family's eating habits without packaging too much meat into one package. You can always thaw out more than one package of meat at a time, and this way you ensure that the meat has a better chance of freezing solid through and through. By packaging the meat into no more than one-quart packages, it is also easier to stack and position it in the freezer. When you place several new unfrozen packages of venison in the freezer at the same time, try to place them in a criss-cross pattern initially until they are totally frozen. By doing this, you allow the cold air to circulate in and around each package better and freeze the meat more evenly.

It is very important to label the meat very accurately. I always try to note if the deer was a young or old buck or doe, the type or cut of meat, and particularly the date it was processed.

SEPARATING THE MEAT FROM THE BONE

First, cut the outside backstraps from the carcass. Do this by first making a horizontal cut across the base of the ham all the way to the backbone.

Beginning cuts for extracting the backstraps.

With your knife held with the blade vertical, cut down each side of the backbone all the way to the shoulder, and with short slicing cuts peel the backstraps down and away from the carcass. This is easier than peeling from the shoulders up, as pictured.

Cutting down the backbone to remove the backstraps.

Illustration showing the actual backstrap area on one side of the backbone.

Now remove the tenderloins from the inside of the carcass or the underside of the lower back area. These are small sections of meat, yet to many they are the most desirable pieces of meat on the entire carcass. If you look carefully in this area, you will notice two strips of meat approximately six to ten inches long, depending on the size of the deer. Take a small knife and gently remove these from the carcass.

Removing the inner tenderloins.

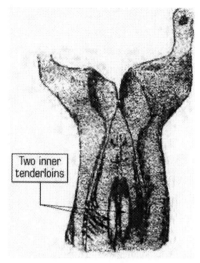

This illustration shows the inner tenderloins.

Next, cut the top half of each of the hindquarters off the bone by letting the hind leg bone and the pelvic bone guide the knife. These cuts give up two very large chunks of meat, perfect for steak cuts.

The first cut to remove the top half of the hindquarter.

The actual removal of the top half of the hindquarter.

Now remove the lower halves of the two hindquarters by the same method. Let the leg bone guide the knife back to the pelvic bone, then cut down to the original cut you made to remove the backstraps. These will be two very large chunks of meat.

The next step is to remove the meat from the front shoulders. To do this, feel the meat with your hands, and let the bone guide your knife to remove the meat. Once you do this the first time, you will learn the physical makeup of the shoulder bone, and the next time you will know how to place your blade to make the necessary cuts. This is done basically like you did the hindquarters, but because of the difference in the physical makeup of the upper front

The removal of the lower half of the hindquarter.

Removing the meat from the front shoulder.

shoulder blade, it presents a little more of a challenge the first time you do it.

Many hunters discard the entire ribcage, but if you choose to salvage this portion, take a saw and cut the ribcage straight down the side of the backbone on each side to remove them from the carcass. Now cut them in half, straight across the rib bones, once more to reduce them to freezer-size lengths. You should now cut the ribs in sections based on the number of ribs you prefer to package for the freezer.

Removing the final part of the shoulder meat.

The final step should be to go over the entire remaining portion of the carcass and carefully remove the various tidbits of meat that were left after you made the previous cuts. You will find a great deal of meat in various places about the carcass that can be removed and used for stew pieces or for grinding up into ground venison. Freeze these in packages marked for whatever you plan to use them for, such as stew meat or maybe ground meat, and so forth.

Be sure to discard the remaining bones in such a way that they will not end up on someone's deck because their dog dragged them there. The best bet is to haul the bones to a dump or take them back to the woods on your next hunting trip and leave them for the buzzards or coyotes.

Removing the ribcage for freezing purposes.

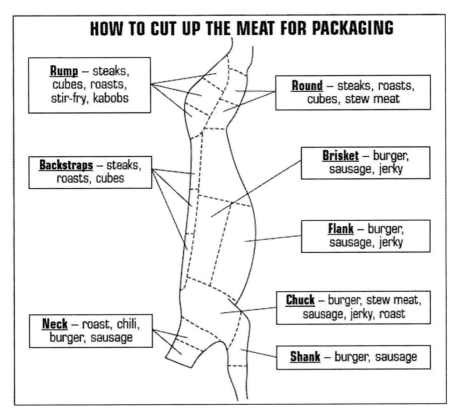

HOW TO CUT UP THE MEAT FOR PACKAGING

Rump – steaks, cubes, roasts, stir-fry, kabobs

Round – steaks, roasts, cubes, stew meat

Backstraps – steaks, roasts, cubes

Brisket – burger, sausage, jerky

Flank – burger, sausage, jerky

Chuck – burger, stew meat, sausage, jerky, roast

Neck – roast, chili, burger, sausage

Shank – burger, sausage

How to Cut up the Meat for Packaging

The packaging process is the last stage of a great deal of work but is well worth the effort. A great deal of venison has been wasted over the years because it was not properly processed or packaged for preservation—either poorly packaged, packaged with water in the meat, incorrectly cut, or not cleaned properly prior to packaging.

The following steps should be taken in the actual packaging process for the most adequate and thorough preservation of the meat:

1. Begin by trimming off any excess or unwanted fat from each cut of meat to be wrapped.

2. Cut each section of meat to be individually wrapped across the grain of the meat. Make the section no larger than one quart, for thorough freezing.

3. Wrap each section of meat tightly in plastic wrap to eliminate any air pockets.

4. Take each package of meat wrapped in plastic wrap and wrap it in freezer wrap with the shiny side toward the meat.

5. Wrap the meat as tightly as possible, and use freezer tape to tape the packages closed.

6. Use a black magic marker and label each package. I usually note the sex, when it was packaged, and what cut of meat it is.

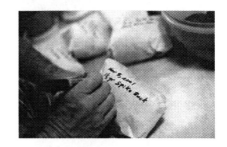

7. The last step is to place each package of meat already double-wrapped into a resealable freezer bag and seal it tightly after squeezing out all the air you possibly can.

8. I sometimes place two or three packages of meat in one large resealable bag.

Photo © by Mary Morris.

ROUGH SCORING YOUR BUCK

Often a hunter will take a nice buck and one of the first things he or she will wonder is if it would score high enough to get into the record books. I am quite sure there have been several nice bucks killed that would have been eligible for the record books had the hunter known how to rough score the deer or had enough curiosity about the buck's score to take it to someone and have it properly scored. You can rough score the deer yourself to get an idea of what you have, and then if you think it qualifies, you can have it officially scored for purposes of a record book score. Scoring your buck unofficially is a fairly simple process, but it definitely allows room for error. You probably won't come up with exactly the same score as an official scorer, but you can at least be in the ballpark. With a good understanding of how to score, you can expect to get close. You can go to the websites of both Pope & Young and Boone & Crockett and print off a copy of their official scoresheet and the instruction sheet. This instruction sheet clearly explains how to score the deer. I have included copies of these scoresheets and the instructions for each at the end of this chapter. When you score the deer yourself, it is considered a rough score. However, when an official who is trained and totally qualified to score your deer does it, the score is considered an official score. In certain situations, there are close calls to be made that only an official can determine.

For the purpose of measuring for yourself, you may use a small metal tape measure or a cloth tape measure.

First, you want to measure the length of the tines. This is done by first establishing the base of the tine in order to have a starting reference. Using a straightedge lined up with the top of the main beam on each side of the tine, draw a line with a pencil across the base of the tine. Now that you have this reference point, measure from this base line up the outside center line of the tine, to the very tip of the tine, and repeat this process for each and every tine. (See the following diagram.)

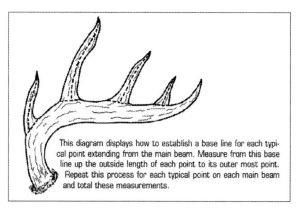

This diagram displays how to establish a base line for each typical point extending from the main beam. Measure from this base line up the outside length of each point to its outer most point. Repeat this process for each typical point on each main beam and total these measurements.

If there were any abnormal or nontypical points, you would measure them in very much the same way. If an abnormal point runs off of a typical point or tine, establish the base line to the typical point. Now you merely measure from this baseline to the tip of the abnormal point, while staying on the outside center line of the point.

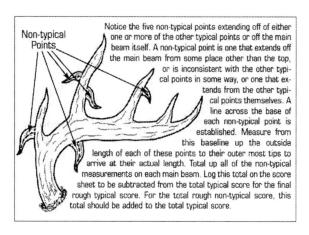

Non-typical Points

Notice the five non-typical points extending off of either one or more of the other typical points or off the main beam itself. A non-typical point is one that extends off the main beam from some place other than the top, or is inconsistent with the other typical points in some way, or one that extends from the other typical points themselves. A line across the base of each non-typical point is established. Measure from this baseline up the outside length of each of these points to their outer most tips to arrive at their actual length. Total up all of the non-typical measurements on each main beam. Log this total on the score sheet to be subtracted from the total typical score for the final rough typical score. For the total rough non-typical score, this total should be added to the total typical score.

Now you will want to measure the main beam. To do this, measure from the base, more specifically the center point on the outside of the base of this beam, while staying on the outside center line, and follow it all the way out to the main beam's outermost tip.

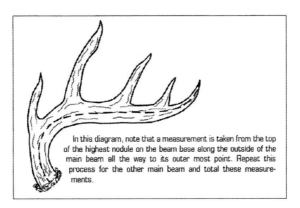

In this diagram, note that a measurement is taken from the top of the highest nodule on the beam base along the outside of the main beam all the way to its outer most point. Repeat this process for the other main beam and total these measurements.

Regardless of how many points a buck has, you are entitled to four circumference measurements on each main beam. This is normally referred to as the buck's mass. These circumference measurements are taken at the smallest points between two tines if the buck has eight points or less, or at designated points along the beam. The first point of measure would be the smallest point between the base of the main beam and the brow tine. The second point of measure would be the smallest point between the brow tine and the first primary or typical point. If the rack only has two points on each side or three counting the main beam, the third point of measure would be one-third of the distance from the last tine to the end of the main beam, and the fourth would be two-thirds of this distance. If the rack has three points or four counting the main beam, then this last point of measure would be one-half the distance from the last tine to the end of the main beam. (See the following diagram.)

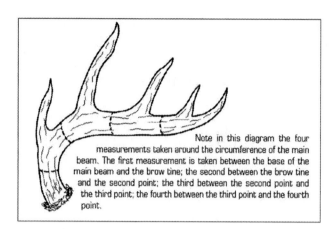

Note in this diagram the four measurements taken around the circumference of the main beam. The first measurement is taken between the base of the main beam and the brow tine; the second between the brow tine and the second point; the third between the second point and the third point; the fourth between the third point and the fourth point.

Measuring the inside spread of the main beams is done at the widest point between the main beams that is parallel to the bases. The tape measure must be parallel to a line straight across the two main beam bases. The way the scoresheet states to officially score your buck, this measurement is on a line at a right angle to the center line of the skull measured from the widest point between main beams. For rough scoring, it will be close in most cases to simply use the parallel line across the main beam bases as mentioned above. This measurement may not exceed the length of the longer antler, and if it does, the length of the longer antler is to be used.

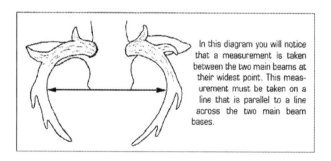

In this diagram you will notice that a measurement is taken between the two main beams at their widest point. This measurement must be taken on a line that is parallel to a line across the two main beam bases.

To arrive at your rough typical score, add the inside spread or longer antler figure to the measurements of the right side antlers and the measurements of the left side antlers, and subtract the differences between the right side and the left side.

To arrive at your rough nontypical score, follow the same procedure as for the typical score, but go one step further and add all of
the nontypical point measurements.

When hunters refer to gross or net scores, they are talking about
the difference between what the deer actually had on his head versus
what an official would add or deduct for points. The nontypical gross
is basically the total rack with no deductions but does not reflect the
true score of the buck.

Rough-scoring your buck is where you score the buck as closely
as you can by the official method. By knowing how the officials will
score your buck, you can get a rough idea of what you have and
whether it would qualify possibly for record book contention.

To be officially scored, a rack must be allowed sixty days to dry
out, but this is not necessary for rough scoring. The minimum score
to be entered into the Pope & Young record book for a typical rack is
125 points, and for a nontypical rack, 155 points.

For the purpose of the scoring system and how it works, the measurements are taken of the basic typical rack first, just as explained
above, and all these measurements are added together. If the buck
has any nontypical or abnormal points, they can either be measured
and added to the total for the gross nontypical score or can be subtracted to reach the gross typical score. This is generally how the
rough scoring system works. Scoresheets that are available through
the record-keeping clubs make this scoring process much easier. The
scoresheets offer a great deal of information to allow anyone to be
able to rough score his or her buck.

Typical and nontypical are the two basic types of racks scored.
Typical scoring places a great deal of priority on symmetry. In the
case of a typical rack, both side-to-side discrepancies and abnormal points will count against the final score. If a buck has at least
one abnormal point, Pope & Young allows the hunter to decide if he
wants the rack to be scored as a typical rack or a nontypical rack. An
abnormal point is any point that does not originate off the top of the
main beam or one that appears to be out of place and doesn't quite
match the tines on the other main beam. The present Boone & Crockett world record typical whitetail buck measured 213⅝ points. This
is the Milo Hanson buck killed in 1993 in Biggar, Saskatchewan. The

present Pope & Young world record typical whitetail buck measured 204⁴⁄₈ points and was killed by Mel Johnson in 1965 in Peoria County, Illinois.

A buck's nontypical score is achieved on top of its typical score. In other words, the nontypical points are either added to or deducted from the typical score. The present Boone & Crockett nontypical whitetail record buck measured 333⁷⁄₈ points. This buck was picked up by a hunter in 1981 in St. Louis County, Missouri. The present Pope & Young nontypical whitetail record buck measured 294⁰⁄₈ points and was killed by Michael Beatty in 2000 in Greene County, Missouri.

Scoring antlers is not a true science and does require judgment calls to be made in the process at times. Sometimes it may be difficult to determine if a certain point is part of the basic typical frame or an abnormal point growing from it.

The Boone and Crockett scoring system uses some basic measurements in inches to the nearest one-eighth of an inch using a flexible steel tape measure. The minimum acceptable score for the all-time record book for a typical rack is 170 points and for a nontypical rack is 195 points. Measure the length of the tines, the over all length of the main beams, the inside spread, and the eight circumferences or mass measurements. Count the number of points on each main beam; each point must be at least one inch long in order to be counted as a point, and its length must exceed its width. The main beam tip is considered a point but is not measured as a point. Measure the inside spread or the greatest distance between the inside edges of the main beams. Calculate the length of all normal points or all points that project upward from the top of the two main beams and are measured along the outer curve of the point. Calculate the length of all abnormal points or points that project from somewhere other than the top of the main beam, such as the side or bottom of the main beam. Now measure the length of the main beam from the lowest outside edge of a burr or nodule at the beams base, along the outer edge to the very tip of the beam. The four circumference measurements for each beam are the last measurements necessary to score the buck.

The scoresheets require other measurements and information that is not computed into the actual score but is useful information in assisting the scoring official as he or she scores the buck. This is also information that is necessary for a complete record of the buck.

Photo © by Kevin Lammi

250 Station Drive
Missoula, MT 59801
(406) 542-1888

BOONE AND CROCKETT CLUB®
OFFICIAL SCORING SYSTEM FOR NORTH AMERICAN BIG GAME TROPHIES

TYPICAL
WHITETAIL AND COUES' DEER

MINIMUM SCORES	AWARDS	ALL-TIME
whitetail	160	170
Coues'	100	110

KIND OF DEER (check one)
- ☐ whitetail
- ☐ Coues'

G2 G3 G4 G5 G6 G7

H4 H3 F E E G1 H2 H1

Detail of Point Measurement

Abnormal Points	
Right Antler	Left Antler

SUBTOTALS		
TOTAL TO E		

SEE OTHER SIDE FOR INSTRUCTIONS			COLUMN 1	COLUMN 2	COLUMN 3	COLUMN 4
A. No. Points on Right Antler		No. Points on Left Antler	Spread Credit	Right Antler	Left Antler	Difference
B. Tip to Tip Spread		C. Greatest Spread				
D. Inside Spread of Main Beams		SPREAD CREDIT MAY EQUAL BUT NOT EXCEED LONGER MAIN BEAM				
E. Total of Lengths of Abnormal Points						
F. Length of Main Beam						
G-1. Length of First Point						
G-2. Length of Second Point						
G-3. Length of Third Point						
G-4. Length of Fourth Point, If Present						
G-5. Length of Fifth Point, If Present						
G-6. Length of Sixth Point, If Present						
G-7. Length of Seventh Point, If Present						
H-1. Circumference at Smallest Place Between Burr and First Point						
H-2. Circumference at Smallest Place Between First and Second Points						
H-3. Circumference at Smallest Place Between Second and Third Points						
H-4. Circumference at Smallest Place Between Third and Fourth Points						
		TOTALS				

ADD	Column 1		Exact Locality Where Killed:		County:	State/Prov:
	Column 2		Date Killed:	Hunter: (Legal Name)		
	Column 3		Trophy Owner: (Legal Name)		Telephone #:	
	Subtotal		Trophy Owner's Address:			
SUBTRACT Column 4			Trophy Owner's E-mail:		Guide's Name:	
FINAL SCORE			Remarks: (Mention Any Abnormalities or Unique Qualities)			

OM I.D. Number ☐☐☐☐

I, _____ , certify that I have measured this trophy on _____

at _____

and that these measurements and data are, to the best of my knowledge and belief, made in accordance with the instructions given.

Witness: _____ Signature: _____ I.D. Number ☐☐☐☐

INSTRUCTIONS FOR MEASURING TYPICAL WHITETAIL AND COUES' DEER

All measurements must be made with a 1/4-inch wide flexible steel tape to the nearest one-eighth of an inch. (Note: A flexible steel cable can be used to measure points and main beams only.) Enter fractional figures in eighths, without reduction. Official measurements cannot be taken until the antlers have air dried for at least 60 days after the animal was killed. The 60-day drying period for a trophy that has been frozen or boiled begins the day it is removed from the freezer or boiling pot, respectively.

A. Number of Points on Each Antler: To be counted a point, the projection must be at least one inch long, with the length exceeding width at one inch or more of length. All points are measured from tip of point to nearest edge of beam as illustrated. Beam tip is counted as a point but not measured as a point. **Point totals do not add into the final score.**

B. Tip to Tip Spread is measured between tips of main beams. **Tip to tip spread does not add into the final score.**

C. Greatest Spread is measured between perpendiculars at a right angle to the center line of the skull at widest part, whether across main beams or points. **Greatest spread does not add into the final score.**

D. Inside Spread of Main Beams is measured at a right angle to the center line of the skull at widest point between main beams. Enter this measurement again as the Spread Credit if it is less than or equal to the length of the longer main beam; if greater, enter longer main beam length for Spread Credit.

E. Total of Lengths of all Abnormal Points: Abnormal Points are those non-typical in location (such as points originating from a point or from bottom or sides of main beam) or extra points beyond the normal pattern of points. Measure in usual manner and enter in appropriate blanks.

F. Length of Main Beam is measured from the center of the lowest outside edge of burr over the outer side to the most distant point of the main beam. The point of beginning is that point on the burr where the center line along the outer side of the beam intersects the burr, then following generally the line of the illustration.

G-1-2-3-4-5-6-7. Length of Normal Points: Normal points project from the top of the main beam. They are measured from nearest edge of main beam over outer curve to tip. Lay the tape along the outer curve of the beam so that the top edge of the tape coincides with the top edge of the beam on both sides of the point to determine the baseline for point measurements. Record point lengths in appropriate blanks.

H-1-2-3-4. Circumferences are taken as detailed in illustration for each measurement. If brow point is missing, take H-1 and H-2 at smallest place between burr and G-2. If G-4 is missing, take H-4 halfway between G-3 and tip of main beam.

MATERIALS RELEASE FORM FOR ALL NON-HUNTER-TAKEN TROPHIES

I certify by my signature that the information I have provided on this form is accurate and correct. I also understand that all my entry materials, including photographs, as well as any additional photographs taken by Boone and Crockett (our representatives or agents) during Awards Programs or Judges Panels, or likenesses rendered from these photographs become the property of the Boone and Crockett Club and may be used to promote the Club, and its records-keeping activities.

Date: _____ Signature of Trophy Owner: _____

ENTRY AFFIDAVIT FOR ALL HUNTER-TAKEN TROPHIES

For the purpose of entry into the Boone and Crockett Club's® records, North American big game harvested by the use of the following methods or under the following conditions are ineligible:

I.   Spotting or herding game from the air, followed by landing in its vicinity for the purpose of pursuit and shooting;
II. Herding or chasing with the aid of any motorized equipment;
III. Use of electronic communication devices to guide hunters to game, artificial lighting, electronic light intensifying devices (night vision optics), sights with built-in electronic range-finding capabilities, thermal imaging equipment, electronic game calls or cameras/timers/motion tracking devices that transmit images and other information to the hunter;
IV. Confined by artificial barriers, including escape-proof fenced enclosures;
V.   Transplanted for the purpose of commercial shooting;
VI. By the use of traps or pharmaceuticals;
VII. While swimming, helpless in deep snow, or helpless in any other natural or artificial medium;
VIII. On another hunter's license;
IX. Not in full compliance with the game laws or regulations of the federal government or of any state, province, territory, or tribal council on reservations or tribal lands;

I certify that the trophy scored on this chart was not taken in violation of the conditions listed above. In signing this statement, I understand that if the information provided on this entry is found to be misrepresented or fraudulent in any respect, it will not be accepted into the Awards Program and 1) all of my prior entries are subject to deletion from future editions of **Records of North American Big Game** 2) future entries may not be accepted. I also certify by my signature that the information I have provided on this form is accurate and correct. I also understand that all my entry materials, including photographs, as well as any additional photographs taken by Boone and Crockett (our representatives or agents) during Awards Programs or Judges Panels, or likenesses rendered from these photographs become the property of the Boone and Crockett Club and may be used to promote the Club, and its records-keeping activities.

FAIR CHASE, as defined by the Boone and Crockett Club®, is the ethical, sportsmanlike and lawful pursuit and taking of any free-ranging wild, native North American big game animal in a manner that does not give the hunter an improper advantage over such game animals.

The Boone and Crockett Club® may exclude the entry of any animal that it deems to have been taken in an unethical manner or under conditions deemed inappropriate by the Club.

Date: _____ Signature of Hunter: _____

(SIGNATURE MUST BE WITNESSED BY AN OFFICIAL MEASURER OR A NOTARY PUBLIC.)

Date: _____ Signature of Notary or Official Measurer: _____

Records of
North American
Big Game

250 Station Drive
Missoula, MT 59801
(406) 542-1888

BOONE AND CROCKETT CLUB
OFFICIAL SCORING SYSTEM FOR NORTH AMERICAN BIG GAME TROPHIES

NON-TYPICAL
WHITETAIL AND COUES' DEER

MINIMUM SCORES		
	AWARDS	ALL-TIME
whitetail	185	195
Coues'	105	120

KIND OF DEER (check one)
☐ whitetail   ☐ Coues'

Abnormal Points

Right Antler	Left Antler
SUBTOTALS	
E. TOTAL	

Detail of Point Measurement

SEE OTHER SIDE FOR INSTRUCTIONS		COLUMN 1	COLUMN 2	COLUMN 3	COLUMN 4
A. No. Points on Right Antler*	No. Points on Left Antler*	Spread Credit	Right Antler	Left Antler	Difference
B. Tip to Tip Spread*	C. Greatest Spread*				
D. Inside Spread of Main Beams	SPREAD CREDIT MAY EQUAL BUT NOT EXCEED LONGER MAIN BEAM				
F. Length of Main Beam					
G-1. Length of First Point					
G-2. Length of Second Point					
G-3. Length of Third Point					
G-4. Length of Fourth Point, If Present					
G-5. Length of Fifth Point, If Present					
G-6. Length of Sixth Point, If Present					
G-7. Length of Seventh Point, If Present					
H-1. Circumference at Smallest Place Between Burr and First Point					
H-2. Circumference at Smallest Place Between First and Second Points					
H-3. Circumference at Smallest Place Between Second and Third Points					
H-4. Circumference at Smallest Place Between Third and Fourth Points					
	TOTALS				

ADD	Column 1		Exact Locality Where Killed:	County:	State/Prov:
	Column 2		Date Killed:	Hunter:	
	Column 3		Trophy Owner:	Telephone #:	
	Subtotal		Trophy Owner's Address:		
SUBTRACT Column 4			Trophy Owner's E-mail:	Guide's Name:	
	Subtotal		Remarks: (Mention Any Abnormalities or Unique Qualities)		
	ADD Line E Total				
	FINAL SCORE			OM I.D. Number	

*A, B, and C do not add into the score.

I, _____ , certify that I have measured this trophy on _____
PRINT NAME   MM/DD/YYYY

at _____
STREET ADDRESS   CITY   STATE/PROVINCE

and that these measurements and data are, to the best of my knowledge and belief, made in accordance with the instructions given.

Witness: _____ Signature: _____ I.D. Number ☐☐☐☐
                                                                                B&C OFFICIAL MEASURER

INSTRUCTIONS FOR MEASURING NON-TYPICAL WHITETAIL AND COUES' DEER

All measurements must be made with a 1/4-inch wide flexible steel tape to the nearest one-eighth of an inch. (Note: A flexible steel cable can be used to measure points and main beams only.) Enter fractional figures in eighths, without reduction. Official measurements cannot be taken until the antlers have air dried for at least 60 days after the animal was killed. If the trophy was bleached, frozen, or boiled, it must dry for 60 days after it is bleached or removed from the freezer or boiling pot.

A. Number of Points on Each Antler: To be counted a point, the projection must be at least one inch long, with the length exceeding width at one inch or more of length. All points are measured from tip of point to nearest edge of beam as illustrated. Beam tip is counted as a point but not measured as a point. **Point totals do not add into the final score.**

    B. Tip to Tip Spread is measured between tips of main beams. **Tip to tip spread does not add into the final score.**

    C. Greatest Spread is measured between perpendiculars at a right angle to the center line of the skull at widest part, whether across main beams or points. **Greatest spread does not add into the final score.**

    D. Inside Spread of Main Beams is measured at a right angle to the center line of the skull at widest point between main beams. Enter this measurement again as the Spread Credit if it is less than or equal to the length of the longer main beam; if greater, enter longer main beam length for Spread Credit.

    E. Total of Lengths of all Abnormal Points: Abnormal Points are those non-typical in location (such as points originating from a point or from bottom or sides of main beam) or extra points beyond the normal pattern of points. Measure in usual manner and enter in appropriate blanks.

    F. Length of Main Beam is measured from the center of the lowest outside edge of burr over the outer side to the most distant point of the main beam. The point of beginning is that point on the burr where the center line along the outer side of the beam intersects the burr, then following generally the line of the illustration.

    G-1-2-3-4-5-6-7. Length of Normal Points: Normal points project from the top of the main beam. They are measured from nearest edge of main beam over outer curve to tip. Lay the tape along the outer curve of the beam so that the top edge of the tape coincides with the top edge of the beam on both sides of the point to determine the baseline for point measurement. Record point lengths in appropriate blanks.

    H-1-2-3-4. Circumferences are taken as detailed in illustration for each measurement. If brow point is missing, take H-1 and H-2 at smallest place between burr and G-2. If G-4 is missing, take H-4 halfway between G-3 and tip of main beam.

MATERIALS RELEASE FORM FOR ALL NON-HUNTER-TAKEN TROPHIES

I certify by my signature that the information I have provided on this form is accurate and correct. I also understand that all my entry materials, including photographs, as well as any additional photographs taken by Boone and Crockett (our representatives or agents) during Awards Programs or Judges Panels, or likenesses rendered from these photographs become the property of the Boone and Crockett Club and may be used to promote the Club, and its records-keeping activities.

Date: _____ Signature of Trophy Owner: _____

ENTRY AFFIDAVIT FOR ALL HUNTER-TAKEN TROPHIES

For the purpose of entry into the Boone and Crockett Club's® records, North American big game harvested by the use of the following methods or under the following conditions are ineligible:

    I.   Spotting or herding game from the air, followed by landing in its vicinity for the purpose of pursuit and shooting;

    II.   Herding or chasing game with the aid of any motorized equipment;

    III. Use of electronic communication devices to guide hunters to game, artificial lighting, electronic light intensifying devices (night vision optics), sights with built-in electronic range-finding capabilities, thermal imaging equipment, electronic game calls or cameras/timers/motion tracking devices that transmit images and other information to the hunter;

    IV. Confined by artificial barriers, including escape-proof fenced enclosures;

    V.   Transplanted for the purpose of commercial shooting;

    VI. By the use of traps or pharmaceuticals;

    VII. While swimming, helpless in deep snow, or helpless in any other natural or artificial medium;

    VIII. On another hunter's license;

    IX. Not in full compliance with the game laws or regulations of the federal government or of any state, province, territory, or tribal council on reservations or tribal lands;

I certify that the trophy scored on this chart was not taken in violation of the conditions listed above. In signing this statement, I understand that if the information provided on this entry is found to be misrepresented or fraudulent in any respect, it will not be accepted into the Awards Program and 1) all of my prior entries are subject to deletion from future editions of Records of North American Big Game and 2) future entries may not be accepted. I also certify by my signature that the information I have provided on this form is accurate and correct. I also understand that all my entry materials, including photographs, as well as any additional photographs taken by Boone and Crockett (our representatives or agents) during Awards Programs or Judges Panels, or likenesses rendered from these photographs become the property of the Boone and Crockett Club and may be used to promote the Club, and its records-keeping activities.

FAIR CHASE, as defined by the Boone and Crockett Club®, is the ethical, sportsmanlike and lawful pursuit and taking of any free-ranging wild, native North American big game animal in a manner that does not give the hunter an improper advantage over such game animals.

The Boone and Crockett Club® may exclude the entry of any animal that it deems to have been taken in an unethical manner or under conditions deemed inappropriate by the Club.

Date: _____ Signature of Hunter: _____
                                                                 (SIGNATURE MUST BE WITNESSED BY AN OFFICIAL MEASURER OR A NOTARY PUBLIC.)

Date: _____ Signature of Notary or Official Measurer: _____

Pope & Young Club

Official Scoring System for Bowhunting North American Big Game

MINIMUM SCORE
whitetail 125
Coues' 65

TYPICAL
WHITETAIL AND COUES' DEER

KIND OF DEER (check one)
☐ whitetail
☐ Coues'

☐ **IN VELVET**

G2 G3 G4 G5 G6 G7
H4
H3
F
E
H2 E
G1
H1

Detail of Point Measurement

C
E B E
D
E

Abnormal Points	
Right Antler	Left Antler

SUBTOTALS	
TOTAL TO E	

SEE OTHER SIDE FOR INSTRUCTIONS			COLUMN 1	COLUMN 2	COLUMN 3	COLUMN 4
A. No. Points on Right Antler		No. Points on Left Antler	Spread Credit	Right Antler	Left Antler	Difference
B. Tip to Tip Spread		C. Greatest Spread				
D. Inside Spread of Main Beams		SPREAD CREDIT MAY EQUAL BUT NOT EXCEED LONGER MAIN BEAM				
E. Total of Lengths of Abnormal Points						
F. Length of Main Beam						
G-1. Length of First Point						
G-2. Length of Second Point						
G-3. Length of Third Point						
G-4. Length of Fourth Point, If Present						
G-5. Length of Fifth Point, If Present						
G-6. Length of Sixth Point, If Present						
G-7. Length of Seventh Point, If Present						
H-1. Circumference at Smallest Place Between Burr and First Point						
H-2. Circumference at Smallest Place Between First and Second Points						
H-3. Circumference at Smallest Place Between Second and Third Points						
H-4. Circumference at Smallest Place Between Third and Fourth Points or half way between Third Point and Beam Tip if Fourth Point is missing.						
		TOTALS				

ADD	Column 1		Location of Kill: (County)	(State/Prov)
	Column 2		Date Killed: Hunter:	
	Column 3		Hunter's Address:	
	Subtotal		City: State: Zip Code: Telephone #: ( )	
SUBTRACT Column 4			Guide's Name and Address:	
FINAL SCORE			Remarks: (Mention Any Abnormalities or Unique Qualities)	OM I.D. Number

I, _____ , certify that I have measured this trophy on _____
              PRINT NAME   MM/DD/YYYYY

at _____
          STREET ADDRESS   CITY   STATE/PROVINCE   ZIP CODE

and that these measurements and data are, to the best of my knowledge and belief, made in accordance with the instructions given.

Witness: _____ Signature: _____
            TO MEASURER'S SIGNATURE   P&Y OFFICIAL MEASURER

                                                                   ADDRESS

                                      CITY   STATE/PROVINCE   ZIP

BRIEF INSTRUCTIONS FOR MEASURING TYPICAL WHITETAIL AND COUES' DEER

Measurements must be made with a flexible steel tape or steel cable and recorded to the nearest one-eighth of an inch. To simplify addition, please enter fractional figures in eighths and in proper fractions. Refer to **P & Y Measurer's Manual** for a detailed description of measuring procedures.

A. Number of Points on each antler. To be counted a point, a projection must be at least one inch long AND, at some location at least one inch from the tip, the length of the projection must exceed its width. Beam tip is counted as a point but not measured as a point.

B. Tip to Tip Spread is measured between tips of main beams.

C. Greatest Spread is measured between perpendiculars at a right angle to the center line of the skull at widest part whether across main beams or points.

D. Inside Spread of Main Beam is measured at a right angle to the center line of the skull at widest point between main beams. Enter this measurement again in "Spread Credit" column if it is less than or equal to the length of longer main beam. If greater, enter longer main beam length for Spread Credit.

E. Total of Length of Abnormal Points. Abnormal points are generally considered to be those non-typical in location (such as points originating from a point or from bottom or sides of main beam). Sketch all abnormal points on antler illustration (front of form) showing location and length. Measure in usual manner and enter in appropriate blanks.

F. Length of Main Beam is measured from the center of the lowest outside edge of burr over outer curve to the most distant point of the main beam. Begin measuring at the location on the burr where the center line along the outer curve of the beam intersects the burr.

G-1-2-3-4-5-6-7. Length of Normal Points. Normal points project from the top of the main beam as shown in illustration. They are measured from the top edge of the main beam (baseline), over their outer curve, to their tip. To establish the appropriate baseline, lay a tape or (preferably) a cable on the top edge of the beam on each side of the point and draw a line under the cable to reflect the top edge of the beam as if the point was not present. Record point lengths in appropriate blanks.

H-1-2-3-4. Circumferences. Circumferences are taken at the smallest place between corresponding normal points, as illustrated. If first point is missing, take H-1 and H-2 at smallest place between burr and second point. If G-4 is missing, take H-4 halfway between the center of G-3 and tip of main beam. Circumference measurements must be taken with a steel tape (a cable cannot be used for these measurements).

ENTRY REQUIREMENTS

1. **Original scoring form** completed by an Official Measurer of the Pope & Young Club or the Boone & Crockett Club.
2. **Completed Fair Chase Affidavit.**
3. **Three photos of antlers, horns, or skull** (a view from the front side, a view from the left side and a view from the right side). A field photo is also requested, if possible.
4. **$35.00 recording fee** (made payable to the Pope and Young Club)

Drying Period: To be eligible for entry in the Pope & Young Records, a trophy must first have been stored under normal room temperature and humidity for at least 60 days after date of kill. No trophy will be considered which has been altered in any way from its natural state.

POPE & YOUNG CLUB

Official Scoring System for Bowhunting North American Big Game

NON-TYPICAL
WHITETAIL AND COUES' DEER

KIND OF DEER (check one)
☐ whitetail ☐ Coues'
☐ IN VELVET

Abnormal Points	
Right Antler	Left Antler
SUBTOTALS	
E. TOTAL	

Detail of Point Measurement

SEE OTHER SIDE FOR INSTRUCTIONS

				COLUMN 1	COLUMN 2	COLUMN 3	COLUMN 4
A. No. Points on Right Antler		No. Points on Left Antler		Spread Credit	Right Antler	Left Antler	Difference
B. Tip to Tip Spread		C. Greatest Spread					
D. Inside Spread of Main Beams		SPREAD CREDIT MAY EQUAL BUT NOT EXCEED LONGER MAIN BEAM					
F. Length of Main Beam							
G-1. Length of First Point							
G-2. Length of Second Point							
G-3. Length of Third Point							
G-4. Length of Fourth Point, If Present							
G-5. Length of Fifth Point, If Present							
G-6. Length of Sixth Point, If Present							
G-7. Length of Seventh Point, If Present							
H-1. Circumference at Smallest Place Between Burr and First Point							
H-2. Circumference at Smallest Place Between First and Second Points							
H-3. Circumference at Smallest Place Between Second and Third Points							
H-4. Circumference at Smallest Place Between Third and Fourth Points or half way between Third Point and Beam Tip if Fourth Point is missing.							
			TOTALS				

ADD	Column 1		Location of Kill:	(County)	(State/Prov)
	Column 2		Date Killed:	Hunter:	
	Column 3		Hunter's Address:		
	Subtotal		City: State: Zip Code: Telephone #: ( )		
SUBTRACT Column 4			Guide's Name and Address:		
	Subtotal		Remarks: (Mention Any Abnormalities or Unique Qualities)		
ADD Line E Total					
FINAL SCORE			OM I.D. Number		

BRIEF INSTRUCTIONS FOR MEASURING NON-TYPICAL WHITETAIL AND COUES' DEER

Measurements must be made with a flexible steel tape or steel cable and recorded to the nearest one-eighth of an inch. To simplify addition, please enter fractional figures in eighths and in proper fractions. Refer to **P & Y Measurer's Manual** for a detailed description of measuring procedures.

A. **Number of Points on each antler**. To be counted a point, a projection must be at least one inch long AND, at some location at least one inch from the tip, the length of the projection must exceed its width. Beam tip is counted as a point but not measured as a point.

B. **Tip to Tip Spread** is measured between tips of main beams.

C. **Greatest Spread** is measured between perpendiculars at a right angle to the center line of the skull at widest part whether across main beams or points.

D. **Inside Spread of Main Beam** is measured at a right angle to the center line of the skull at widest point between main beams. Enter this measurement again in "Spread Credit" column if it is less than or equal to the length of longer main beam. If greater, enter longer main beam length for Spread Credit.

E. **Total of Length of Abnormal Points**. Abnormal points are generally considered to be those non-typical in location (such as points originating from a point or from bottom or sides of main beam). Measure in usual manner and enter in appropriate blanks.

F. **Length of Main Beam** is measured from the center of the lowest outside edge of burr over outer curve to the most distant point of the main beam. Begin measuring at the location on the burr where the center line along the outer curve of the beam intersects the burr.

G-1-2-3-4-5-6-7. **Length of Normal Points**. Normal points project from the top of the main beam as shown in illustration. They are measured from the top edge of the main beam (baseline), over their outer curve, to their tip. To establish the appropriate baseline, lay a tape or (preferably) a cable on the top edge of the beam on each side of the point and draw a line under the cable to reflect the top edge of the beam as if the point was not present. Record point lengths in appropriate blanks.

H-1-2-3-4. **Circumferences**. Circumferences are taken at the smallest place between corresponding normal points, as illustrated. If first point is missing, take H-1 and H-2 at smallest place between burr and second point. If G-4 is missing, take H-4 halfway between the center of G-3 and tip of main beam. Circumference measurements must be taken with a steel tape (a cable cannot be used for these measurements).

ENTRY REQUIREMENTS

1. **Original scoring form** completed by an Official Measurer of the Pope & Young Club or the Boone & Crockett Club.
2. **Completed Fair Chase Affidavit.**
3. **Three photos of antlers, horns, or skull** (a view from the front side, a view from the left side and a view from the right side). A field photo is also requested, if possible.
4. **$35.00 recording fee** (made payable to the Pope and Young Club)

Drying Period: To be eligible for entry in the Pope & Young Records, a trophy must first have been stored under normal room temperature and humidity for at least 60 days after date of kill. No trophy will be considered which has been altered in any way from its natural state.

Scoresheets reproduced courtesy of Boone and Crockett Club, 250 Station Drive, Missoula, MT 59801. (406) 542-1888, boone-crockett.org

* The reference source for this chapter was the Boone & Crockett Club official scoresheet instruction page and the Pope & Young Club official scoresheet instruction page, both published by the Boone and Crockett Club. You can visit Boone & Crockett Club's website at http://www.boone-crockett.org/ and visit http://www.boone-crockett.org/pdf/SC_whitetail_typical.pdf to download a copy of the whitetail typical scoresheet and scoring instructions, or visit http://www.boone-crockett.org/pdf/SC_whitetail_nontypical.pdf on their site to download a copy of their whitetail nontypical scoresheet and scoring instructions. You can also visit the Pope & Young Club's website at: http://www.pope-young.org/pdfs/ScoreSheets/wtc_typical_r6-2008.pdf to download a copy of the typical whitetail scoresheet and scoring instructions, or visit http://www.pope-young.org/pdfs/ScoreSheets/wtc_nontypical_r6-2008.pdf to download the nontypical whitetail scoresheet and scoring instructions.

DETERMINING THE AGE OF YOUR DEER

The first thing you should understand about deer aging is why we always refer to a deer's age as one-and-a-half, two-and-a-half, three-and-a-half, and so on. The reason for this is that most fawns are born in the spring, and by the time we go deer hunting in the fall, the deer are either six months old, one year and six months old if they were born the previous year, or two years and six months old if they were born the year before that—and so on.

The average age of the highest percentage of deer harvested every year is two-and-a-half years old or younger—which is much younger than most people might think. In some states, this percentage may run as high as 80 percent. Most serious hunters and game managers would acknowledge that a good buck is three-and-a-half years old or older. Most trophy hunters will not harvest any buck that they feel to be less than four-and-a-half years old. In most hunted deer populations, less than 2 percent of the deer are more than five-and-a-half years old.

There are a few ways to generally judge an older buck on the hoof prior to making the decision whether to harvest him or not. Even though good nutrition can affect this characteristic to the point of making a younger buck look older than he actually is, exceptionally large racks are more common on older bucks. The main beams of such a rack will extend almost all the way out to the end of the nose or be very tall on the head. The diameter of his main beam at the skull will be approximately two inches or greater. His G2s (the second vertical point running off the main beam) and G3s (the third vertical point running off the main beam) will be much longer. The older buck's stomach and back will sag slightly, and he will have a more massive body size as well as being broader at the shoulders. His neck will be more swollen during the rut, and his entire body will be very stocky, much like an old bull. Younger bucks will be sleeker, like a racehorse. The hoof tracks of older bucks will normally be at least four inches or longer and because of his size and weight will leave a deeper than normal impression than that left by average-size deer in the same terrain. Many older bucks have more gray around their face and forehead. Big, older bucks will rub large and small trees, while the younger bucks will only rub the smaller trees. These are some basic guidelines to use when you have to make a fairly quick decision as to whether or not to harvest a particular buck. The way to gain proficiency in aging deer accurately on the hoof is to observe a large number of deer so that when you do harvest one you will be able to more accurately determine his or her age. Just as most of us get very good at putting people we see in ten-year age groups, like twenty-something, thirty-something, forty-something, and so on, we can do the same thing with deer. The reason we develop that skill with people, almost subconsciously, is that we see lots of people that we know. Our knowledge of those people we know usually includes their age, at least within a year or two. Each of us can learn to develop that skill with deer as well.

The science of aging a deer is based on tooth development and replacement. This is a very visually accurate method of aging deer up to two-and-a-half years old. After that, to accurately age a deer requires the use of forensic science (which I will explain later). Deer replace their baby, or milk, teeth at a fairly set rate, much like humans do. As surely as a six-year-old child will soon lose his or her baby teeth, an eighteen- to twenty-two-month-old buck will lose his third premolars, or at least begin to. By the age of two-and-a-half years, a deer has all of his or her permanent teeth.

A few basics apply to a deer's two sets of teeth. One set is in the very front of the mouth, and is called the incisors; further back in the mouth is a second set, the premolars and molars. The front teeth are used for collecting food, and the second set for grinding it up. The first three on each side are called premolars, and the three back teeth on each side of the jaw are called molars.

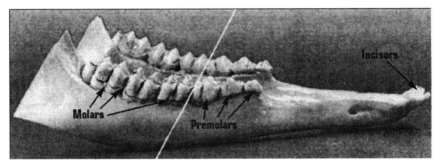

Your basic deer jaw. Incisors in the front, premolars and molars in the back, and a big space between.

The front two middle incisors are replaced at four to six months of age, and the rest of the front teeth are replaced at about the tenth or eleventh month: the lateral incisors and canine teeth. Unlike horses, deer do not have upper incisors, but only lower ones.

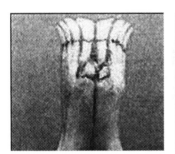

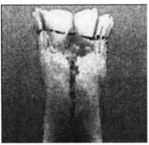

Front teeth of a six-month-old deer (fawn). Permanent incisors are emerging from below the middle two teeth.

Fawn jaw with permanent front teeth fully emerged, but not yet in final position.

Front teeth all permanently in place. Deer is at least 1½ years old.

Besides the obvious visual characteristics like the nose and muzzle of a six-month-old deer appearing short and stubby compared to an older deer and their body size appearing smaller, it is also possible to determine if a deer is a fawn by looking at its teeth. The central two incisors may still be erupting. Notice the photo at the far left on the previous page. The incisors may appear twisted as they emerge through the gums.

Deer grow two sets of premolars. The first set appears in fawns and lasts until the deer is about one-and-a-half years old, at which time the permanent adult premolars push out the baby or milk premolar teeth. Generally there are only four cheek teeth showing in a six-month-old deer, with only one molar on each side by the fall hunting season. Therefore, six-month-old deer have only four cheek teeth: three premolars and one molar on each side. The key here is that if the deer has less than six cheek or jaw teeth, it is a fawn that was born this spring. Notice the photo below.

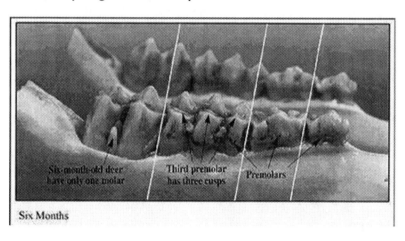

Six-month-old deer have only one molar   Third premolar has three cusps   Premolars

Six Months

By the time the deer reaches one-and-a-half years of age, or by the second hunting season, all three of the molars have come in, although the third one back may have the last cusp still just below the gumline. One very important aging characteristic of the first set of premolars is that if the third premolar has three crowns or cusps and the deer has all six jaw teeth present, it is a one-and-a-half-year-old deer. The next photo is an example of a one-and-a-half-year-old deer.

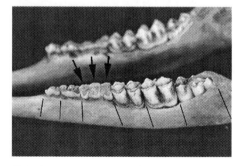

This is a one-and-a-half-year-old deer.

When the permanent teeth come in and all of the premolars have two cusps as shown in the photo to the right, this deer is at least two-and-a-half years old.

Deer grow only one set of the fourth, fifth, and sixth cheek teeth, the molars. A two-and-a-half-year-old deer will have all six molars and premolars fully developed. Look closely at the fourth

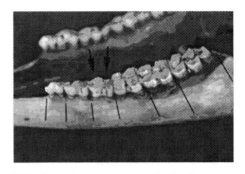

This is at least a two-and-a-half-year-old deer.

cheek tooth (first molar). The cusps are sharp and show little or no wear, and the enamel (white portion) of the lingual crest shows well above the dentine (brown portion). The enamel portion of the cusp is wider than the dentine.

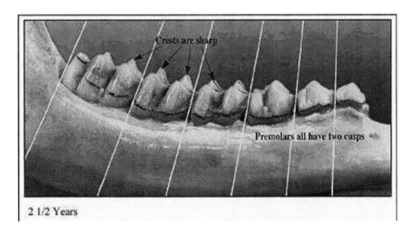

Crests are sharp

Premolars all have two cusps

2 1/2 Years

Just about the time we think we know how to properly do something, science comes along and throws us a curve, makes us wonder what we were thinking. When you understand how accurate the new method of aging your deer is, you'll be unable to understand how you ever thought you could accurately guess the age of deer over two-and-a-half years of age. I'm sure that some people were better at getting close to the exact age than others, but no one could guarantee the accuracy.

The following teeth examples located on the next page were aged using the tooth-wear method. In example A, notice that this set of teeth could really be anything from a two-and-a-half-year-old buck or older. The third premolar now has two cusps, indicating that the deer is at least two-and-a-half years old. Based on tooth wear, you can't be sure how close to two-and-a-half years of age he actually is. As for the other two examples, B and C, notice how you are strictly attempting to determine which one has the most wear. Keep in mind that even though example C is supposed to be a five-and-a-half-year-old deer, he may have been exposed to the types of food sources that were much more abusive to his teeth than example B. If this were the case, he could actually be the same age as example B or even younger.

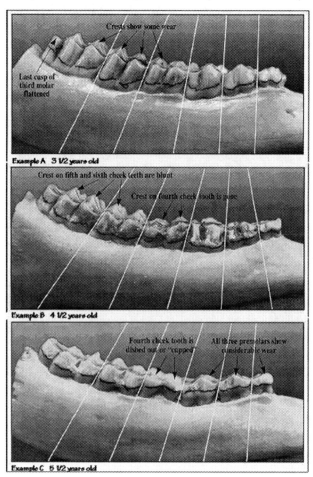

Crests show some wear

Last cusp of
third molar
flattened

Example A 3 1/2 years old

Crest on fifth and sixth cheek teeth are blunt

Crest on fourth cheek tooth is gone

Example B 4 1/2 years old

Fourth cheek tooth is
dished out or "cupped"

All three premolars show
considerable wear

Example C 5 1/2 years old

Here again, the following set of teeth were aged at nine-and-a-half years old using the tooth wear method. Notice how all of the cheek teeth are cupped and worn nearly to the gumline. Because of the vast differences in geological locations and food sources that this deer may have been exposed to, his exact age is uncertain. How can we be sure whether this deer is seven-and-a-half or anything older up through nine-and-a-half years old if we are strictly looking at the amount of wear involved?

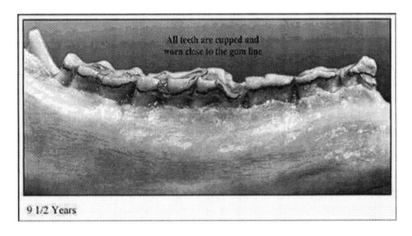

All teeth are cupped and worn close to the gum line

9 1/2 Years

As deer hunters, we have all tried to guess the age of our deer, and most of us have been taught and used this jawbone tooth-wear technique for many years. If you're like me, it was always guesswork beyond two-and-a-half years of age. I never felt 100 percent sure about the accurate age. Many years ago, there were many different claims of how to age deer. Some people claimed that the number of points on a buck's rack determined his age, and others guessed the age by the size of the horns or body size. The tooth-wear method was first proposed in 1949, and there have been several studies since then to attempt to verify the accuracy of this technique. There has never been a study that was able to substantiate the accuracy of this method, however. A good analogy to the difficulties in determining age by tooth wear could be the amount of rubber left on a used tire. Would you attempt to determine how many miles were traveled on a used tire, or how many years old it was, by measuring the remaining tread depth? Of course you wouldn't, because there is no way to be accurate about it. Common sense and experience tells us too many factors can affect the type of wear the tires received. The same thing applies to deer.

Different geological locations and food sources will affect the amount of tooth wear a deer will sustain during a given period. It is also true that the relative hardness of the tooth enamel varies among individuals as well as forces applied in the chewing process, just like it does in humans. It is now known that tooth wear is not an accurate method for aging deer, but visual tooth development and replacement can be accurate for deer up to two-and-a-half years old. I will reemphasize that if you analyze the teeth of your deer and find that the deer has six teeth on one side of his jawbone, we know that the deer is at least one-and-a-half years old. If he has only four or five teeth, we know he was born that spring and is closer to six months old. Once you determine that there are six teeth present, you should now look at the third jaw tooth back, or premolar. If this tooth has three cusps, we know this is a one-and-a-half-year-old deer, but if this tooth has only two cusps, it is a two-and-a-half-year-old deer or older. This is an accurate method to age deer up through two-and-a-half years of age. Beyond this age is where things are always fuzzy or plain guesswork.

Then scientists discovered that there is a physiological mechanism that occurs in all mammals, including deer—and, yes, even humans. Every year, a layer of cementum is deposited around the portion of the teeth located beneath the gum. They also discovered that a forensic laboratory method allows histologists to prepare these teeth so that the rings of cementum can be counted under a high-powered microscope as easily and accurately as counting the growth rings of a tree. What this means is that it is now possible to determine exactly how long the teeth have been in the deer's mouth, thus telling us how old he is. The two teeth that should be used for this process are the two front center incisors, because these teeth are in place by the time the fawn is four to six months old and remain in place throughout the deer's life. If you know your deer is over two-and-a-half years old but sus-

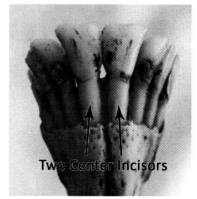

Two Center Incisors

pect him to be even older and desire to know exactly how old he is, you can extract the two front lower incisors and send them off for analysis.

Care should be taken in removing the teeth so that you don't damage the roots. The cementum layers form beneath the gumline around the root in annual rings or layers called annuli. The bottom third of the root is actually the part of the tooth that is most important for analysis. It is for this reason that this method of aging is called the Cementum Annuli method. It is believed that the reason that mammals have this annual deposit of cementum is that it provides a new surface for the flesh in the jaw to attach to the tooth.

Collecting the incisor teeth from freshly killed deer can be very easy, actually much easier than removing the jaw bone for the much less accurate eruption wear technique. First open the deer's mouth then take a sharp, thin-bladed knife and make a cut between the two

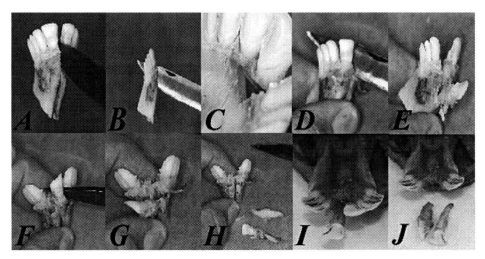

From left to right, top to bottom. Step A: First cut down between the two center teeth, all the way to the bone. Step B: Next, cut down the outside of the right, center tooth, all the way to the bone. Step C: Now cut down the outside of the left, center tooth, all the way to the bone. Step D: Now go back to the center of the two front teeth and work your knife gently with a tilting side-to-side motion to loosen the two teeth. Next, move the knife to the outside of each of the two center teeth and do the same thing. Step E: It should be fairly easy now to gently separate the teeth from the bone, leaving only tissue holding them together. Step F: Separate the teeth from the bone by cutting the tissue.

center incisors on the inside of the deer's mouth. The knife in the pic-
ture is from a Leatherman tool. The easiest way to make these cuts is
by pushing down with the knife, making a gentle rocking motion until
the knife will go no further (Photo A & B). The cut should extend back
into the deer's mouth and about three times the distance that these
teeth extend above the gum line. Make another cut on each other side
of these center incisors using the same technique (Photo C & D).

Now, apply downward (outward) pressure to one of the incisors
until it starts to come loose. In photo K we show the bottom of the
front jaw of a whitetail with all the flesh removed (not necessary for
incisor removal). As you can readily see there is very little bone/
cartilage supporting the underside of these incisors, which is why
this downward pressure works without breaking off the root. You
may need to apply a pulling and twisting force and use your knife to
completely detach this tooth from the jaw. Trim any large chunks of
flesh away from the tooth and discard. Remove the other incisor in
the same manner. Place both of these teeth in a small paper envelope
and mark the envelope with your identification nomenclature (i.e.,
Jim's 8 point 2011; Joe's doe 2010 Hill Country, etc.)

Once you have removed these two incisors, you will be unable to
see the cementum layers or rings with the naked eye. The teeth must
be packed carefully into an envelope and mailed to a special laboratory like Wildlife Analytical Laboratories (PO Box 295, Burnet TX
78611; 512-756-1989). They also offer a kit to aid in this removal process on their website (http://www.deerage.com/). The kit instructs
you on the proper way to extract the teeth and what exactly to do
with them prior to shipping them to their lab for analysis. The cost
for this type of analysis will vary based on how long you are willing to wait for your results. The standard 120-day waiting period kit
costs $19.95 plus shipping and handling. If you have any questions
or doubts, just give them a call. I have found them to be passionate
about aging deer and other game mammals, good people who also
love to help folks out.

You must take special care not to damage the root of the teeth,
especially the tip since this is the portion of the tooth that is used for
the aging process. If you have any problem with any aspect of this

process, feel free to call or contact Wildlife Analytical Laboratories at (512) 756-1989 or go on line to www.deerage.com.

Once these teeth are received at the laboratory, they are first placed in an acid solution for about a week to remove all the calcium. After this process, they are no longer hard like a bone, but more like a pencil eraser. They are then placed in a mold and covered with a special wax to fully support the tooth root. Using the proper equipment, thin layers are shaved off until they reach the center of each tooth. They use a couple of the center slices of each tooth and stain these slices to make the cementum rings or layers visible under a high-powered microscope at about 150× magnification.

The cementum layers are now completely visible and counted for an exact age of your deer.

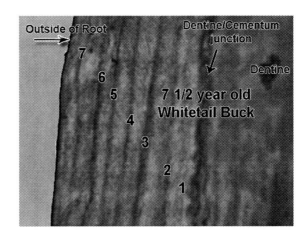

Portions of the previous information can be obtained from the USGS website, as well as certain photographs. The specific page on their website is http://www.npwrc.usgs.gov/resource/mammals/ deerteeth/ages.htm. Information on the Cementum Annuli method for aging deer can be found at the Wildlife Analytical Laboratories website (http://www.deerage.com). I wish to thank USGS for allowing me to use their photos and information, and to thank Henry Chidgey of Wildlife Analytical Laboratories for his contribution as well. Henry devoted a great deal of his time and photos and research information to this chapter of the book. I highly recommend Wildlife Analytical Laboratories and Henry's staff to accurately age your deer.

WHITETAIL OVERPOPULATION VERSUS POTENTIAL EXTINCTION

A great deal of thought and positive action must go into a solution to the present overpopulation problem that is tempered with the present conditions that are exposing a road to possible extinction in some areas.

In certain parts of the country, the annual roadkill number is almost as high as the annual hunting harvest in those areas. The encroachment of humans deeper and deeper into the whitetail's habitat as a result of the driving desire to work in the city but live in the country where it is peaceful and quiet is certainly taking a toll on the whitetail. Subdivisions are being built in more and more serene settings, and the narrow highways that are built right through the forest to access them promote a great deal more whitetail roadkills. The deer are on the roads constantly, and the drivers have little or no warning of their presence until it is too late. In some cases, high fences or electric fences are utilized in an effort to prevent a portion of these situations, but for the most part, it is a futile effort. The deer will find ways through, over, or around these fences.

Other than the increased road kills, the development of these sub-divisions has aided the development of the local deer herds. Humans move in and plant flowers, fruit trees, gardens, and so on, and the deer suddenly realize that they never had it so good.

The homeowners become quite put out with the deer situation as a result of this type of activity, and many of those who were originally against deer hunting begin to seek some type of assistance to rid themselves of this problem.

The problem, however, is that these are now residential areas where legal hunting is not permitted without some type of local authority intervention. In some cases, special hunts are set up that are well organized and well supervised. On a much wider scale in these types of areas, the local wildlife management authorities are attempting to monitor these herd populations and increase the quotas,

Often deer are quite comfortable in heavy subdivisions.

lengthen the seasons, and move herds, where possible, in an effort to contain these problems.

In the above problem areas, a new subdivision or a newly built shopping center has not deteriorated the whitetails' food sources. These situations may have altered these food sources, but in most cases, they have improved them to the point of increasing herd sizes.

The other end of the spectrum would be those situations where subdivisions, shopping malls, industrial plants, and other structures have eliminated critical food sources and had a negative impact on the herd size. There are many of these situations as well. After construction is completed, modifications to the property should be made to re-create natural food sources for the whitetail deer that were there before the construction came—building in harmony with nature.

There are other negative influences on the various deer herds in certain areas, such as tremendous numbers of young and unhealthy deer and fawns taken by predators each year. More should be done to maintain better control over these predator numbers in certain areas.

Another negative influence is insufficient herd management and a lack of monitor-

Coyotes take a heavy toll on deer herds.

ing by local officials, private clubs, and landowners. There are some areas where all the mature bucks in a given area have been depleted by hunters to the point of creating an extreme overpopulation of doe as well as a genetically inferior herd.

Generally speaking, when managed properly, hunting has proven to be the best conservation method to adequately maintain the balanced herd capacities. Without good conservation tactics, many deer would perish from starvation, and many would weaken from starvation to the point of being mauled to death by their predators. There would be many more roadkills, and as a result, more human safety hazards. There would be greater crop damage, more residential encroachment by the deer, and more disease among the herds.

This deer was hit by a train and propelled up on top of this power line pole.

To take a stand against deer hunting is, in my mind, to be in favor of all of this. We need to attempt to educate the public as much as we can about the overwhelming benefits of professional whitetail herd management. We need to show them that we hunters are sincere, caring professionals with the ultimate goal of securing the survival of the whitetail deer and preventing their extinction.

Predators such as these coyotes regularly prey on young and weakened deer.

Photo © by Mary Morris.

THE CLOSE OF A SUCCESSFUL HUNT

Now that the hunt has come to an end and you have the time to reflect on all the wonderful moments and camaraderie involved, you find gratification in the knowledge that this is only the close of one of many more to come. The realization of just how much closer these outings have brought you and your sons or daughters or other friends or loved ones make these events priceless. When you can gaze up at the full camp pole of hanging deer and know that everyone hunted ethically and responsibly and understood the conservation aspect of what had taken place on the hunt, there's a feeling of contentment. Each hunter focusing on good shot placement for a quick, clean kill, appreciative of the reward of venison for the table to feed their families for many days to come is, to a great extent, coming full circle with our forefathers.

It is my hope that each of us can serve as role models not only for the younger generation of hunters following in our footsteps, but also for our fellow hunters. If we each dedicate ourselves to good hunting ethics and reflect this attitude on others, we can all enjoy whitetail deer hunting even more. Just about all of the deer-hunting members of my family and my hunting buddies, some related and some not, are very successful at it. These photographs merely reflect a few hunts out of the many we have enjoyed over the years. I share a common bond with all the individuals in these photographs and will treasure that bond always.

A successful hunt's bounty.

As long as I am physically able and the good Lord blesses my days, when September rolls around you will find me in the woods or on a deer stand once more. It is my hope and prayer that I have done this book justice, and that all who read it will do so with the confidence that I have tried to help them in my own small way.

Any hunt that yields a deer is a successful hunt.

Photo © by Mary Morris

TWENTY-FIVE GREAT VENISON RECIPES

I've mentioned before how much I enjoy preparing and eating venison almost as much as I enjoy whitetail deer hunting itself. There's nothing like a well-prepared venison meal that pleases the entire family. If you put a little tender love and care into it, you will amaze even yourself, unless you happen to already be a chef. Try to be creative with venison, and write down exactly what steps and ingredients you use. Venison is a very healthy meat product and very low in fat content, so for these reasons it would be wise for all of us to include venison in our diet. My wife and I have been preparing venison for years and have developed a genuine love for the taste. This is very easy to do if you take the necessary steps to prepare it properly. We plan to put together a complete venison recipe book in the near future, but for now I am including twenty-five of my favorite recipes in this chapter. Each recipe clearly explains what steps should be taken for the best result. I feel confident that any one who tries these recipes will enjoy them as much as we do.

1 ◆ VENISON MEATLOAF

1 1/2 lbs. of ground venison
1 1/2 teaspoon of salt
1 tablespoon of beef stew
  seasoning
1/4 cup of chopped onions

1/2 cup of ketchup
1/2 teaspoon of pepper
1/2 cup of salsa
1/4 cup of bread crumbs or
  oats

Mix well and press into a baking dish. Bake at 350° for about 45 minutes. Spread a thin layer of ketchup on top. Makes 4 to 6 servings.

2 ◆ VENISON CHILI

2 lbs. of ground venison
1 tablespoon of chili powder
1/2 medium onion, chopped
1 can of kidney beans
1/2 cup of tomato ketchup

1 cup of cooked macaroni
1 teaspoon of Tabasco sauce
1 teaspoon pepper
2 cups of water

Cook and brown the ground venison, and then pour off the fat. Mix in all ingredients in a large stew pot and cover. Cook at 325° to 350° for at least 45 minutes or until the venison and vegetables are tender and lightly browned. Makes 4 to 6 servings.

3 ◆ VENISON SPAGHETTI

1 1/2 lbs. of ground venison
1 small onion, chopped
1/2 green pepper, chopped
1/4 cup of butter
1/4 cup of bacon drippings

1 can of tomato paste
1 tablespoon of beef stew
  seasoning
2 or 3 stalks of celery

Cook chopped onion, chopped green peppers, and ground venison until lightly brown in the butter and bacon drippings. Pour off the fat and add finely chopped celery and tomato paste. Cover and cook slowly for 45 minutes. Serve over well-cooked and drained spaghetti. Sprinkle with parmesan cheese. Makes 4 to 6 servings.

4 ◆ VENISON HAMBURGERS IN BARBEQUE SAUCE

2 lbs. of ground venison
1 medium onion, chopped
1 minced green pepper
1/3 cup of sweet pickle relish
1/3 cup of vinegar
1 medium size chopped onion
1 cup of ketchup
1 minced green pepper

2 teaspoons of prepared
  mustard
1/3 cup of sweet pickle relish
  mustard
2 tablespoons of brown sugar
1/4 teaspoon of Tabasco sauce
1 small can of mushrooms

First, make venison patties by mixing ground venison with chopped onion, green pepper, and sweet pickle relish. Flatten into patties. Combine all of the other ingredients in a saucepan. Bring to a boil and then reduce the heat and simmer for 10 minutes. Now add the venison patties and simmer for an additional 25 minutes. Makes 6 servings.

5 ◆ VENISON AND RICE

1 cup of rice
2 cups of water
1 package of Lipton Dry Onion
 Soup
1 1/2 lbs. of venison sliced very
 thin

2 cans of undiluted mushroom
 soup
1/2 cup of salsa

Grease a casserole dish and spread dry rice on the bottom. Put water over the rice then sprinkle dry onion soup over the rice. Place sliced venison over the Rice mixture and spread mushroom soup over the venison. Bake 1 1/2 to 2 hours at 350°. Top with salsa if desired. Makes 4 servings.

6 ◆ VENISON PEPPER STEAKS

2 tablespoons of bacon drippings
 or canola oil
1 lb. of venison, cut into thin,
 narrow strips
2 tablespoons of minced onions
1 small clove garlic, chopped
1 bouillon cube
1/2 cup of hot water
1 teaspoon of salt

1/8 teaspoon of pepper
2 large green peppers, cut into
 strips
1 cup of celery, sliced diagonally
2 tablespoons of minced
 pimentos
2 tablespoons of cornstarch
2 tablespoons of water
1 tablespoon of soy sauce

Heat bacon drippings or canola oil in skillet then add venison and brown well. Add onion, garlic, and bouillon cube dissolved in 1/2 cup of hot water with salt and pepper. Cover, cook on low heat for 15 minutes. Add green peppers, celery, and pimentos. Cook until tender. Combine cornstarch, 2 tablespoons of water, and soy sauce, and add to venison. Simmer for five minutes to thicken gravy. Serve with rice and additional soy sauce if desired. Makes 4 servings.

7 ◆ VENISON CHILI CON CARNE

1 tablespoon bacon drippings or canola oil
1 onion, diced
2 lbs. of ground venison
1 can of tomato soup
1 can of tomatoes

1 can of kidney beans
1 tablespoon of salt
6 to 8 stalks of celery, diced
1/4 teaspoon of pepper
chili powder to taste

Brown onions in bacon drippings or canola oil and add ground venison. Cook until venison is brown. Add remaining ingredients. Simmer approximately one hour. Dilute with water or tomato juice if desired. Makes 6 to 8 servings.

8 ◆ VENISON AND CHOW MEIN NOODLE CASSEROLE

1 lb. of ground venison
2 tablespoons of butter
1 green pepper, diced
1 onion, chopped
1 cup of diced celery

1 teaspoon of salt
1 cup of water
1 can of mushroom soup
1 can of chow mein noodles

Brown venison in butter. Add green pepper. Simmer until green pepper is tender. Cook celery, onion, water and salt until celery is tender. Add mushroom soup and blend well. Add to venison mixture. Add 2/3 of the noodles to the venison mixture. Pour into a buttered casserole dish. Sprinkle remaining noodles on top. Bake uncovered at 350° about 30 minutes. Makes 4 to 6 servings.

9 ◆ COPENHAGEN VENISON BALLS

1 lb. of ground venison
1/2 cup of cold water
1/2 lb. of ground beef
1/4 teaspoon of pepper
3/4 cup of fine, dry

breadcrumbs
1 egg, well beaten
2 tablespoons butter or
drippings for frying

Combine all of the ingredients except the fat for frying and mix well. Shape 1 level teaspoonful of meat mixture into balls the size of large marbles. Heat butter or drippings in large skillet. Brown meatballs well on all sides and remove them from the skillet as they brown. Prepare Brown Sauce.

BROWN SAUCE:
3 onions, thinly sliced
1 tablespoon of butter
2 1/2 cups of water
1/2 cup cream or milk
1/3 cup Sherry

3 tablespoons of flour
1/2 teaspoon Worcestershire
sauce
3 tablespoons of bacon drippings
1 1/4 teaspoons salt
1/4 teaspoon pepper

Cook onions slowly in 1 tablespoon of butter until dark brown. Blend flour into drippings remaining in the skillet. Add water and cook until mixture boils and thickens. Stir consistently. Add remaining ingredients and blend well. Return the meatballs to the sauce and cover and simmer gently for about 30 minutes. Stir occasionally. Makes 6 to 8 servings.

10 ◆ BAKED VENISON STROGANOFF

3 lbs. of venison, cut in 3/4-inch cubes
1 cup of water
1 teaspoon of salt
1/2 teaspoon pepper
1/2 teaspoon of ginger
1/2 teaspoon of curry

1 jar of sliced mushrooms, undrained
3 cups of low-fat sour cream
1 package of onion soup mix
1/4 cup of shortening
1 teaspoon of paprika

Brown venison in approximately one quarter cup of bacon drippings or canola oil until well browned on all sides. Mix in salt, pepper, ginger, curry powder and water. Cover and simmer about one hour and 15 minutes or until meat is almost tender. Add mushrooms. Blend in sour cream and onion soup mix. Stir 1/2 of the sour cream mixture into the venison and juices in the skillet. Pour into a buttered 2-quart casserole dish. Spread remaining sour cream mixture on top. Sprinkle lightly with paprika. Cover. Bake at 325° about one hour or until the meat is tender. Serve with buttered noodles. Makes 8 servings.

11 ◆ VENISON MEDALLIONS

3 lbs. of venison tenderloin
1 tablespoon of pepper
1 teaspoon of garlic salt
1 1/2 cups of flour

2 tablespoons of Mrs. Dash for batter seasoning
1/2 teaspoon of salt
1 onion, minced

Cut venison tenderloin into very thin, approximately 2-inch medallions. Mix the flour, salt, pepper, garlic salt, and seasoning into a batter and spread on to a large plate. Before battering, sprinkle meat tenderizer on both sides of the medallions. Deep fry in a skillet of heated canola oil or vegetable oil. Sprinkle minced onions over the venison as it is cooking. Cook over medium to medium high heat and turn meat as needed to promote even cooking/browning. This recipe is also great without the flour batter but simply sprinkle everything over both sides of the meat prior to cooking. The flour is the only thing you would omit. Makes 6 to 8 servings.

12 ◆ VENISON AND WINE CASSEROLE

2 tablespoons of salad oil
2 tablespoons of butter or sherry
2 lbs. of venison, cut into thin strips
3 tablespoons of flour
3/4 teaspoon of salt
1/4 teaspoon of pepper

1 cup of beef broth
1 cup of dry white wine
1 small bay leaf
1/4 cup of minced parsley
1 (1 lb.) jar of small white onions, drained
2 (4 oz) cans of button mushrooms, drained

Heat oil and butter in a skillet. Cook the venison strips until browned. Mix in flour, salt, and pepper. Add beef broth and wine. Cook at a medium heat until the mixture boils and is thickened. Stir constantly and add bay leaf and parsley. Pour into a 2 1/2-quart casserole and cover. Bake at 325° for 45 minutes. Add onions and mushrooms and cover. Bake for another 25 minutes at same temperature or until meat is tender. Serve with buttered noodles. Makes 6 servings.

13 ◆ CHECKERBOARD VENISON LOAF

1 (8 ounce) package of herb-seasoned bread stuffing
2 lbs. of ground venison
1/2 cup of finely diced celery
2 teaspoons of seasoned salt

1 tablespoon of grated onion
Green pepper rings and tomato wedges
1 egg

Combine stuffing mix with butter and water according to the package directions, and add onions. Blend ground venison, egg, celery and seasoned salt. Place 2/3 of the venison mixture into a 9 × 5 × 3" pan. Make a lengthwise strip of the mixture to cover only half of the bottom of the pan. Fill in the other half of the pan with 1/3 of the stuffing mixture. Make two more layers of each, alternating the strips of venison and stuffing each time to form the checkerboard pattern. Cover the pan with aluminum foil. Bake at 375° for 45 minutes. Remove the foil and bake about 30 minutes longer or until brown. Let stand for 15 minutes. Invert pan on a platter and remove the venison loaf. Garnish with green pepper rings and tomato wedges. Makes 6 servings.

14 ◆ VENISON SAUERBRATEN HAMBURGERS

1 1/2 lbs. of ground venison
1/3 cup of milk
1 tablespoon instant minced onions
1 egg, slightly beaten
1/4 cup of fine, dry bread crumbs
1/2 teaspoon of grated lemon rind

1 1/2 teaspoons of salt
1 can of beef gravy
1/4 cup of water
2 tablespoons of vinegar
1/2 teaspoon of ginger
1/4 cup of brown sugar, packed
2 tablespoons of shortening
Dash of cloves

Combine first seven ingredients and mix lightly. Shape into six large patties. Melt shortening in large skillet and brown venison patties on both sides. Remove from skillet. Mix remaining ingredients in skillet and bring to a boil. Add patties and cover. Simmer about 30 minutes and turn several times for even cooking. Serve with buttered noodles. Makes 6 servings.

15 ◆ OVEN-BAKED VENISON STEW

1 beef bouillon cube
2 lbs. of venison, cut in 1-inch cubes
2 1/2 teaspoons of salt
2 cups of diced onions
8 medium carrots, peeled and cut in large pieces
1/2 cup of boiling water

1 can of tomato soup
6 stalks Pascal celery, cut in large pieces
1 tablespoon of sugar
2 tablespoons of quick-cooking tapioca
6 medium potatoes, cut in halves

Dissolve bouillon cube in boiling water. Mix with remaining ingredients. Pour into an ungreased 3 1/2 quart casserole dish and cover. Bake covered at 250° about 4 1/2 hours. Makes 8 servings.

16 ◆ VENISON LASAGNA

1 lb. of ground venison
2 tablespoons of shortening
1 clove garlic, minced
1 tablespoon of chopped parsley
1 tablespoon of basil
1 teaspoon of salt
1 can of Roma tomatoes
2 (6 ounce) cans of tomato paste
3 cups of cream-style cottage cheese

2 eggs, slightly beaten
1/2 teaspoon of pepper
1/2 cup grated parmesan cheese
8 ounces lasagna noodles, cooked and drained
3/4 lb. of Mozzarella cheese, thinly sliced

Cook ground venison in shortening. Stir in next 6 ingredients and cook uncovered until mixture is thick. Stir occasionally. Combine cottage cheese, eggs, salt, pepper, parsley and Parmesan cheese. Place half of the noodles in a buttered 13 x 9 x 2" baking dish. Cover with half of the cottage cheese mixture, half of the cheese slices, and half of the venison mixture. Repeat layers. Bake uncovered at 350° for approximately 40 minutes. Let stand for 10 minutes before serving. Makes 8 servings.

17 ◆ BURGUNDY VENISON

3 cups of thinly sliced onions
1/4 cup bacon drippings
2 lbs. venison cut in 1-inch
   cubes
1 1/2 tablespoons all-purpose
   flour
1/8 teaspoon marjoram

1/8 teaspoon thyme
1 teaspoon salt
1/4 teaspoon pepper
1/2 cup beef consumé
1 cup Burgundy wine
1/2 lb. mushrooms, sliced

Cook onions in bacon drippings until brown. Remove from drippings and set aside. Brown venison in drippings and add a little more fat if necessary. Sprinkle flour and seasonings over venison. Stir in consume and wine. Cover and bring to a boil. Turn to a low heat and simmer for 11/2 hours. Add onions and mushrooms. If gravy is too thick, add a little water. Simmer about 1 hour longer. Makes 8 servings.

18 ◆ PIZZA VENISON LOAF PIE

1/8 teaspoon of pepper
1 lb. of ground venison
1/2 cup dry bread crumbs
1/4 cup finely chopped onion
1 (8 ounce) can tomato sauce
1/4 cup diced green pepper

1/2 cup water
1 teaspoon of oregano, crushed
1 unbaked 9-inch pie shell
1 teaspoon salt
3/4 cup shredded cheddar
   cheese

Combine venison, onion, green pepper, oregano, salt, pepper, bread crumbs, tomato sauce and water. Mix lightly. Spread venison mixture evenly into the pie shell. Bake at 400° for 15 minutes. Reduce temperature to 350°. Bake 30 minutes longer then remove from the oven. Sprinkle cheese over top and bake about 5 minutes or until cheese is melted. Makes 6 servings.

19 ◆ BARBECUED VENISON LOAVES

1 lb. of ground venison
1 cup fine, dry bread crumbs
1 lb. of ground beef or ground pork
2 eggs, slightly beaten
1 1/2 teaspoons of salt

1/2 cup of milk
3/8 teaspoon black pepper
2 raw carrots, shredded
2 raw potatoes, shredded
1 teaspoon baking powder
1/2 teaspoon grated onion

Combine all ingredients and mix well. Shape into 10 individual loaves and place in a baking dish or pan. Pour half of the barbecue sauce over meat loaves and cover. Use aluminum foil as a cover. Bake at 350° for 40 minutes. Uncover and add the remaining barbecue sauce. Bake uncovered for 30 minutes longer.

BARBECUE SAUCE
2 tablespoons chopped onion
1 tablespoon shortening
3 tablespoons Worcestershire sauce
2 tablespoons brown sugar

1 cup of ketchup 1/2 teaspoon salt
2 tablespoons of vinegar
1/8 teaspoon black pepper
1/4 cup lemon juice

Cook onion in shortening until golden brown. Add remaining ingredients and simmer for 5 minutes.

20 ◆ VENISON-STUFFED GREEN PEPPERS

8 green peppers
1/4 cup of cracker crumbs
1 lb. ground venison
1/2 cup tomato soup
1/2 lb. ground beef
1/2 teaspoon of salt

1/2 lb. ground pork
1/8 teaspoon pepper
1 small egg, slightly beaten
1/2 small onion, finely chopped
1/4 cup of water
1/2 cup browned bread crumbs

Wash and cut off stem and remove seeds from green peppers. Cook uncovered in boiling, salted water for about 5 minutes. Drain upside down. Mix meat, egg, onion, cracker crumbs, soup, salt and pepper all together. Fill green peppers with meat mixture and top with browned bread crumbs. Place in shallow baking dish and add 1/4 cup of water. Bake at 350° about 45 minutes.

21 ◆ VENISON AND VEGETABLE DINNER

1 lb. of venison cut in 1-inch
  cubes
1/4 cup of butter
1/2 cup chopped onions
2 cups soup stock
Worcestershire sauce

2 cups uncooked, broad noodles
1/2 cup diced celery
6 carrots, cut in 2-inch pieces
1 green pepper, diced
1 teaspoon of salt and pepper
1 package frozen peas

Brown venison in butter then add onions and brown them lightly. Add soup stock, Worcestershire sauce, noodles, celery, carrots and green pepper. Season with salt and pepper and cover. Bring to the boiling point at a high heat. Simmer about 30 minutes then add peas and cook about 10 minutes longer. Makes 6 servings.

22 ◆ CHRISTMAS VENISON STEW

3 lbs. of venison, cut into 1-inch cubes
6 green onions, chopped, including the green tops
1 red onion, chopped
1/3 cup parsley flakes or 2/3 cup fresh parsley, chopped
1 red pepper or 1 small jar of pimentos
1 green pepper, diced
1 can Italian tomato sauce
1 can or 1 frozen package of La Seur green peas
1 can tomato paste or Mexican tomato sauce
1 package spinach noodles
2 or 3 fresh tomatoes or 1 large can stewed tomatoes
4 sticks of celery, chopped
1 teaspoon of salt
1 1/2 to 2 teaspoons of black pepper
1 small jar of stuffed green olives
1 teaspoon of white sugar
1 tablespoon of brown sugar
1 tablespoon of fresh minced garlic or garlic powder
1 teaspoon of paprika
1 teaspoon of chili powder
1 teaspoon of oregano
2 teaspoons of Mrs. Dash seasoning
1 teaspoon of sweet basil
2 tablespoons of parmesan cheese
Worcestershire sauce

Brown the venison cubes in canola or vegetable oil and add all of the seasonings except the brown and white sugar. Add the onions and sauté with the venison. Add all the remaining ingredients except for the noodles and the green peas. Bring this mixture to a boil, then turn down and let simmer for approximately 1 hour covered until the venison and the vegetables are tender. Add the green peas to the mixture the last 20 minutes of cooking time. Cook the noodles in accordance with the instructions on the package. Serve the mixture over the noodles and top with Parmesan cheese. Makes 6 servings.

23 ◆ FIVE-CHEESE VENISON STROGANOFF

3 lbs. of venison, cut in 1-inch
cubes
4 celery stalks, chopped fine
1/2 cup Colby-Jack shredded
cheese
1 can water chestnuts,
1 can mushrooms
1/2 cup Swiss cheese, (or
Mexican-style shredded
cheese)
1 can cream of celery soup
1 can golden cream mushroom
soup
1 teaspoon salt
1 medium white or yellow onion,
chopped
1 1/2 teaspoon pepper
2 teaspoons Mrs. Dash
seasoning

1 (16 ounce) container of sour
cream
1 teaspoon onion salt or onion
powder
1/2 cup Mozzarella cheese,
shredded
1/2 cup milk
1/2 cup cheddar cheese,
shredded (mild or medium)
1 clove garlic or 1 teaspoon of
fresh garlic
1 teaspoon of dry or prepared
mustard
1/3 cup parmesan-romano
cheese, grated or shredded
1 teaspoon of celery salt

Brown the venison cubes in Canola or vegetable oil and add all of the seasonings. Add the onions and celery and sauté with the venison until they are tender. Add the mushrooms next and brown. Add the two cans of soup with 1/2 can of water and 1/2 can of milk and stir in. Add the water chestnuts and the sour cream and mix to a creamy consistency. Add additional water and or milk if mixture is too thick. Simmer covered for 20 to 30 minutes until venison is tender. Add all the cheeses except the parmesan cheese and then cover for an additional 10 to 20 minutes or until the cheeses melts. Spoon the hot mixture over hot noodles or hot rice. Prepare the noodles or rice in accordance with the instructions on the package. Top with the parmesan cheese and extra sour cream if desired. Makes 6 servings.

24 ◆ FAR EAST VENISON

3 lbs. of venison, cut in 1/2- to 3/4-inch cubes
1/4 cup of water
1 can of cream of mushroom soup
2 teaspoons black pepper
1/2 to 3/4 cup of water
2 teaspoons of Butter Buds
1 teaspoon garlic salt
1 teaspoon nutmeg
1 teaspoon of dried mustard or prepared Dijon mustard
1/2 teaspoon cinnamon
1 teaspoon ginger
2 teaspoons of spicy brown mustard
1 teaspoon of turmeric
1 teaspoon of Mesquite Liquid Smoke
1 (12 oz.) box of Skinner Angel Hair Pasta (Roasted Garlic and Red Bell Pepper)
2 teaspoons of Mrs. Dash seasoning
2 teaspoons of Maggi seasoning (onion and herb)
1 (8 ounce) container of sour cream (light or no-fat)

Brown venison in olive oil sprinkled with black pepper and 1 teaspoon of garlic salt. Add dried mustard, turmeric, Butter Buds, Mesquite Liquid Smoke, Maggi seasoning, Mrs. Dash, and 1/4 cup of water. Bring this mixture to a slight boil or until the mixture achieves a golden color. Simmer covered for 45 minutes or until venison is tender. Add mushroom soup, 1/2 to 3/4 cup water, 2 teaspoons black pepper, nutmeg, cinnamon, sour cream, ginger and spicy brown mustard. Cook until you achieve a creamy mixture. Prepare the pasta in accordance with the instructions on the box. Serve the mixture hot over the pasta and top with grated parmesan cheese and sour cream. Makes 6 servings.

25 ◆ CULTURED BUTTERMILK VENISON MARINADE

(will lessen the gamy flavor of
  antlered animals)

2 cups of buttermilk or 2
  pressed cloves of garlic
yogurt

Season to taste with salt and pepper, curry powder, cinnamon, or ginger. Mix marinade in a glass or stainless steel container and use a wooden spoon to turn or stir the venison occasionally. Place the venison in the marinade and place in the refrigerator for 12 to 48 hours depending on the age of the deer while turning from time to time.

Photo © by Mary Morris.

POPULAR WHITETAIL DEER AND OTHER OUTDOOR OR HUNTING-RELATED WEBSITES

Like many other whitetail deer enthusiasts, I spend a great deal of my spare time online searching the many related whitetail deer sites. You can learn a great deal by searching the Internet for answers to your questions about whitetails. I have listed many of my favorite sites that I feel will be very helpful in a variety of ways. Many of these sites are quite good to help you learn more about whitetail deer and how to hunt them. Many of the other sites will interest you because, in this author's opinion, they are the type of sites that are interesting to most people who are drawn to deer hunting. We as deer hunters actually have a great deal more in common with each other than just deer hunting. Use the Internet to stay current on modern technology, equipment, clothing, maps, moon phases, weather conditions, available leases, and other tools available to us hunters. As you learn of a new interesting website, add it to this list.

POPULAR WHITETAIL DEER AND OTHER RELATED SITES

WHITETAILDEER.COM
www.whitetaildeer.com
WHITETAILS.COM
www.whitetails.com
WHITETAIL DEER
www.whitetail-deer.org
QUALITY DEER MANAGEMENT
ASSOCIATION
www.qdma.com
LEGENDARY WHITETAILS
www.legendarywhitetails.com
HUNTERSNET
www.huntersnet.com
WHITETAIL MASTERS
www.whitetailmasters.com
DEERHUNTING.COM
www.deer-hunting.com
DEER HUNTING.NET
www.deerhunting.net
TRAILCAM
www.trailcam.com
TENNESSEE DEER.COM
www.tndeer.com
AMERICAN-HUNTER.COM
www.american-hunter.com/toc.
html
HUNTERS CORNER
www.hunterscorner.com
THE WILDLIFE COMPANY
www.wildlifecompany.com
THE JUMP
www.thejump.net
POPE AND YOUNG
www.pope-young.org
BOONE AND CROCKETT
www.boone-crockett.org
WHITETAILS UNLIMITED
www.whitetailsunlimited.com
DEER.COM HUNTING DIRECTORY
www.deer.com

WHITETAIL INSTITUTE
www.deernutrition.com
THE DEER DOMAIN
www.deerdomain.com
DEER LEASES NATIONWIDE
www.agsites.net/links/
huntingleases.html
NORTH AMERICAN HUNTING CLUB
ONLINE
www.huntingclub.com
HUNTING SWEEPSTAKES
www.huntingsweepstakes.com
HUNTING LOG.COM
www.huntinglog.com
INVENT A NEW HUNTING PRODUCT
www.franklinforge.com
THE WAY WHITETAIL DEER HUNTING
REALLY IS
www.white-taildeer.com
THE HUNTING TRAIL NETWORK
www.thehuntingtrail.net
WHITETAIL HUNTING STRATEGIES
www.shooters.com/Harris
AUCTIONS FOR HUNTING PRODUCTS
www.gearbay.com
GUN TALK
www.guntalk.com
ONE STOP SITE FOR HUNTING/
FISHING SEARCH ENGINES
www.huntseek.net
DEER MANAGEMENT
www.angelfire.com/hi/
deerhuntingqdm
DEER HUNTING STORIES
www.deer-hunt.com
THE HUNTING NETWORK
www.hunting.net
TIPS
www.hunting.net/tips
HUNTING INFORMATION SYSTEMS
www.huntinfo.com
JOHN EBERHART'S WHITETAILS
www.deer-john.com

EDERS HUNTING AND WHITETAIL
DEER SOURCE
www.edershunting.com
AWESOME ANTLERS
www.awesomeantlers.com
WHITETAIL DEER HUNTING AND
BREEDING
www.whiteoakwhitetail.com
LEASEHUNTING.COM
www.leasehunting.com
DEER AND BIG GAME HUNTING LINKS
www.hunting.about.com/cs/
deerhunting
ROGER RAGLIN-AMERICA'S
WHITETAIL DEER HUNTER
www.rogerraglin.com
HUNTERS FOR THE HUNGRY
www.h4hungry.org
HUNTING HOT SPOTS
www.huntinghotspots.com
ALL ABOUT WHITETAILS
www.whitetaildeer.com
NORTHLAND IMAGES
www.northlandimages.com
ETHICS AND HUNTING
www.american-hunter.com/
Articles/cn_0898.html
AMERICAN TROPHY WHITETAIL LINKS
www.americantrophywhitetail.
com/Links.html
EVERYTHING ABOUT DEER HUNTING
IN THE USA
www.hunt4deer.com
HUNTING REGULATIONS U.S. STATES
www.thebowman.com/tb_
huntreguls.html
BEST DEER HUNT
www.bestdeerhunt.com
INTERNET SHOOTING DIRECTORY
www.shootguns.info/hunt.html
WHITETAILS UNLIMITED
www.whitetailsunlimited.org

MONSTER MULEYS
www.monstermuleys.com
AMERICAN WHITETAIL DEER
HUNTING RESOURCES
www.americanwhitetaildeerhuntin
gresources.com
PERMISSION TO HUNT
www.p2hunt.com
TRACKER OUTDOORS
www.tracker-outdoors.com/
wildlife.htm
WEST WIND WHITETAILS
www.westwindwhitetails.com/
index.html
WHERE TO HUNT.NET
www.where2hunt.net
WHITETAILS.COM
www.whitetails.com
WHITE-TAIL DEER DENSITY MAP
www.deer-departed.com/deer-
density-map.html
WHITETAIL DOMAINS
www.whitetaildomains.com
WHITETAIL HEAVEN
www.whitetaileddeer.ca
WHITETAIL HUNTING GUIDES AND
OUTFITTERS
www.outfitterpros.com
WHITETAIL SOLUTIONS
www.whitetailsolutionsllc.com
WILD ANIMAL INFORMATION
www.wildanimalinfo.com
WILDLIFE FOREVER
www.wildpa.com
WILDLIFEREADY.COM
www.wildlifeready.com
WORLD CLASS OUTDOORS HUNTING
www.worldclassoutdoors.com/
index.htm
ADVANCED WHITETAIL HUNTING
www.advanced-whitetail-hunting.
com

ADVENTURE VIDEO
www.adventurevideo.org
ARTISTIC ANTLERS
www.artisticantlers.com
BACK FORTY WILDLIFE
MANAGEMENT, LLC
www.backfortywildlife.com
BACKWOODS WHITETAILS
www.backwoodswhitetails.com
CAMTRAKKER
www.camtrakker.com
CENTURY INTERNATIONAL
www.centuryarms.com
CROOKED HORN OUTDOOR VIDEO
PRODUCTIONS
www.crookedhornoutdoors.com
CUDDE BACK DIGITAL
www.cuddeback.com/indexb.html
DECAL JUNKY STICK 'EM UP!
www.decaljunky.com
DECALS FOR ARCHERS
www.decalsforarchers.com/home.
html
DEER
www.westwindwhitetails.com/
page-deer-5.html
DEER ANATOMY
www.deerhunting.ws/
deeranatomy.htm
DEER DEER DEER
www.deerdeerdeer.com
DEER FEVER.COM
www.deerfever.com
DEER HUNTER 2 SOCIETY
www.angelfire.com/sports/
deerhunter2
DEERHUNTERSCLUB.COM
www.deerhuntersclub.com
DEER HUNTING ADVENTURE CLUB
www.deerhuntingadventureclub.
com

DEER MANAGEMENT PROFESSIONALS
OF SOUTHEASTERN
PENNSYLVANIA
www.deerprofessionals.com/index.
html
DEER TRACKING.COM
www.deertracking.com
DEER T-SHIRTS
www.ezmerchandise.com/
deertshirts.html
DEFENSE MASTER.COM
www.defensemaster-knives.com/
index.htm
DOC'S HORNY STUFF, THE ULTIMATE
HUNTING SCENT ELIMINATOR
www.docshornystuff.com
FARMERS ALMANAC
www.almanac.com
FOGGY BOTTOM OUTDOORS
www.foggybottomoutdoors.com
FROM BEAR CREEK
www.frombearcreek.com
HAYNES HUNTING SYSTEMS
www.hayneshunting.com/catalog
HUNTER'S GUIDE
www.thehuntersguide.com
HUNTER'S INFORMATION SERVICE
www.fordinfo.com
HUNTER'S SPECIALTIES
www.hunterspec.com
HUNTERSPRO
www.hunterspro.com
HUNT FAIR CHASE
www.huntfairchase.com/index.php
HUNT FISH CAMP WISCONSIN
www.huntfishcampwisconsin.com/
Links.html
HUNT STATS.COM
www.huntstats.com/deer.html
HUNT THE OUTDOORS
www.hunttheoutdoors.com
HUNTING EXPO USA
www.huntingexpousa.com

HUNTING FOOTAGE.COM
www.huntingfootage.com
HUNTING GEAR REVIEW
www.hunting-fishing-gear.com
HUNTING GUIDE
www.huntingworldtop100.com
HUNTING IN ALBERTA, CANADA
www.abhunting.com
HUNTING INFORMATION
www.huntinginfo.org
HUNTING NAVIGATOR
www.huntingnavigator.com
HUNTINGNET.COM
www.huntingnet.com
HUNTING NETWORK
INTERNATIONAL, LLC
www.huntingnetwork.org
HUNTING PA
www.huntingpa.com
HUNTING SQUARE huntingsquare.com
IBEOUTDOORS.COM
www.ibeoutdoors.com/index.html
INTERNET HUNTING SOCIETY
www.huntingsociety.org
MOUNTAIN MAN TRAP SUPPLY
www.mountainmantraps.com/
main.htm
MPHUNTCONSULTING.COM
mphuntconsulting.com/Home_
Page.php
MULE DEER FOUNDATION
www.muledeer.org
MULEYMADNESS.COM
www.muleymadness.com
OUTDOOR HITS
www.outdoorhits.com
OUTDOOR RINGS
www.outdoorrings.com
OUTDOOR SAFE
www.outdoorsafe.com
OUTDOORS EXPERIENCE
www.outdoorsexperience.com
OUTDOORS UNLIMITED
www.outdoorsunlimited.net

OUTFITTER FOCUS
www.outfitterfocus.com/index.
shtml
PABUCKS.COM
www.pabucks.com
PHEASANTS FOREVER INC.
www.pheasantsforever.org
PREDATOR MASTERS
www.predatormastersforums.com
QUAILS UNLIMITED
www.qu.org
RACKMAX.
www.rack-max.com
REFLEX, INC.
www.reflexbow.com
ROCKY MOUNTAIN ELK FOUNDATION
INC.
www.rmef.org
RYNOSKIN.
www.rynoskin.com
SAFARI CLUB INTERNATIONAL
FOUNDATION
www.safariclubfoundation.org
SAFARIS INTERNATIONAL
www.safarisinternational.com
SIERRA CLUB
www.sierraclub.org
SIMPLE SURVIVAL
www.simplesurvival.net
SPORTSMAN'S CHOICE
www.sportsmanschoice.com/
index.htm
SPORTSMAN'S EDGE
hus.parkingspa.com/hc3.asp
STAGES OF ANTLER DEVELOPMENT
www.tpwd.state.tx.us/huntwild/
wild/game_management/deer/
antler_growth
STATELINE OUTDOORS
www.statelineoutdoors.com
STORY CREEK, INC.
www.storycreekinc.com

SUB SPECIES OF DEER.
www.deerhunting.ws/
classifications.htm
SURVIVE THE OUTDOORS
www.survivetheoutdoors.com
TED NUGENT
www.tednugent.com
TERRASERVER-USA (TOPO MAPS)
www.terraserver.com
THE BUCKSKINNER
www.thebuckskinner.com
THE HUNTING WIRE
www.thehuntingwire.com
THE OUTDOOR LODGE
www.theoutdoorlodge.com
THE OUTDOOR PRESSROOM.
www.outdoorpressroom.com
THE WILDLIFE RANCH
www.thewildliferanch.com/index
.htm
THE WILDLIFE SOCIETY
joomla.wildlife.org
TIGHTTRACK.COM
www.tighttrack.com
TOO MANY DEER.
www.riverdeep.net/
current/2002/01/012102t_deer
.jhtml
TRACKER-OUTDOORS
tracker-outdoors.com/tso/index
.htm
TRAILMASTEROUTDOORS.COM
www.trailmasteroutdoors.com
TROPHY BUCK NEWS
wwwtrophybucknews.com
TROPHY ROCK
www.trophyrock.com
UNDERBRUSH
www.leafycamo.com
VALUABLE DEER INFORMATION
animaldiversity.ummz.umich.edu/
site/accounts/information/
Odocoileus_virginianus.html

VARMINT AL'S
www.varmintal.com
VENOM.
www.venompeepsight.com
VORTEX
www.vortexbroadheads.com

CHISTIAN SPORTSMAN

T.R. MICHELS' TRINITY MOUNTAIN
OUTDOORS
www.trmichels.com
GOD'S GREAT OUTDOORS INC
www.ggoutdoors.org
CHRISTIAN DEER HUNTERS
ASSOCIATION
www.christiandeerhunters.org
CHRISTIAN OUTDOORSMAN
www.christianoutdoorsman.com

SUNRISE / SUNSET / MOON PHASES / WEATHER/TIME / TIME

SUN AND MOON DATA
aa.usno.navy.mil/data/docs/RS_
OneDay.html
TIMEANDDATE.COM.
www.timeanddate.com/calendar
LUNAR INFO
www.onhiatus.com/Moon.html
CHECK THE WEATHER
www.msnbc.com
TALK ABOUT THE WEATHER
groups.msn.com
NOAA NATIONAL WEATHER SERVICE
www.nws.noaa.gov
THE WEATHER CHANNEL
www.weather.com
ACUUWEATHER
www.accuweather.com

THE WEATHER NETWORK
www.theweathernetwork.com
WEATHER UNDERGROUND
www.wunderground.com
INTELLICAST
www.intellicast.com
CNN WEATHER
www.cnn.com/weather
WORLD CLIMATE
www.worldclimate.com
RAIN OR SHINE WEATHER
www.rainorshine.com
SUN OR MOON RISE AND SET TABLE
aa.usno.navy.mil/AA/data/docs/
RS_OneYear.html
DATA SERVICES
aa.usno.navy.mil/AA/data
SUNRISE AND SUNSET COMPUTATION
tycho.usno.navy.mil/srss.html
THE OLD FARMERS ALMANAC RISE
AND SET
www.almanac.com/rise/index.php
FIND SUN AND MOON RISE AND SET
TIMES
www.40-below.com/sunmoon
ARI'S TODAY PAGE
www.aristoday.com
SUNRISE AND SUNSET CALCULATOR
www.sunrisesunset.com/sun.html
SUNRISE/SUNSET
www.sunrisesunset.com
TIME AND DATE
www.timeanddate.com/worldclock
WORLD TIME
www.worldtime.com
MOON PHASES
tycho.usno.navy.mil/vphase.html

OUTFITTERS AND GUIDES

BLACKWATER HUNTING SERVICES
www.blackwaterhunting.com

ARCHERY UNLIMITED OUTFITTERS
www.subee.com/led/ledhome.html
HUNTING AND FISHING GUIDES IN
U.S. AND CANADA
www.hunting-fishing-guides.com
NORTH AMERICAN GUIDED HUNTS
www.where2hunt.net
WHITETAIL DEER HUNT AT LARSON'S
CAMP
www.larssonscamp.com
ARCHERY HUNTING FOR MATURE
WHITETAIL
www.trophywhitetaildeer.com
EASTERN WHITETAIL DEER HUNTING
www.americantrophywhitetail.com
SPRUCE WOODS OUTFITTERS
www.sprucewoodsoutfitters.com
ELKHORN CREEK OUTFITTERS
www.huntingelkhorncreek.com
SOUTHHAMPTON OUTFITTERS
www.southamptonoutfitters.com
BIG ANTLER OUTFITTERS
www.big-antler-outfitters.com/
deer.html
FOREST OF ANTLERS WHITETAIL
DEER HUNTING OUTFITTERS
www.forestofantlers.com
BIGHORN OUTFITTERS OF IDAHO
www.huntidaho.com
BOWHUNT BLACK BEAR, CARIBOU,
MOOSE, WHITETAIL DEER,
AND ELK
www.bowhunts.com
GUIDED HUNTS IN WYOMING
www.thehideout.com
OLD STONE FENCE TROPHY ELK AND
WHITETAIL DEER HUNTING
www.fobarehunting.com
BLACKWATER HUNTING SERVICES
www.blackwaterhunting.com
ARCHERY UNLIMITED OUTFITTER
www.subee.com/led/ledhome.html

HUNTING AND FISHING GUIDES IN
U.S. AND CANADA
www.hunting-fishing-guides.com
ALL HUNTERS-WHITETAIL DEER, ELK,
TURKEY, BEAR HUNTING
www.allhunters.net
MOUNTAIN OAK OUTFITTERS
www.mountainoakoutfitters.com
SAGE CREEK OUTFITTERS
www.sagecreekoutfitters.com

A FEW OTHER STATE HUNTING SITES

WELCOME TO GLOBAL HUNTING
www.globalhunting.com
MISS. HARRISWOOD PLANTATION-
WHITETAIL DEER HUNTING
www.huntinfo.com/harriswood
DEER HUNTING GUIDES FROM
ACROSS THE U.S.
www.huntfind.com
ADIRONDAK MOUNTAIN AND
STREAM GUIDE SERVICE
www.adirondackhuntingfishingand
canoeing.com
CARMEN MOUNTAIN WHITETAIL
DEER
www.cazacimarron.com
VIRGINIA GUIDE SERVICE WHITETAILS
AND TURKEY
www.virginiaguideservice.com
HUNTING INFO FOR ENTIRE USA
www.hunt4deer.com
ALABAMA DEER HUNTING.
www.aldeer.com
MAINLAND HUNTING IN ALA. FOR
WHITETAIL AND HOG
www.mainlandhunting.com
AUSTRALIAN DEER ASSOCIATION
www.angelfire.com/nt/
deerqueensland

DEER HUNTING IN ALASKA
www.alaska.net/~captpete/deer.
html
ALBERTA CANADA DEER HUNTING
www.ihuntalberta.com/gallery/
deer2002
SASKATCHEWAN WHITETAIL HUNTS
www.bigdeer.org
NORTH WEST ONTARIO CANADA
WHITETAILS.
www.gopickerel.com
CANADA WHITETAIL DEER WITH BOW
www.skifflakeoutfitters.com
YOUR CANADIAN BOW HUNTING
SITE
www.bowzone.com
ALBERTA WHITETAIL AND MULE DEER
ASSOCIATION
www.albertadeer.com
ARKANSAS DEER HUNTING
www.ardeerhunting.com
WHITETAILS IN ARKANSAS.
www.wildlifefarms.com
ARKANSAS DEER HUNTING
www.ardeerhunting.com
CALIFORNIA DEER HUNTING.
www.californiadeerhunting.com
GEORGIA DEER HUNTING
www.sgawarriors.com
HAWAII DEER HUNTING
www.american-hunter.com/
stateinfo/hawaii.asp
INDIANA DEER HUNTING
www.american-hunter.com/
stateinfo/indiana.asp
KENTUCKY WHITETAIL DEER HUNTS
www.whiteoaklake.com
KANSAS DEER HUNTING
www.ksdeerhunting.com
KANSAS AND MISSOURI HUNTING
www.ks-mo-hunt.org

ILLINOIS WHITETAIL DEER AND
TURKEY HUNTING
www.trophydeerhunt.com
IDAHO DEER HUNTING
www.idahodeerhunting.com
IOWA DEER HUNTING.
www.iowadeerhunting.net
IOWA WHITETAILS
www.iowawhitetail.com
LOUISIANA DEER HUNTING
www.loudeer.com
MAINE TROPHY WHITETAIL DEER
HUNTING OUTFITTERS
www.mainedeerhunting.com
NORTH COUNTRY LODGE IN MAINE
www.northcountrylodge.com
MAINE DEER HUNTING
www.dri-ki.com/deer.html
MARYLAND DEER HUNTING
www.biggamehunt.net/sections/
Maryland
MASSACHUSETTS DEER HUNTING
www.american-hunter.com/
StateInfo/massachusetts.asp
MICHIGAN DEER HUNTING
www.msu.edu/ ~ leciejew/
deerhunting.html
MINNESOTA DEER HUNTING
www.vdl.com/hunting/deer.html
MINNESOTA DEER HUNTERS
ASSOCIATION.
www.mndeerhunters.com
MISSISSIPPI DEER HUNTING
www.msdeer.com
NEBRASKA GAME AND PARKS
COMMISSION-WHITETAIL
DEER
www.ngpc.state.ne.us/wildlife/
wtdeer.html
NEW HAMPSHIRE DEER HUNTING
www.wildlife.state.nh.us/Hunting/
hunting.html

HUNTING IN MEXICO, NEBRASKA,
ALABAMA, AND KANSAS
www.huntingtop10.com
NEW MEXICO DEER HUNTING
www.newmexicodeerhunting.com
NORTH CAROLINA DEER HUNTING.
www.ncdeer.com
NORTH DAKOTA DEER HUNTING.
www.northdakotadeerhunting.com
OHIO DEER HUNTING.
www.american-hunter.com/
stateinfo/ohio.asp
OKLAHOMA DEER HUNTING
www.american-hunter.com/
stateinfo/oklahoma.asp
CEDARTOP OUTFITTERS OF
OKLAHOMA.
www.cedartopoutfitters.com
PENNSYLVANIA DEER HUNTING.
www.penndeer.com
CHERRY RIDGE TROPHY WHITETAIL
DEER HUNTING IN PENN.
www.cherryridge.com
RHODE ISLAND HUNT
www.huntri.com/home.shtml
SCOTLAND'S PREMIER HUNTING
AGENCY
www.scothunt.co.uk
SOUTH CAROLINA DEER HUNTING
www.biggamehunt.net/sections/
South_Carolina
SOUTH DAKOTA DEER HUNTING
www.southdakotadeerhunting.com
TENNESSEE DEER HUNTING
www.tndeer.com
TEXAS DEER HUNTING.
www.texasdeerhunter.com
2000 ACRE DEER HUNTING RANCH IN
TEXAS
www.wbranch.com
WHITETAIL DEER HUNTING IN TEXAS
www.sweetwatercreekbowhunt.
com

MUSTANG CREEK RANCH-
WHITETAILS OF TEXAS
www.whitetailbuck.com
MAGNUM GUIDE SERVICE IN TEXAS.
www.magnumguideservice.com
TEXAS DEER HUNTING.
www.deertexas.com
SALT FORK HUNTS-TEXAS
www.saltforkhunts.com
UTAH DEER HUNTING
www.american-hunter.com/
stateinfo/utah.asp
VERMONT'S WHITETAIL DEER
HUNTING
www.scenesofvermont.com/
hunting
VIRGINIA DEER HUNTING
www.virginiadeerhunters.org
WASHINGTON DEER HUNTING
www.american-hunter.com/
StateInfo/washington.asp
WEST VIRGINIA DEER HUNTING
www.wvsportsmen.com/license_
hunting.cfm
DREAMMOUNTAIN IN WEST
VIRGINIA.
www.dreammountain.net
CHRONIC WASTING DISEASE IN
WISCONSIN WHITETAILS
www.caids-wi.org
WDNR-DEER HUNTING IN
WISCONSIN
www.dnr.state.wi.us/org/land/
wildlife/hunt/deer
WISCONSIN DEER HUNTING
www.wisconsindeerhunting.com
WYOMING DEER HUNTING
www.wyomingdeerhunting.com
DEER HUNTING ON PRIVATE
WYOMING RANCH.
www.bar-nunn.com
WYOMING DEER HUNTING
www.huntwwth.com

DEER FARMERS AND LAND MANAGEMENT

DEERFARMER.COM
www.deerfarmer.com
NORTH AMERICAN DEER FARMERS
ASSOCIATION
www.nadefa.org
LAKE WHITETAIL DEER FARM
www.angelfire.com/ok3/
Lakewhitetails
MQUADS TROPHY WHITETAIL FARM
www.trophy-whitetail-deer.com
MORGAN'S BIRCHWOOD WHITETAIL
DEER FARM
www.deerfarmer.net/Birchwood
DEER FARM DIRECTORY
www.deerfarms.com/farms.shtml
FIELD OF DREAMS WHITETAIL DEER
FARM.
www.deerfarmer.net/
Fieldofdreams
WHITETAIL DEER FARMER
whitetaildeerfarmer.com
WHITETAIL DEER MANAGEMENT AND
HUNTING
www.whitetaildeer-management-
and-hunting.com
NORTH AMERICAN DEER FARMERS
ASSOCIATION
www.nadefa.org

FISH AND FOWL

FISHING WORLD.COM
www.fishingworld.com
BASS PRO SHOPS
www.basspro.com
GAME AND FISH-WHITETAIL DEER
www.gameandfish.about.com/cs/
whitetaildeer

TARGET COMMUNICATIONS, DEER
AND TURKEY EXPOS
www.deerinfo.com
TURKEY HUNTING SECRETS
www.turkeyhuntingsecrets.com
TURKEY HUNTING
www.portlandlanding.com/turkey.
html
BLACKWATER DECOYS
www.duckdecoys.com
DELTA WATERFOWL FOUNDATION
www.deltawaterfowl.org
DUCK HUNTERS REFUGE
www.duckhunter.net
HOOSIER JIM'S COUNTRY STORE AND
DUCK MARSH.
www.duckblind.net
DUCKS UNLIMITED
www.ducks.org
QUAILS UNLIMITED
www.qu.org
PHEASANTS FOREVER.
www.pheasantsforever.org
FISHING IN TENNESSEE
www.state.tn.us/twra/fishmain.
html
QUAILS UNLIMITED
www.qu.org
DUCKS UNLIMITED
www.ducks.org
NATIONAL WILD TURKEY
FEDERATION
www.nwtf.com
NATIONAL TURKEY FEDERATION
www.turkeyfed.org
FISH AND HUNT NOW
fishandhuntnow.com
HUNTING FISHING SUPPLIES
www.huntingfishingdirect.com/
sites/addsite.html

WILDLIFE AND OTHER OUTDOOR SITES

AMERICAN RIVERS-PLEASANT RIVER
www.amrivers.org/rivers/
pleasantriver.html
UNITED SPORTSMAN OF AMERICA
www.tnugent.com
EASTERN MOUNTAIN SPORTS
www.emsonline.com
ESPN OUTDOORS.
www.espn.go.com/outdoors
AGRICULTURE AND THE OUTDOOR
WORLD
www.agsites.net/links/
deerhunting.html
TRACKER OUTDOORS
www.tracker-outdoors.com
NORTHERN OUTDOORS
www.mainedeerhunting.com
OUTDOORS NETWORK
www.outdoors.net
THE ONLINE SPORTSMAN.
www.onlinesportsman.com
ANIMAL RIGHTS
www.animalrights.net
ALL OUTDOORS HUNTING AND
FISHING TIPS AND
TECHNIQUES
www.alloutdoors.com
WILDLIFE TRACKER
www.wildlifetracker.com
NAT. REPTILE AND AMPHIBIAN ADV.
COUN
www.nraac.org
WILDLIFE FOREVER
www.wildlifeforever.org
CAMPING
www.campinglinks.com
AMERICA OUTDOORS.COM
www.americaoutdoors.com
LYME DISEASE
www.whitetaildeer.com/howto/
lyme

TICKS
www.ent.iastate.edu/
ImageGallery/ticks
DEER TICK
www.ent.iastate.edu/
ImageGallery/ticks/deertick.
html
MONGO AND TARD'S OUTDOOR
SHACK
www.mongoandtard.com
UNITED OUTDOOR STORES
www.campunited.com
GREEN MOUNTAIN SPORTS
www.greenemountain.net
MPI OUTDOORS
www.mpioutdoors.com
WILD LIFE TREASURES
www.wildlifetreasures.com
MCKENZIE SPORTS PRODUCTS INC
www.mckenziesp.com
AGRICULTURE AND THE OUTDOOR
WORLD
www.agsites.net
FARMERS AND HUNTERS FEEDING
THE HUNGRY
www.fhfh.org

SOMETHING MORE FOR KIDS

BENEFIT4KIDS
benefit4kids.org
KIDS LEARN WHAT TVA DOES FOR
THE OUTDOORS
www.tvakids.com
KID'S CORNER
www.ran.org/ran/kids_action
SMOKEY BEAR-SPLASH PAGE
www.smokeybear.com
OUTDOOR SKILLS EDUCATION
www.dfw.state.or.us/outdoor_
skills

24 HOUR CAMPFIRE.COM
www.24hourcampfire.com

OUTDOOR WOMEN

BRENDA VALENTINE
www.brendavalentine.com
WELCOME TO MY STAND (BRENDA
VALENTINE)
www.bowhunting.net/
brendavalentine/default.htm
BECOMMING AN OUTDOOR WOMAN
www.uwsp.edu/cnr/bow
MS OUTDOOR WOMAN
www.msoutdoor.com
THE OUTDOOR WOMAN
www.theoutdoorwoman.com
OUTDOOR WOMAN
www.myoan.net/woman
WOMAN HUNTING FISHING
OUTDOORS
www.women-outdoors.com
TOMBOY
www.tomboy-womenoutdoors.
com
WOMAN HUNTERS
www.womenhunters.com
WILD WOMAN EXPEDITIONS
www.wildwomenexp.com
MOUNTAIN WOMAN.
www.mountainwoman.com
NATURE NORTH ZONE.
www.naturenorth.com
OUTDOORS NETWORK
www.outdoors.net
WOMAN OUTDOORS
www.womenoutdoors.org
BECOMING AN OUTDOORS WOMAN
www.uwsp.edu/cnr/bow
TOMBOY
www.tomboy-womenoutdoors.
com

WOMEN HUNTERS.
www.womenhunters.com
ARMED FEMALES OF AMERICA
www.armedfemalesofamerica.com
LEADING LADIES OUTDOORS.
www.leadingladiesoutdoors.com

FEDERAL, STATE, AND LOCAL GOVERNMENT/ ORGANIZATIONS

NRA INSTITUTE FOR LEGISLATIVE
ACTION.
www.nraila.org
REFUGE NET
www.refugenet.org
US STATE AND TERRITORY ANIMAL
IMPORT REG
www.aphis.usda.gov/vs/sregs
WILD TURKEY FEDERATION.
www.nwtf.org
NATIONWIDE ST. PARKS
www.tracker-outdoors.com/state-parks
NAT. REPTILE AND AMPHIBIAN ADV.
COUN
www.nraac.org/agencies.html
NATIONAL RIFLE ASSOCIATION.
www.nra.org
FOUNDATION FOR BLACKTAIL DEER
www.blacktail.org
QUALITY DEER MANAGEMENT
ASSOCIATION.
www.qdma.org
LICENSE PLATE.
www.tpwd.state.tx.us/plate/whitetail_deer.html
MASTERS OF DEER HOUNDS
ASSOCIATION
www.countryside-alliance.org/cfh/mdha
GUN OWNERS OF AMERICA
www.gunowners.org

US FISH AND WILDLIFE SERVICE
www.fws.gov
THE WILDLIFE LEGISLATIVE FUND OF
AMERICA
www.wlfa.org
ENVIRONMENTAL PROTECTION
AGENCY
www.epa.gov
NATIONAL WILDLIFE FEDERATION
www.nwf.org
USGS (US GEOLOGICAL SURVEY)
www.usgs.gov
US CORP OF ENGINEERS
www.usace.army.mil
FORESTRY.COM.
www.forestry.com
USDA FOREST SERV. RESEARCH AND
DEV
www.fs.fed.us/research
LINKS TO OTHER STATE GAME, FISH
AND PARKS.
www.state.sd.us/gfp/links.html
NATIONAL WILDLIFE FEDERATION
www.nwf.org/campusecology
BUREAU OF LAND MANAGEMENT
www.blm.gov
US FORESTRY SERVICE
www.fs.fed.us
TENNESSEE WILDLIFE RESOURCES
AGENCY
www.state.tn.us/twra/huntmain.html
NATIONAL AUDUBON SOCIETY
www.audubon.org
AUDUBON INSTITUTE
www.auduboninstitute.org
WILDLIFE CONSERVATION SOCIETY.
www.wcs.org
TENNESSEE VALLEY AUTHORITY
www.tva.gov
US FISH AND WILDLIFE SERVICE
www.fws.gov

NATIONAL PARK SERTVICE
www.nps.gov
BUREAU OF LAND MANAGEMENT
www.blm.gov/nhp
NATIONAL DROUGHT MONITOR
www.drought.unl.edu/dm/monitor.html
NATIONAL ENDANGERED SPECIES
ACT REFORM COALITION.
www.nesarc.org
NATIONAL FIRE NEWS
www.nifc.gov/fire_info/nfn.htm
NATIONAL FISH AND WILDLIFE
FOUNDATION
www.nfwf.org
NATIONAL GRASSLANDS
www.fs.fed.us/grasslands
NATIONAL PARKS CONSERVATION
ASSOCIATION.
www.npca.org
NATIONAL PARK SERVICE
www.nps.gov
NATURAL RESOURCES DEFENSE
COUNCIL
www.nrdc.org
NATIONWIDE STATE PARKS
www.usparks.about.com
NATIONAL TAXIDERMISTS
ASSOCIATION
www.nationaltaxidermists.com
NATIONAL WEATHER SERVICE
www.weather.noaa.gov
NATIONAL WILD TURKEY
FEDERATION
www.nwtf.org
STATE AGENCIES AND LINKS
TO WHITETAIL DEER
ASSOCIATIONS
www.whitetailquest.com/old/stateagencies.html
STATE FISH AND GAME
DEPARTMENTS.

www.outdoorsunlimited.net/linkcust/fishandgame.html
TENNESSEE DEER
www.tndeer.com
TENNESSEE DEPARTMENT OF
ENVIRONMENT AND
CONSERVATION
www.state.tn.us/environment
TENNESSEE SPORTSMAN
www.tennesseesportsman.com
TENNESSEE WILDLIFE FEDERATION.
www.tnwf.org
TEXAS DEER ASSOCIATION
www.texasdeerassociation.com
TEXAS DEER HUNTING.
www.1atexasdeerhunting.com
TEXAS HUNTING LEASE.
www.texashuntinglease.com
TEXAS OUTDOORSMAN.COM
www.texasoutdoorsman.com/links.htm
THE CONGRESSIONAL SPORTSMAN'S
FOUNDATION
www.sportsmenslink.org
THE FEDERALIST PATRIOT
www.patriotpost.us
THE HOUSE OF REPRESENTATIVES
www.writerep.house.gov/writerep/welcome.shtml
THE NATURE CONSERVANCY
www.nature.org
THEODORE ROOSEVELT
CONSERVATION PARTNERSHIP
www.trcp.org
THE PEOPLES RIGHTS ORGANIZATION
(PRO)
www.peoplesrights.org
UNITED BOWHUNTERS OF
KENTUCKY
www.unitedbowhuntersofkentucky.org
ALL STATE DNR OFFICES
www.deerhunting.ws/allstatesregs.htm

BILL OF RIGHTS
www.archives.gov/exhibits/
charters/charters.html
CONSTITUTION OF THE UNITED
STATES.
www.archives.gov/exhibits/
charters/charters.html
DECLARATION OF INDEPENDENCE
www.archives.gov/exhibits/
charters/charters.html
DEPARTMENT OF VETERANS AFFAIRS.
www.va.gov
DISABLED SPORTSMAN OF AMERICA.
www.disabledsportsmenofamerica.
org
FIRSTGOV.GOV.
www.usa.gov
HUNTERS HELPING HUNTERS
www.hhh.client.techpro.com
HUNTERS FOR THE HUNGRY
www.h4hungry.org
HUNT FOR THE HUNGRY.
www.huntforthehungry.com
HUNT OF A LIFETIME
www.huntofalifetime.org
INTERNATIONAL HUNTER
EDUCATION ASSOCIATION
www.ihea.com
KEEP AND BEAR ARMS
www.keepandbeararms.com
LIBERTY BELLES.
www.liberty-belles.org
STUDENTS FOR THE SECOND
AMENDMENT
www.sf2a.org
TEAMING WITH WILDLIFE
www.teaming.com
SECOND AMENDMENT SISTERS
www.2asisters.org
DEER HUNTING INFO. BY STATE.
www.deerhunting.ws/
stateinfopage.htm

THE VARMIT HUNTERS ASSOCIATION
www.varminthunter.org

HUNTING/HUNTING SUPPLIES/PRODUCTS

OUTLAW.COM-WHITETAIL DEER
HUNTING GEAR.
www.outlaw.com
BASS PRO SHOPS.
www.basspro.com
HUNTING PRODUCTS.COM.
www.huntingproducts.com
THE HUNTERS MALL
www.huntersmall.com
BUCK KNIVES.
www.buckknives.com
SCHRADE KNIVES
www.schradeknives.com
GAMALIEL SHOOTING SUPPLY
www.gamaliel.com/deer-hunting.
html
WHITETAIL MAGIC SCENT
DESTROYING DETERGENT
www.whitetailmagic.com
OUTDOOR PRODUCTS
www.outdoor-products.com
HUNTER SPECIALTIES.
www.hunterspec.com
DEER CRACK HUNTING PRODUCTS
www.deer-crack.com
HUNTER'S BUDDY INDEX
www.huntersbuddy.com
MOSSY OAK SAFETY GLASSES
www.safetyglassesusa.com
WING SUPPLY HUNTING SUPPLIES
www.wingsupply.com
A-WAY HUNTING PRODUCTS
www.awayhunting.com
ONLINE OUTDOOR RESOURCE
www.hunting.com
DEER HUNTING PRODUCTS
www.deerhuntingstore.com

HUNTING TOP 10
www.huntingtop10.com
HUNTER'S SHOOTING ASSOCIATION.
www.huntershooter.com
HUNTER SPECIALTIES.
www.hunterspec.com
COMPARISON SHOPPING FOR
DEER AND DEER HUNTING
PRODUCTS
www.epinions.com/
content_33616531076
KNIFE DEALERS AND RETAILERS
www.cutlerscove.com/links/
knifedealers-retailers.html
THE KNIFE AND EDGED WEAPONS
SOCIETY
www.huntingsociety.org/knives.
html
ALLFISHERMAN.COM-LINKS
www.links.allfishermen.com/lists/
all_38.html
WALKERS GAME EAR.
www.walkersgameear.com
GPS PRODUCTS
www.delorme.com
TRACK MASTER
www.TrackMasterATS.com
POLAR WRAP
www.polarwrap.com
BACK COUNTRY INC
www.backcountryinc.com
A. POLYDOROU AND SON
www.polydorou.com.cy
DUOFOLD
www.duofold.com
EXCHANGER
www.polarwrap.com
BRATEMANS INC
www.bratemans.com
EQUIPPED TO SURVIVE
www.equipped.com
MIDWAY USA.
www.midwayusa.com

HUNTER OUTFITTER.COM
www.hunteroutfitter.com
DEER CAM
www.deercam.com
BIG GAME PRO SHOP
www.biggameproshop.com
BIG WOODS BUCKS
www.bigwoodsbucks.com
BLACKTAIL COUNTRY.
www.blacktailcountry.com
BOOKING NW GUIDES
www.bookingnwguides.com
BOONE AND CROCKETT CLUB
www.boone-crockett.org
BOSSBUCK.COM
www.bossbuck.com
BPBULLETS
www.muzzleloadingbullets.com
BP-OUTDOORS
www.bp-outdoors.com
BRENDA VALENTINE
www.brendavalentine.com
BUCK GRUB
www.buckgrub.com
BUCKMASTERS.
www.buckmasters.com
BUCKPOLE.NET
www.buckpole.net
CABELA'S
www.cabelas.com
CAMPING GEAR.
www.campingequipmentworld.
com
COLEMAN CAMPING GEAR
www.summitcampinggear.com
DRD OUTDOOR SPORTS
www.drdoutdoorsports.webs.com
EXPLORE PRODUCTS
www.exploreproducts.com
FAMILY TENT CAMPING
www.familytentcamping.com
GANDER MOUNTAIN
www.gandermountain.com

GRAYBEARD OUTDOORS
www.go2gbo.com/forums//index.
php
HAT COUNTRY
www.hatcountry.com
HUNTERS BARN
www.huntershogbarn.com
HUNTING DEPOT
www.hunting-depot.com
HUNTING SUPPLIERS
www.huntingsuppliers.com
J & M SUPPLY
www.shootnhunt.com
KING'S OUTDOOR WORLD
www.kingsoutdoorworld.com
L.L.BEAN.
www.llbean.com
OUTDOOR GB
www.outdoorgb.com
OUTDOOR GEAR
www.outdoorequipmentshop.net
PENN'S WOODS PRODUCTS, INC
www.pennswoods.com
PETERSON OUTDOORS.
www.petersonoutdoors.org
SPORTSMAN'S SHOPPING GUIDE.
COM—THE GUIDE TO
BUYING HUNTING, FISHING
AND CAMPING GEAR ONLINE
www.sportsmans-shopping-guide.
com/links.htm
THE OUTDOOR SHACK
www.outdoorshack.com
THE OUTDOOR STORE
www.camping4less.com/index.htm
THE TENT CAMPSITE
www.thetentcampsite.com
T J GENERAL STORE.
www.tjgeneralstore.com
TRAIL TENTS.COM
www.trailtents.com

BOW HUNTING/ARCHERY/EQUIPMENT

ARCHERY EXCHANGE
www.archeryexchange.com
ARCHERY INFORMATION
www.archeryinfo.info
ARCHERY OUTPOST
archeryoutpost.com/bot.htm
ARCHERY-RESEARCH.COM
www.archery-research.com
BOWSITE.COM
www.bowsite.com
BROKEN ARROW DESIGNS
www.brokenarrowdesigns.net
BROWNING-ARCHERY
www.browning-archery.com
CROSSBOWS
www.xbowsplus.com
EASTON ARCHERY
www.eastonarchery.com
EXCALIBUR CROSSBOWS INC
www.crossbow-hunting-
crossbows-excalibur.com
INTERNATIONAL BOWHUNTING
ORGANIZATION
www.ibo.net
MARTIN ARCHERY
www.martinarchery.com
PARKER COMPOUND BOWS
www.parkerbows.com/pb/2007
PSE-ARCHERY
www.pse-archery.com
ROCKY MOUNTAIN ARCHERY
www.rmarchery.com
NOCK POINT
www.nockpoint.com
NORTH AMERICAN BOWHUNTERS
www.hunting.net/nab
ARCHERY AUCTIONS.
www.archeryauctions.com
BOWHUNTING.COM
www.bowhunting.com

BOWHUNTING.NET
www.bowhunting.net
INTERNET ARCHERY INFORMATION
www.archeryinfo.info
BOW TECH
www.bowtecharchery.com
TRUEFLIGHT
www.trueflightfeathers.com
TRUGLO ARCHERY
www.truglosights.com
ARCHERY TRADITIONS
www.archerytraditions.com
ASAHI ARCHERY
www.asahi-archery.co.jp
BOWHUNTING SUPERSITE FOR REAL
BOWHUNTERS
www.bowsite.com
BRAVE YOUTH BOWS
www.beargoldeneagle.com/bear
DARTON ARCHERY
www.dartonarchery.com
DIAMOND ARCHERY
www.diamondarchery.com
FORGE BOWS
www.forgebow.com
HIGH COUNTRY ARCHERY
www.highcountryarchery.com
ONEIDA EAGLE BOWS
www.oneidaeaglebows.com
PARKER BOWS
www.parkerbows.com
REFLEX BOWS
www.reflexbow.com
RENEGADE ARCHERY.
www.renegadearchery.com
BOWSITE.COM
www.bowsite.com
BEN PEARSON
www.benpearson.com
WHITETAIL BOWHUNTING DAYS.
www.members.tripod.com/
Bowbucks

HOYT USA.
www.hoytusa.com
MATHEWS INC.
www.mathewsinc.com
ALPINE ARCHERY
www.alpinearchery.com
WASP ARCHERY PRODUCTS
www.wasparchery.com
BOWHUNTING SUPPLIES AND
EQUIPMENT.
www.lancasterarchery.com
THE ARCHERY MALL
www.archerymall.com
THE BOW SHOP
www.bow-shop.com
BOWHUNTING PRICES
www.centralmdoutfitters.com/id3.
html
MERLIN BOWS
www.merlin-bows.co.uk
BEAR ARCHERY
www.fulldraw.net/bear
THE ARCHERY NETWORK
www.archerynetwork.com
CASCADE ARCHERY
www.cascadearchery.com
HORTON MANUFACTURING
www.crossbow.com
JIM FLETCHER ARCHERY
www.fletcherarchery.com
MUZZY PRODUCTS CORP
www.badtothebone.com
SPECIALTY ARCHERY
www.specialtyarch.com
ALLEGHENY MOUNTAIN ARROW
WOODS
www.arrowwoods.com
GOLDEN EAGLE ARCHERY.
www.gearchery.com
BARNETT CROSS BOWS
www.barnettcrossbows.com
BEMAN ARCHERY.
www.beman.com

BINGHAM PROJECTS, INC. ARCHERY.
www.binghamprojects.com
ALLARCHERY.COM—THE ARCHERY
COMMUNITY
www.archersworld.com
BIRDSONG ARCHERY.
www.birdsongarchery.com
BEAR PAWS BOWS.
www.bpbows.com
BOW SIGHTS BY ERADICATOR
www.eradicator.com
TALK.ALL ARCHERY.COM
www.talk.allarchery.com
INTERNATIONAL BOW HUNTING
ORGANIZATION.
www.ibo.net
BOW HUNTING AND ARCHERY WITH
RICKEY WELCH
www.1-dakota-bowhunting.com
THE BOWSITE
www.bowsite.com
BOWHUNTING INFORMATION FOR
THE HUNTER
www.tracker-outdoors.com/
bowhunting.html
BOW AND ARCHERY INFORMATION
www.bowhuntinginfo.com
BOWHUNTING LINKS.
www.bowhuntinglinks.com
TRACKER OUTDOORS
www.tracker-outdoors.com/
archery-p.html
CLASSIFIEDS BOWHUNTING
EQUIPMENT
www.spav.com/sa/basecamp/
classifieds/classifieds/class_
Bow.html

MUZZLELOADER / MUZZLELOADER EQUIPMENT

MUZZLELOADER
www.muzzleloader.com
SAVAGE ARMS
www.savagearms.com/
muzzleloader
WDNR LAW ENFORCEMENT
MUZZLELOADER
www.dnr.state.wi.us/org/es/
enforcement/safety/muzzleqa.
html
MUZZLELOADER
www.southforkrifleclub.
homestead.com/muzzleloader.
html
MUZZLELOADER BUILDERS SUPPLY
www.muzzleloaderbuilderssupply.
com
MAINTAINING YOUR MUZZLELOADER
www.owlhollowgunclub.org/
stories/ml-maint.html
MUZZLELOADE QUIZ
www.tpwd.state.tx.us/edu/
homestudy/muzzl/muzzlquiz.
html
MUZZLELOADER MANUFACTURERS
www.bigbuckrack.com/
Muzzleloaders.html
MUZZLELOADER HUNTS
www.bitterrootelk.com/html/
muzzleloader_hunts.html
MUZZLELOADER NIPPLE WITH A
VALVE
www.directfirearms.com
THE HOG HEAVEN MUZZLELOADER
www.hogheavenmuzzleloaders.
com
MUZZLELOADER BUILDERS SUPPLY
www.muzzleloaderbuilderssupply.
com

NATIONAL MUZZLELOADING RIFLE
ASSOCIATION
www.nmlra.org
THE GUN WORKS MUZZLELOADING
EMPORIUM
www.thegunworks.com
THE BLACKPOWDER RIFLE SOCIETY
www.huntingsociety.org/
muzzleloaders.html
PYRODEX.
www.pyrodex.com
MUZZLELOADING-SHOOTING SKILLS
www.agctr.lsu.edu/parish/bossier/
Outdoor_Skills/muzzleloading.
html
CVA MOUNTAIN STAULKER
MUZZLELOADER
www.outdoorsite.com/site/go.cfm/
owner/024EDD91-BBAC-4055-
98D2E1DA501AA7C8
MUZZLELOADER TRAJECTORY
TABLES   www.clcweb.net/
Muzzleloading/Trajectory_
Tables/trajectory_tables.html
R & P MUZZLELOADING
www.muzzleloadingbullets.com

WEAPONS AND AMMO MANUFACTURERS AND RELATED SITES

AMERICAN FIREARMS NETWORK
www.amfire.com
SAVAGEARMS
www.savagearms.com
NATIONAL RELOADING
MANUFACTURERS
ASSOCIATION
www.reload-nrma.com
RIFLES, CARTRIDGES, SCOPES, ETC
www.wildgoose.com
RIFLE GUARD
www.rifleguard.com

DAN WESSON FIREARMS COMPANY
www.danwessonfirearms.com
DIXIE GUN WORKS
www.dixiegun.com
FREEDOM ARMS INC.
www.freedomarms.com
GLOCK
www.glock.com
HI-POINTFIREARMS
www.hi-pointfirearms.com
ITHACA GUN.
www.ithacagun.com
BERETTA
www.berettausa.com
BROWNING
www.browning.com
CHARTER
www.charterfirearms.com
PRECISION RELOADING INC
www.precisionreloading.com
BARTLETT RELOADERS
www.gibrass.com
GUN WEB.
www.gunweb.com
MARLIN
www.marlinfirearms.com
BALLARD RIFLE AND CARTRIDGES
www.ballardarms.com
RIFLE MANUFACTURERS.
www.shootersolutions.com/
rifleman.html
FIRE ARM MANUFACTURERS
www.gunnerynetwork.com
GREEN MOUNTAIN
www.gmriflebarrel.com
RUGER, STURM AND COMPANY
www.ruger-firearms.com
SMITH & WESSON
www.smith-wesson.com
REMINGTON
www.remington.com
SPRINGFIELD ARMORY
www.springfield-armory.com

COLT
www.colt.com
RUGER.
www.ruger-firearms.com
WINCHESTER
www.winchester-guns.com
CHARTER ARMS
www.charterfirearms.com
THOMPSON CENTER ARMS.
www.tcarms.com
KNIGHT RIFLE.
www.knightrifles.com
MAUSER ARMS
www.mauser.com
AMERICAN FIREARM INDUSTRY
www.amfire.com
PRIVACY – FIREARM RIGHTS – PRO
GUN – ANTI CONTROL
www.xmission.com/~ranthon/
america.html
LONG RIFLES
www.longrifles.com
SIGHTING IN.
corpsoflongriflemen.homestead.
com/sightingin.html
DAISY MANUFACTURING
www.daisy.com
MANNLICHER
www.steyr-mannlicher.com
HORNADY
www.hornady.com
SKS INDUSTRIES
www.sskindustries.com
CVA
www.cva.com
REPUBLIC
www.republicarms.com
MOSSBERG.
www.mossberg.com
WEATHERBY.
www.weatherby.com
LONGHUNTERS MERCANTILE INC
www.longhunters.com

SHOTGUN MUZZLELOADER AND
COMPACT SCOPES
www.leupold.com/products/Info_
Shotgun_Compact.html
BEST CARTRIDGES FOR WHITETAIL
www.wildgoose.com
2ND AMENDMENT (specializing
in custom AND obsolete
ammunition)
www.ammunitions.com
ACCURATE ARMS RELOADING
www.accuratepowder.com
ALLIANT POWDER
www.alliantpowder.com
THE AMMO BANK
www.ammobank.com
THE AMMO DEPOT
www.ammodepot.com
BARNES BULLETS
www.barnesbullets.com
SIERRA BULLETS
www.sierrabullets.com
BERGER BULLETS INC
www.bergerbullets.com
BEST SHOT AMMO
www.bestshotammo.com
FEDERAL AMUNITION
www.federalcartridge.com
WINCHESTER AMMUNITION.
www.winchester.com
HODGDON POWDER
www.hodgdon.com
THE ARMORY
www.the-armory.com
UNIQUE SHOT SHELLS
www.uniqueshotshells.com
INTERACTIVE HANDLOADING
www.gunuts.com
AMERICAN WESTERN ARMS.
www.awaguns.com
BERSA
www.bersafirearmsusa.com

CHARTER ARMS
www.charterfirearms.com
CVA
www.cva.com
CZ
www.cz-usa.com
DAKOTA ARMS
www.dakotaarms.com
DISCOUNT RELOAD.
www.discountreload.com
GALLERY OF GUNS.COM.
www.galleryofguns.com
GUN BROKER.COM.
www.gunbroker.com
GUN-DATA.COM
www.gun-data.com
GUN OWNERS OF AMERICA
www.gunowners.org
GUN DEALERS ONLINE
www.gundealersonline.com
GUN FORUMS
www.hk94.com
GUNS LOCAL.COM
www.gunslocal.com
GUN OWNERS INFORMATION
www.gunsinfo4u.com
GUN SAFES AND GUN CABINETS.
www.gunsafes.com
GUNSHOPS.COM.
www.gunshop.com
GUN STOCKS
www.gungearusa.com
HENRY REPEATING ARMS
www.henryrepeating.com
KNIGHT RIFLES
www.knightrifles.com
LEATHER HOLSTERS
www.oldtradingpost.com
MOSSBERG.
www.mossberg.com
NUMRICH GUN PARTS CORP
www.gunpartscorp.com
OLD TREE GUN BLANKS

www.oldtreegunblanks.com
SHARPS ARMS
www.csharpsarms.com
SHOOTER SOLUTIONS
www.shootersolutions.com
SHOOTING GLASSES.
www.extremeeyewear.com/
shooting-glasses/shooting-
glasses.html
SPORT HEARING
www.sporthearing.com/home.html
SPORTSMEN'S ASSOCIATION FOR
FIREARMS EDUCATION, INC..
www.nysafe.org
STURDY GUN SAFE MFG.
www.sturdysafe.com
THE GUN INCYCLOPEDIA
www.gunsinfo.org
THE GUN INDEX
www.gunsnstuf.com
THE GUN-LOCKS-SAFES STORE
www.gun-locks-safes.com/index.
asp
THOMPSON CENTER ARMS
www.tcarms.com
WICHITA ARMS
www.wichitaarms.com
FIREARM AND SELF DEFENSE
PRODUCTS
www.xfighterdefense.com
FIREARMSTALK.COM.
www.firearmstalk.com/forums

TARGETS AND DECOYS

RINEHART 3-D ARCHERY TARGETS
www.rinehart3-d.com
3-D TARGETS.
www.featherfast.com
WHITETAIL DEER DECOYS
www.hintontargets.com/
Deerdecoy.html

AMERICAN TARGETS.
 www.americantargets.com
DELTA TARGETS.
 www.deltatargets.net
MAUSER
 www.mauserwaffen.de
METAL SPINNING TARGETS
 www.metaltargets.com
MYTARGETS.COM
 www.mytargets.com

ALL OPTICS

PIONEER OPTICS
 www.pioneer-research.com
ZEISS OPTICS
 www.zeiss.com
TRIJICON OPTICS
 www.trijicon-inc.com
SWAROVSKI OPTICS
 www.Swarovskioptics.com
SWIFT OPTICS.
 www.SwiftOptics.com
TASCO OPTICS
 www.tascosales.com
VIVITAR OPTICS.
 www.vivitar.com
LEUPOLD OPTICS
 www.leupold.com
STEINER OPTICS
 www.pioneer-research.com
BAUSCH & LOMB
 www.bushnell.com
ADCO OPTICS
 www.adcosales.com
BURRIS OPTICS
 www.burrisoptics.com
PENTAX OPTICS
 www.pentax.com
HAWKEYE OPTICS
 www.hawkeyes-intl.com

WEAVER OPTICS
 www.weaveroptics.com
LIGHT FORCE OPTICAL
 www.lightforce.com
NIKON OPTICS.
 www.nikonusa.com
R & R INTER. TRADE NIGHT OPTICS
 www.nightoptics.com
1 ABOVE THE REST–YOUR LAZER
 SUPER STORE (SCOPES).
 www.1above.com
AIMPOINT (SCOPES)
 www.aimpoint.com
B JONES SIGHT SYSTEMS.
 www.bjonessights.com
ITT INDUSTRIES NIGHT VISION
 OPTICS
 www.ittnv.com
BINOCULAR REVIEWS.
 www.buyers-guide-to-binoculars.
 com
CRIMSON TRACE LASER SIGHTS.
 www.crimson-trace-laser-grips.
 com
ICU BINOCULARS
 www.icubinoculars.com
NIGHT VISION EQUIPMENT BY ATN
 www.atncorp.com
NIGHT VISION RIFLE SCOPES
 www.nightvisionplanet.com/night-
 vision-rifle-scopes.html
RIFLESCOPE-SHOP.COM
 www.riflescope-shop.com
RIVERSIDEOPTICS.COM.
 www.riversideoptics.com

DEER STANDS AND BLINDS

BLACK SHADOW DEER STANDS
 www.deerandtreestands.com
DEER STANDS OF YOUR CHOICE
 www.angelfire.com/sc/

huntingstands
TREE STANDS
www.allhuntingsupplies.com/on-deer-hunting-tree-stands.html
AWSOME TREESTANDS
www.awesometreestands.com
TREELOUNGE DEER STANDS.
www.treelounge.com
BUCKFINDER PRODUCTS (STANDS)
www.buckfinder.com
LONE WOLF STANDS
www.lonewolfstands.com
AUSTIN OUTDOORS TREE STANDS.
www.austintreestands.com
BIG GAME HUNTING ACCESSORIES STANDS.
www.big-gameusa.com
BUCK SHOT TREE STANDS
www.buckshot-stands.com
CRANFORD MANUFACTURING INC. (STANDS).
www.ezyclimb.com
OL' MAN TREE STANDS
www.olmanoutdoors.com
SUMMIT STANDS
www.summitstands.com
LADDER STANDS
www.deerstandsusa.com
TRAILHAWK TREE STANDS
www.trailhawk.com
TREE CLIMBER TREE STANDS.
www.treeclimber.com
STEPLADDER
www.steppladder.com
HIDEOUT TREE STAND AND FIELD BLIND.
www.hideouttreestand.com
GAME TAMER TREE STANDS
www.gametamers.com
DEER HUNTER TREE STANDS
www.deerhunterstands.com
AMACKER TREE STANDS
www.amacker.com

HIDE OUT TREE STANDS
www.hideouttreestand.com
TREE STANDS FOR THE DEER HUNTER
spillwaysportsman.com
TSC TREE STANDS
www.tsctreestands.com
LOGGY BAYOU TREE STANDS
www.loggybayou.net
OUT LAW TREE STANDS
www.outlaw.com
TREE STAND WAREHOUSE
www.eders.com
DEER STANDS USA
www.deerstandsusa.com
AMERISTEP
www.ameristep.com
BIG GAME TREESTANDS.
www.biggametreestands.com
DEER BLINDS
www.deerblinds.net
GORILLA TREESTANDS
www.gorillatreestands.com/cms
HUNTING BLINDS.
www.milestactical.com/huntingblinds.html
INNOVATIVE TREESTANDS, INC
www.itstreestands.com
STRONGBUILT TREE STANDS
www.strongbuiltinc.com
TREESTAND.COM
www.treestand.com

CAMOFLAGE CLOTHING AND ACCESSORIES

NATURAL GEAR CAMOUFLAGE.
www.naturalgear.com
ADVANTAGE CAMOUFLAGE
www.advantagecamo.com
CAMOVISION CAMOUFLAGE
www.camovision.com
CUSTOM CONCEALMENT CAMOUFLAGE

www.ghillie.com
DOWN WIND 3D CAMOUFLAGE
www.downwind3dcamo.com
GHILLIE SUITS CAMOUFLAGE.
www.ghilliesuits.com
IMAGE COUNTRY CAMOUFLAGE
www.imagecountry.com
MOSSY OAK CAMOUFLAGE
www.mossyoak.com
PORTMIDWEST INTERNATIONAL
CAMOUFLAGE
www.coversystem.com
PREDATOR CAMOUFLAGE
www.predatorcamo.com
PROHOOD CAMOUFLAGE.
www.prohood.com
RANCHO SAFARI CAMOUFLAGE
www.ranchosafari.com
REALTREE CAMOUFLAGE.
www.realtreeoutdoors.com
SLEEPING INDIAN DESIGNS INC.
CAMOUFLAGE
www.woolcamo.com
TRU-WOODS CAMOUFLAGE.
www.truwoods.com
SCENT-LOK CAMOUFLAGE
www.scentlok.com
TREBARK CAMOUFLAGE
www.trebark.com
BRIARBUSTER CAMOUFLAGE
www.briarbuster.com
HOP-A-LONG OUTDOOR PRODUCTS
CAMO
www.hopalongoutdoors.com
KING OF THE MOUNTAIN CLOTHING
www.kingofthemountain.com
KOBUK WADERS
www.kobukwaders.com
POINTER BRAND OVERALLS
www.pointerbrand.com
RUGGED CLOTHING
www.ruggedclothing.com
WRANGLER.

www.wrangler.com
10X WEAR CLOTHING
www.10xwear.com
AB EMBLEM AND CAPS
www.abemblem.com
HATCH GLOVES
www.hatch-gloves.com
REALTREE
www.realtree.com
HIGH DESERT.
www.hdesert.com
PRO HOOD
www.prohood.com
RACOE INC.
www.racoe.com
ICE BREAKER PRODUCTS
www.icebreakerinc.com
SCENTLOK
www.scentlok.com
CAMO CARPET
www.camocarpet.com
CAMOUFLAGE GHILLIE SUITS
www.milestactical.com/
ghilliesuits.html
GHILLIES AND STUFF
www.ghilliesandstuff.com
GORE-TEX.
www.gore.com
HUNTING CLOTHES UNLIMITED.
www.ranchwearunlimited.com
LONGLEAF CAMO
www.longleafcamo.com
THE CAMO COALITION
www.camocoalition.com
THE HEATER BODY SUIT
www.heaterbodysuit.com/index.
htm

COVER SCENTS AND LURES

WHITETAIL SPECIALTIES OUTDOOR
PRODUCTS SCENTS
www.deer-scent.com
DEER SCENTS AND LURES.
www.loweswhitetail.com
CREEKSIDE WHITETAIL AND
KILLBUCK SCENTS
www.creeksidewhitetail.com
NORTHERN WHITETAIL SCENTS
www.northernwhitetail.com
HARMON DEER SCENTS
www.harmondeerscents.com
BEAR SCENTS
www.bearscents.com
BUCK MAGIC
www.buckmagic.com
BUCK STOP SCENTS
www.buckstopscents.com
BUCKEYE SCENTS
www.buckeyescents.com
BUCKS N DOES HSE SCENTS.
www.bucksndoes.com
BUCKWOODS LLC SCENTS
www.ebuckwoods.com
MRS. DOE PEE'S BUCK LURE
www.mrsdoepee.com
DOC'S DEER FARM AND SCENTS
www.docsdeerscent.com
IN-SCENTS
www.In-scents.com
BUCKSKIN INDUSTRIES
www.deerscent.com
CREEKSIDE WHITETAIL KILLBUCK
SCENT
www.killbuck.com
NORTHERN WHITETAIL SCENTS
www.northernwhitetail.com
SCENT SHIELD.
www.scentshield.com
WHITETAIL MAGIC SCENTS
www.whitetailmagic.com

SCENTS
www.hunterspec.com
ALL HUNTERS DEER HUNTING
SCENTS AND COVERS.
www.allhunters.net/id41.html
CODE BLUE HUNTING SCENTS
www.codebluescents.com
KISHEL SCENTS
www.kishelscents.com
TINGLEYS NORTHLAND HUNTING
LURES
www.tingleysnorthland.com
TINKS SCENTS AND LURES
www.tinks69.com

GAME CALLS

BERRY GAME CALLS
www.berrygamecalls.com
PRIMOS HUNTING CALLS
www.primos.com
CACHE RIVER DUCKALL CALLS
www.duckall.com
GREG KEATS CUSTOM CALLS.
www.gregkeats.com
CALL PURRFECT CALLS
www.callpurrfect.com
HAYDEL'S GAME CALLS
www.haydels.com
TIMBER MALLARD DUCK CALLS
www.timbermallard.com
OAK LEAF GAME CALLS AND GUIDE
SERVICE
www.oakleafguideservice.com
PENN'S WOODS GAME CALLS
www.pennswoods.com
FAULKNER WATERFOWL CALLS
www.qualityhunter.com
HUNTERS SPECIALTIES CALLS
www.hunterspec.com
PAUL'S CALLS
www.paulscalls.com

QUAKER BOY GAME CALLS
www.quakerboygamecalls.com
SOUTHERN GAME CALLS
www.southerngamecalls.com
KNIGHT & HALE PRODUCTS.
www.knight-hale.com
DEER CALLS BY EXTREME
DIMENSION.
www.phantomcalls.com
GAME CALLS
www.gamecalls.net
ALLPREDATORCALLS.COM.
www.allpredatorcalls.com
BIG BUCK 4N2 RATTLING ANTLERS
www.bigbuckrattlingantlers.com
MOUNTAIN SCREAMER GAME CALLS.
www.mountainscreamer.com
RATTLEMASTERS OF TEXAS.
www.rattlemasters.com/home.htm
WILSON GAME CALLS.
www.wilsongamecalls.com
WOODS WISE PRODUCTS
www.woodswise.com

GAME FEED AND SEED PRODUCTS

FOOD PLOTS
www.americaoutdoors.com
JACKSON'S WHITETAIL DEER FOOD
PLOT SEED.
www.whitetaildeerfoodplot.com
RACKMAX BIOSTIMULANT.
www.rack-max.com
FOOD SOURCE SYSTEMS.
www.fssystem.com
WHITETAIL SUPPLY AND FEED/DEER
LURES
www.whitetailsupply.com
BUCK MAGIC
www.buckmagic.com
LAMCO AUTOMATIC FEEDERS
www.lamcofeeders.com

WHITETAIL HABITAT
www.whitetailhabitat.com
PRAIRIE WILDLIFE
www.prairiewildlife.org
AMERICAN HUNTER FEEDERS
www.americanhunterfeeders.com
WHITETAIL INSTITUTE
www.deernutrition.com
TECOMATE SEED COMPANY
www.tecomate.com
ANTLER KING
www.antlerking.com
FIFIELD SEED AND FEED STORE
www.fifieldseednfeed.com/index.
html

TAXIDERMY AND TROPHY CARE

ANIMAL HOUSE TAXIDERMY
www.taxidermyusa.com/
animalhouse
JIM ALLRED TAXIDERMY SUPPLIER
www.jimallred.com
REALISTIC TAXIDERMY WEBSITE
www.taxidermy.org
T & L FURS
www.tandlfurs.com
TAXIDERMY
www.taxidermy.net
TROPHY CARE INTERNATIONAL
www.fordinfo.com/trophycare
TAXIDERMY NET
www.taxidermy.net/link.html

SPORT UTILITY VEHICLES AND BOATS

YAMAHA ATV'S
www.yamaha-motor.com
RANGER BOATS
www.rangerboats.com

ATV SOURCE.COM
www.atvsource.com
ATV SALVAGE.
www.atvsalvage.com

MAPS AND TRAVEL INFORMATION

MAP QUEST
www.mapquest.com
MAP STORE
www.mapstoremn.com
DELORME MAPS.
www.delorme.com
MAP TECH
www.maptech.com
HUNTING TRAVEL INFORMATION
www.huntinfo.com
TERRA SERVER.
www.terraserver.com
DEER DENSITY MAP
www.deerhunting.ws/densitymap.
htm
MYTOPO.COM
www.mytopo.com/index.cfm

MAGAZINES AND OTHER PUBLICATIONS

NATIONAL RIFLE ASSOCIATION
www.nra.org
NORTH AMERICAN HUNTER
MAGAZINE
www.visitors.huntingclub.com/
magazine.asp
FARMERS ALMANAC.
www.farmersalmanac.com
TAXIDERMY TODAY MAGAZINE
www.taxidermytoday.com
HUNT REPORT.COM
www.huntreport.com

BIG BUCKS MAGAZINE
www.bigbuckmag.com
EDERSBO
wwww.edersbow.com
FIELD AND STREAM
www.fieldandstream.com
DEER AND DEER HUNTING
MAGAZINE
www.magazinecity.net
WHITETALES MAGAZINE
www.mndeerhunters.com
MUZZLELOADER MAGAZINE
www.muzzmag.com
THE DEER FARMERS MAGAZINE
www.deerfarmer.co.nz
TAXIDERMY TODAY MAGAZINE
www.taxidermytoday.com
OUTDOOR LIFE.
www.outdoorlife.com
BEAR HUNTING MAGAZINE
www.bear-hunting.com
OUTDOOR TIMES
www.outdoortimes.com
GUNS AND GEAR MAGAZINE
www.gunsandgear.com
HUNTING LEASES MAGAZINE.
www.huntinglease.com
SPORTS AFIELD
www.sportsafield.com
BOWHUNTER
www.bowhunter.com
DEER HUNTING.
www.safaripress.com
AMERICAN SHOOTING MAGAZINE
www.americanshooting.com
THE GREAT OUTDOORS.
www.icc2.com/greatoutdoor
THE AMERICAN HUNTER
www.theamericanhunter.com
NORTH AMERICAN HUNTER
www.americanhunter.com
RACK MAGAZINE ONLINE
www.rackmag.com

RIFLE MAGAZINE
www.riflemagazine.com
RIFLE SHOOTER MAGAZINE
www.loveleaf.net/magazine/
RIFLESHOOTER.html
WOODS AND WATERS MAGAZINE.
www.woodsandwatersmagazine.
com
BOW AND ARROW HUNTING
MAGAZINE
www.bowandarrowhunting.com
TEXAS HUNTING MAGAZINE
www.texashunting.com
THE WHITETAIL FANATIC MAGAZINE
www.whitetailfanatic.com
WATER AND WOODS
www.waterandwoods.net

CATALOGS

HUNTING GEAR AND CATALOG LINKS.
www.hunters-haven.com
KRAUSE PUBLICATIONS PRODUCTS
www.deeranddeerhunting.com
CHAGNON'S OUTDOOR CATALOGUE
(TRAPPING)
www.outdoorcatalog.com
ADIRONDACK OUTDOORS CATALOG
www.adirondackoutdoor.com
CAMPMAN CATALOG
www.campman.com
DROPTINE OUTDOORS CATALOG
www.droptine.com
DUNNS SUPPLY CATALOG.
www.dunnscatalog.com
REI
www.rei.com
BASS PRO SHOP
www.bassproshops.com
GAMALIEL SHOOTING SUPPLY
CATALOG
www.gamaliel.com

GRAFS AND SONS CATALOG
www.grafs.com
HUNTERS RIDGE OUTDOORS
CATALOG
www.huntersridgeoutdoors.com
LL BEAN CATALOG.
www.llbean.com
LEBARON OUTDOOR PRODUCTS
CATALOG
www.lebaron.ca/english
LION COUNTRY SUPPLY CATALOG
www.lcsupply.com
ORVIS CATALOG.
www.orvis.com
THE OUTPOST CATALOG.
www.theoutpostmall.com
QUAKERBOY GAME CALLS CATALOG.
www.quakerboygamecalls.com
REDDING-RELOADING SUPPLY
CATALOG
www.redding-reloading.com
HERTERS.
www.herters.com
SCOTT'S DOG SUPPLY CATALOG
www.scottsdog.com
SPORTSMAN GUIDE CATALOG
www.sportsmansguide.com
STAFFORD'S CATALOG
www.stafford-catalog.com
SURPLUS OUTPOST CATALOG
www.surplusoutpost.com
WILDERNESS ADVENTURES CATALOG
www.wildadv.com
WINGSET CATALOG
www.wingset.com
CABELA'S CATALOG
www.cabelas.com
USEFUL FIREARM RELATED LINKS
www.huglushotguns.com/links.
html
THE GUN SHOP
www.gunshop.com

GUNHOO GUN PAGES CENTRAL
www.gunsgunsguns.com/gunhoo
EDERSBOW CATALOG
www.edersbow.com/catalog

EDUCATIONAL RESOURCES

HUNTING VIDEOS
www.huntingvideos.com
RIFLE REVIEW CHART
www.fieldandstream.com/
deergear/dg96.rifles.chart.html
WHITETAIL DEER PRINTOUT   www.
enchantedlearning.com/
subjects/mammals/deer/
whitetailprintout
HUNTER EDUCATION
www.tpwd.state.tx.us/edu/hunted
INTERNATIONAL HUNTER
EDUCATION
www.ihea.com
HUNTING AND FUR TRAPPING
www.indians.org
OUTDOOR ADVENTURE VIDEOS
www.oavideo.com
DOLEY'S WILDLIFE ENCYCLOPEDIA
www.nvmedia.com/Doley/wildlife.
html
WILD HARVEST VIDEOS.
www.wildharvestvideos.com
WILDLIFE RESEARCH
www.wildlife.com
THE DEER SHACK HUNTING VIDEOS
www.deershack.com
SHOOT BALLISTIC SOFTWARE
www.pinsoft.com.au
DEER HUNTING EXPERT SOFTWARE
www.st-tech.com
NORTH AMERICAN HUNTING CLUB-
LIBRARY.
www.huntingclub.com

DEER HUNTING GAMES.
www.qualityinks.com/deerhunting.
php
SOFTWARE FOR WHITETAIL DEER
HUNTING.
www.st-tech.com

KNIVES

BLADE TRADER.
www.bladetradder.com
GERBER KNIVES AND TOOLS.
www.gerberknivesandtools.com
HUNT 4 KNIVES
www.hunting4knives.com
HUNTING BLADES.COM
www.huntingblades.com
HUNTINGKNIFEDEPOT.COM
www.thehuntingknifedepot.com
HUNTING KNIVES A
www.fernknives.com
HUNTING KNIVES B.
www.banditsbuckknives.com
KNIVES AND ACCESSORIES AT
POCKETKNIVESUSA.COM
www.pocketknivesusa.com
KNIVES FOR POCKET, HUNTING,
CAMPING, FISHING, MILITARY
AND MORE!
www.ebladestore.com
KNIVES TOWN
www.knivestown.com
HUNTING POCKET AND FIXED BLADE
KNIVES
www.huntingpocketknives.com

MISCELLANEOUS SITES OF INTEREST

DIAMONDBACK CANNONS HOME
    PAGE
    www.diamondbackembroidery.
        com/cannon
JACKSON HOLE BUFFALO MEAT
    www.buybuffalomeat.com
ROSEMARY MILLETTE PRINTS
    www.snowgoosegallery.com
SNOW GOOSE GALLERY.
    www.snowgoosegallery.com
KRITTERS IN THE MAILBOX
    www.krittersinthemailbox.com
BUCKHEAD GOURMET
    www.buckheadgourmet.com
OPHIOLOGICAL SERV
    www.ophioservices.com
TICK ENTOMOLOGY WEBSITE
    atum.isis.vt.edu
LYME DISEASE NETWORK.
    www.lymenet.org
AMERICAN LYME DISEASE
    FOUNDATION
    www.aldf.com
WEATHER CHECK
    www.accuweather.com
TREE PRO
    www.treepro.com
CANADIAN WILDLIFE SERVICE
    www.cws-scf.ec.gc.ca
THEODORE ROOSEVELT
        CONSERVATION ALLIANCE.
    www.trca.org
HOT GUNS FRONTLINE
    www.pbs.org/wgbh/pages/
        frontline/shows/guns
SPORTSMAN'S CONNECTION
    www.outdoortalknetwork.com
SMOKY MTN. SCAN FREQ
    www.seviercounty.org

POISON IVY, OAK, AND SUMAC
    INFORMATION CENTER
    www.poisonivy.aesir.com
ZAP MOSQUITOS
    www.zapmosquitos.com
EIDNES FURS
    www.eidnesfurs.com
ENVIROLINK
    www.envirolink.org
HUNTING DOG INFORMATION.
    www.doginfo.org
KISKY PRODUCTIONS
    www.kisky.com
LOST HUNTER.COM
    www.losthunter.com
AMERICAN LYME DISEASE
    FOUNDATION
    www.aldf.com
WILDERNESS SURVIVAL
    www.wilderness-survival.net
COMMUNITY EMERGENCY RESPONSE
    SUPPLY
    www.cpr-savers.com/emergency/
        cert-kits-equipment.html
EMERGENCY SURVIVAL KITS
    www.survivorind.com/packages.
        html
EMERGENCY SURVIVAL PACKS
    www.survivalpacks4u.com
CAPTAIN DAVE'S SURVIVAL
    www.survival-center.com
URBAN SURVIVAL
    urbansurvival.com/week.htm
WELCOME TO HOODS WOODS
    www.survival.com
SURVIVAL INTERNATIONAL
    www.survivalinternational.org/
        home
SURVIVAL SKILLS
    www.en.wikipedia.org/wiki/
        Survival_skills

SURVIVAL AND SELF-SUFFICIENCY
LINKS
www.greatdreams.com/survival.
htm

WILDLIFE GOURMET

BUCK HEAD GOURMET
www.buckheadgourmet.com
ONE STOP JERKY SHOP
www.onestopjerkyshop.com
SAUSAGE SOURCE
www.sausagesource.com
MOUNTAIN HOUSE FREEZE DRIED
FOODS | SURVIVAL FOOD L
www.survival-warehouse.com
GOURMET WILD GAME
www.gourmetwildgame.com

WILD GAME GOURMET
wwwdnr.state.il.us/recipes
THE GAME GOURMET
www.stoneywolf.com/
gamegourmet.htm
GOURMET HEALTH RECIPES
www.e-gourmet-recipes.com/
gourmet-recipes/gourmet-
recipes.php?cat = 14
VALLEY GAME AND GOURMET.
www.valleygame.com
GOURMETSLEUTH
www.gourmetsleuth.com/
Gourmet/List/Wild-Game-
584aspx

A LITTLE ABOUT THE AUTHOR

Having spent the youth of my life in a small community called Only, Tennessee, where my parents lived at the time I was born, I received a valuable foundation block for my life. I knew that I would always prefer and try to remain as close to my roots as possible. The simple, down to earth, honest-to-goodness country way of life, would always be me at heart. My love for the outdoors and deer hunting stems from these early years I spent in Only, Tennessee. I began hunting at about 10 years of age with an old single shot 22 rifle. I developed a real appreciation for the ability to bring home meat for the table. There was a feeling of doing my part for the family, and it felt good.

I guess one of my favorite places in the entire world to be is in the deep woods of Tennessee, whitetail deer hunting. Over the years, I have spent thousands of hours in the woods, scouting, tracking and observing, photographing, hunting, and harvesting whitetail deer. Over the years, I have endured all types of weather in order to be out there when the deer were active. When you spend a great deal of time doing anything, you naturally will get good at it if you apply what you learn. You will get even better at it if you truly love to do it. This is the way I feel about whitetail deer hunting and why I feel qualified to write this book. I have taken some nice, racked bucks over the years, and for probably the last 30 of those, as many deer for the freezer as I needed every year.

A LITTLE ABOUT THE GRAPHIC
ARTIST AND DESIGNER

My daughter Melanie, the original designer of this book has been in the printing industry for the past 19 years and in digital prepress for the last 13 of those. Graphic art, and design, computer graphics, and photo re-touching is what she does. Her work is always challenging but very rewarding, and that's why she loves it so. She spent over two years in the design, layout, and digital production of "American Whitetail Deer Hunting Tips and Resources". This book is over 500 pages, 39 chapters with hundreds of photos and illustrations. Since it took over six years researching and writing the book, Melanie worked with me during that period to make the finished product the high quality creation that it turned out to become. All this is why it took so long to produce and during the process she learned a great deal about the whitetail deer, deer hunting, and everything that it entails, but more importantly for me, we learned a lot about each other. I am extremely impressed and proud of her and her ability to do high quality graphic art work and her dedication to each project she undertakes. Melanie is very detailed and precise, a perfectionist,

501

and as a result her work reveals this type of approach. The experience of working with my daughter on this project has been priceless and I am so very proud that she has been a part of it all. I know that she feels that this book is one of the most challenging and rewarding things she's ever done professionally.

BIBLIOGRAPHY

My appreciation to all those who provided their opinion of this work in the form of their own testimonials. These folks include John L. Sloan, Brenda Valentine, Terry Higginbotham, Jimmy Holt, Jason Cruise, Bryan White, Gary L. Benton, Donald R. Blizzard, Howard J. Lux, David Salman, John E. MacEwan, Jerry Wilson, Tom Tann, Mary Morris.

I want to honorably mention those deceased family members who assisted with the creation of this work in some way and they include my uncle Loyal McClanahan, My cousin Spence McClanahan, and my nephew Will McClanahan. More recently these family members also include my precious mother Mary Brown Townsend, and my aunt Anne Stutts.

TECHNICAL ASSISTANCE/WEB HOSTING:
◆ Melanie Townsend, Fred Halfpap, Gary Benton

EDITING:
◆ Linda Townsend

RECIPES:
◆ Linda Townsend, Mary Brown Townsend, Joy Hogan

ORIGINAL LAYOUT & GRAPHIC DESIGN & PHOTO RETOUCHING
◆ Melanie Townsend, melwolf13@aol.com

PHOTO SOURCES:

Terry and Linda Townsend · Melanie Townsend · Mary Brown Townsend · Barry Stutts · Rick Stutts · Mike Stutts · Mary Carolyn McClanahan · My late cousin Spence McClanahan · My late uncle Loyal McClanahan · Kathie McClanahan · Tommy McClanahan · Canita Campbell · Cindy and Tommy Parker · Artie Slinker · Greg Slinker · Jerri Stutts · Mary Morris (wildlife photographer for tndeer.com) · Dennis Goldsby (designer/creator of the web site www.tndeer.com) · Northland Images, Kevin Lammi (nature photographer/creator of www.northlandimages .com) · Eric Van Eck · J. Cokendolpher · Matthew Choate · Larry Bell · Kurt Welch (The Deer Domain, www.deerdomain.com) · Larry Gilbert · Peter Eades (nature photographer/provider of book cover photos as well as others) · Jack Izard (www.deerdomain.com) · Jerry Vanis (www.deer domain.com) · Howard J. Lux with Wildlife Buffet (www. wildlifebuffet .com and his personal site www.wildlifefoodplots-made-ez.com) · CamTrakker ("The Big Buck Surveillance System," www.camtrakker. com/www.trailcam.com) · Rick Long (Whitetail Hunter, www.white tailhunter.zzn.com) · Mardi Snipes for most of the snake photos, (www.coastalreptiles.com, email: atheris@coastalreptiles.com) · Troy & Marla Hibbitts for Trans-Pecos Copperhead (e-mail: alterna@flash.net) · Terry Hibbitts for Western Pigmy Rattlesnake · Jeremy & Angel Coates for Broad Band Copperhead; Great Basin Rattlesnake; & Midget Faded Rattlesnake (Exotic Gems Reptile, www.exoticgemsreptile.com) · Mike Mahanay for Grand Canyon Rattlesnake (mike@grandcanyontreks.org) · Red Diamond Rattlesnake (www.sdnhm.org) · American International Rattlesnake Museum for Twin Spotted Rattlesnake · Western Coral Snake (www.desertusa.com/mag98/may/papr/du_westcoral.html). · Geoffrey A. Hammerson for the Midget Faded Rattlesnake · Dr Brenda Gilmore for Brown Recluse Spider · Micha L. Rieser for Yellow Sac Spider · Troy Lilly, ForestWander.com · Beth Andrus, Nature of New England, www. nenature.com · John Munt, Wiseacre Gardens · Larry Brown, http:// www.flickr.com/photos/lwbrown/ · U.S. Fish & Wildlife Service · D. Gordon E. Robertson, PhD, Fellow of Canadian Society for Biome- chanics, Professor, School of Human Kinetics, University of Ottawa, Ottawa, Canada · Paul Frank · Steve Van Riper · Matthew Isanski

· Dave Bishop, http://treasuresofoz.org/treasures/preserves/donges-bay-gorge, Photo gallery - http://treasuresofoz.org/photo-galleries/nature-preserves/donges-bay-gorge
· Scott Bauer · Tom Tann · Robert Kraft · http://www.wpclipart.com/animals/D/deer/deer_3/approaching_deer_by_Paul.jpg
· Matt Grady with Batguys · Bruce Macqueen · David Wagner
· Heather Henkel, US Geological Survey
· Tony Campbell · John Stehn · Veikko Rihu · Philip K. White, U.S. Fish & Wildlife Service
· Michael S. Price, Director of the San Angelo Nature Center
· Gary Nafis · Tim Vickers ·Chris Brown · Jim Rorabaugh, US Fish & Wildlife Service
· Luther C. Goldman, US Fish & Wildlife Service, Steve Van Riper, US Fish & Wildlife Service, Bobby Mikul.

ARTISTS:

Terry Townsend · Melanie Townsend · Andrew Demarest · The artists whose work is displayed on the National Arbor Day Foundation web site (www.arbordayfoundation.org/trees) for the significance that my drawings of their work lends to this publication as whitetail food sources.

INFORMATION SOURCES:

◆ The author's 35 years of actual whitetail deer hunting experience, plus six years of research.

Henry Chidgey, Wildlife Analytical Laboratories, http://deerage.com/

"Whitetail Deer Signpost and Their Role as a Source of Priming Pheromones," a paper originally presented by Larry Marchinton, W. Matt Knox, and Karl Miller, University of Georgia Researchers, where they also referenced a number of recent works they published in the Journal of Wildlife Management and in the Journal of Mammology.

"For Big Bucks Only," by Jeff Murray, published by Mark LaBarbera of The North American Hunting Club. (A good tip from Noble Carlson.)

Information was obtained from a report on a scientific study conducted at the University of Georgia by Karen Alexy, wildlife biologist.

John Sloan, freelance writer/lecturer and veteran whitetail hunter.

Thomas Hooker, freelance writer and veteran whitetail hunter.

Rick Stutts, veteran forest ranger and veteran whitetail hunter.

Barry Stutts, former forest ranger and veteran whitetail hunter.

"Anatomy of The Whitetail," The Hunting.Network, www.huntingnet.com

"Hunting Whitetails Successfully," by J. Wayne Fears, published by The North American Hunting Club.

Boone and Crockett Club and Pope and Young Club "Official Score Sheet and Instruction Page," reproduced courtesy of Boone and Crockett Club, 250 Station Drive, Missoula, MT 59801, 406/542-1888, www.boone-crockett.org.

"The Deer of North America," by Leonard Lee Rue, III, published by Outdoor Life-Crown Publishers, Inc.

The Whitetail Institute of North America, www.members.aol.com/deerclover

USGS web site, www.usgs.gov, USGS, Northern Prairie Wildlife Research Center, and USGS representative and friend, Don League and wife Helen.

"Whitetail Deer Hunting," by Mike Strandlund, Richard P. Smith, Jim Zumbo, and Bill Bynum, published by The National Rifle Association of America, www.whitetaildeer.com/hunting/weaponsrifle.asp.

"The Modern Deer Hunter," by John O. Cartier, published by Book Division, Times Mirror Magazines, Inc.

"How to Track and Find Game," by Clyde Ormond, published by Book Division, Times Mirror Magazine, Inc.

"Whitetail Fundamentals and Fine Points for the Hunter," by George Mattis, published by Popular Science/Outdoor Life Book Division.

"Bowhunting," by Mike Strandlund, M.R. James, Karl J. Gunzer Jr., published by The National Rifle Association of America.

Mossy Oak Bio-Logic, www.mossyoak.com

The Sportsman's Interactive website, www.thesi.com/habitatqa5.html

Aron Jeffries, on food plots, www.brick.net/~deerhunt/magazine/forages.html

SNAKEBITE EMERGENCY WEBPAGE, www.xmission.com/~gastown/herpmed/snbite.html

HOBO SPIDER WEBSITE, and the research by Mr. Darwin Vest, www.hobospider.org

US Forestry Service, www.fs.fed.us

Information was obtained from a public service pamphlet by Pfizer Global Research & Development with the assistance of Drs. Louis A. Magnarelli and Kirby C. Stafford III, Department of Entomology, Connecticut Agricultural Experiment Station, New Haven, CT; Dr. Robert T. Schoen, Department of Rheumatology, Yale School of Medicine, New Haven, CT; Dr. Joseph J. Gadbaw, Jr., Infectious Diseases Department, Lawrence & Memorial Hospital, New London, CT; and Dr. Steven A. Levy, Durham Veterinary Hospital, Durham, CT. · PHOTO/ART CREDITS: M. Fergione, B. Tucker, L. Zernel, J. Stratton. Designed by: S. Badgett and J. Crandall, Pfizer Research Graphics. Website developed by Jeffrey Wheeler, www.lyme.org/gallery/other_diseases.html

Tennessee Wildlife Resources Agency, www.state.tn.us/twra

National Rifle Association, www.nra.org

Tree Lounge Stands, www.treelounge.com

The Jump, www.thejump.net/hunting

Deer.Com Hunting Directory, www.deer.com

Whitetail Institute, www.deernutrition.com

Quality Deer Management Association, www.qdma.org